LADIES' NIGHT

75 Excuses to Party with Your Girlfriends

Penny Warner

Polka Dot press®

Avon, Massachusetts

Published by

Polka Dot Press, an imprint of Adams Media, an F+W Publications Company

57 Littlefield Street, Avon, MA 02322. U.S.A.

www.adamsmedia.com

ISBN 13: 978-1-59869-578-6

ISBN 10: 1-59869-578-9

Printed in the United States of America.

J I H G F E D C B A

Library of Congress Cataloging-in-Publication Data

is available from the publisher.

This publication is designed to provide accurate and authoritative information with regard to the subject matter covered. It is sold with the understanding that the publisher is not engaged in rendering legal, accounting, or other professional advice. If legal advice or other expert assistance is required, the services of a competent professional person should be sought.

—From a *Declaration of Principles* jointly adopted by a Committee of the American Bar Association and a Committee of Publishers and Associations

Many of the designations used by manufacturers and sellers to distinguish their product are claimed as trademarks. Where those designations appear in this book and Adams Media was aware of a trademark claim, the designations have been printed with initial capital letters.

This book is available at quantity discounts for bulk purchases.

For information, please call 1-800-289-0963.

Dedication

To my husband, Tom, who carries out all my wildest party plans.
To my kids, who never know what to expect.

"Well-behaved women rarely make history." ~ *Laurel Thatcher Ulrich*

Acknowledgments

Thanks to all the party chicks, divas, and hens who shared their party themes and tips for the book: Jamie Beers, Jennifer Belair, Rhys Bowen, CJ Box, Deb Burgess, Taffy Cannon, Stephanie Carmichael, Colleen Casey, Melissa Cerletti, Amber Collins, Debra Costa, Karen Dyer, Cheryl Edgren, Gina Hernandez, Vanessa Hodge, Mary Keenan, Sienna Kidd, Rena Leith, Maria Lima, Betty McBroom, Tracy McBroom, Joanne McCarthy, Pauline Meilsoe, Ann Parker, Annie Pearson, Courtney Rapa, Jody Repstad, Vicki Rose, Susie Sloan, Sue Stephenson, Barbara Swec, Pam Thomson, Diana Todd, Kelly Vasquez, Elaine Viets, Suzanne Vann, Susan Warner, Jenny Wong, and Sue Yura. Party on, girls!

A special thanks to my agents, Lilly Ghahremani and Stefanie Von Borstel, and my editor, Andrea Norville, for accepting the invitation!

Contents

Introduction

"You just reminded me of what's really important in life, friends, best friends."

~ Fried Green Tomatoes

We women love to gather with our friends. In fact, we'll use just about any excuse to get together and have a party. When we party without the men, we can let our hair down, gorge on chocolate, snort when we laugh, and generally be ourselves. But when it comes to hosting a party, we want it to be fresh, original, creative, and personal. Yet with our busy lifestyles, we don't have a lot of time—or money—to spend on celebrating the special events in our friends' lives.

So what do you do when another friend is pregnant—and you've already been to several showers this year. (In fact, if you never play the "Steal the Clothespin" game again it will be too soon.) So how do you plan a baby shower that your girlfriends will actually enjoy? Or a milestone birthday party that hasn't been done to death? Or any other occasion that calls for a party with flair?

Ladies' Night is here to help. Whether you have an upcoming book club meeting, a bachelorette party, a bride-to-be in need of a girls' night out, or a PMS-ing pal who just needs a good time, it's all here—more than seventy-five parties to choose from, all planned and ready to go! In *Ladies' Night*, you'll not only find popular parties such as wedding and baby showers, but you'll also discover cutting edge themes—everything from Red Hat to Redneck parties, Poker Night to Pity/Pamper parties. Plus, there's a bonus section filled with suggestions for offbeat holidays to celebrate throughout the year, such as Chocolate Day, Wear Something Gaudy Day, Swap Ideas Day, and Have a Bad Day Day.

Each party helps you combine your personal style while celebrating the guest of honor's individuality. It's a Do-It-Yourself-meets-*Sex and-the-City* guide to girl time, complete with intriguing invitations, dazzling decorations, creative costumes, cool games and activities, fun food, and festive favors. At the end of each party, you'll find a Party Plus with bonus tips and alternatives, when you want your party to go the extra mile. If you're like me, you'll want to host a party that's different, creative, and full of your own personal touches—like a mysterious night with Nancy Drew wannabes, a Wacky Wake to celebrate the death of singlehood, a Men-Are-Pigs party to get over a breakup, or a Crop 'Til You Drop scrapbooking gala.

Ladies' Night will show you how to bring your own flair to the parties you throw, no matter what the occasion. You'll find hundreds of ideas you can use interchangeably between parties to make each one unique and memorable. All you have to do is bring the spirit—*Ladies' Night* will do the rest.

So get your game on, girl. It's party time!

CHAPTER 1

Party Plans to Prep for Success

"The more you praise and celebrate your life, the more there is in life to celebrate."
~ *Oprah Winfrey*

All successful parties are based on good planning. You don't need to start the preparations months in advance, but the more time you have to pull together the party elements, the better. And even if you're short on time or want to throw together an impromptu gathering, take a few minutes to look over the following suggestions for planning the perfect party. That way you won't forget any of the important details that make a party so memorable and unique!

Who's Who Guest List

The first step in planning a good party is creating a compatible guest list. Opposites don't always attract, so don't include feuding friends or guests with agendas, aggressive personalities, or bad attitudes or you may find your party divided, or worse, under siege. And remember—you don't have to invite everyone. Keep the numbers manageable for the type of party you're hosting, so it remains comfortable and companionable.

Consider hosting separate parties if you have very different friends. You may want to have a sexy shower for your down-home girls to celebrate the upcoming nuptials, and a more sedate soiree for the guest of honor's relatives. That way everyone will have fun and be comfortable, and you'll be undisputed queen of wedding showers.

When planning your list, take into account your space. A crowded room doesn't lend itself to a comfortable event, so think about your space as you prepare your guest list. Likewise, a room that's too large makes a party feel less successful, even if it isn't. It's a fine balance between too many guests and too few, as well as too large a room and too small.

Finally, consider inviting a "special guest"—someone the guest of honor may not be expecting—for an extra surprise. That might be a distant relative, someone who has moved away, a favorite teacher or mentor, or other unexpected friend.

The Subject Is Themes

Bring the party into focus with a creative theme personalized to the guest of honor, event, or occasion. You can turn even the most common gathering, such as a baby or wedding shower, into a unique celebration, by using a little imagination when choosing a theme. Consider making your baby shower a "Big Mama" party where everyone wears padded tummies and maternity clothes, making your bridal shower a "Wacky Wedding" prenup party with guests dressed in old bridesmaid gowns, or making an over-the-hill birthday a "Wild Wake," and ask guests to wear black and veils to honor the death of another year—and the beginning of a new one. A theme gives your party a foundation for the invitations, decorations, games, and refreshments, and makes the details come together easily. Let your imagination go wild as you plan your party theme.

Fussy Budgets

I'm always on a budget, but I still want my parties to be special, so I'm a big fan of DIY (do it yourself). It's easy—and less expensive—if you brainstorm ways to provide great food that you've prepared ahead of time, such as mini-quiches made in cupcake tins; festive decorations that fit the theme, such as related posters, bold banners, colorful balloons, and crepe paper swags; and entertainment with creativity that doesn't involve taking out a loan, such as group games and crafty activities. Then once in a while you can afford to splurge on something spectacular when called for, such as a hired limo, spectacular centerpiece/cake, or special entertainer. You can also ask the guests to chip in for some of the special touches, or contribute to the party by helping with the food, decorations, favors, and gifts. Preparing for the party can be almost as much fun as the party itself, so get your friends to help out.

Set Design

Think of your party as theater, and add drama with detail in the decorations. If you're hosting a tropical theme party, add imaginative touches such as coconut place markers, sand pail serving bowls, and fishnet decorations on the walls. If it's a sexy bachelorette party, include some naughty decorations such as skimpy lingerie, pinups of male underwear models, and colorful condoms lollipops. Or if you're planning a bon voyage party, include decorations that fit the destination, so the guests can feel as if they're traveling too! Simple decorations, such as balloons and crepe paper, can be made to suit any theme, with a little creativity. You can make balloon bouquets to match your Wedding Rehearsal Shower, swag black crepe paper for a scary Halloween web entryway, or create sexy placemats using tabloid pictures of hot stars, depending on your theme. Just keep in mind that your party backdrop sets the stage for fun, creates an authentic atmosphere, and is key to a successful party.

Engaging Invitations

The party really starts when the invitations arrive, so send your guests creative cards with fun fillers. For example, for a High Tea Party, use doily decorated invitations, and add tea bags to the envelopes, so the guests will get a "taste" of what's coming. If you're hosting a Red Hat Party, cut out little hat shapes from red felt, decorate them with sequins and feathers, and write the party details on the back in permanent black marker. Then insert them into red envelopes. For a Welcome to the Neighborhood Party, write the party details on a map of the area. Label the houses of the invited guests, and include some important points of interest, such as the closest Starbucks! Then include a coffee gift card with each invitation! If you don't have time, you can always keep it easy with online e-vites.

Clothes and Costumes

Encourage the guests to dress for the occasion, whether it's fancy frocks or kooky costumes. You can go formal, with your best jewels and beautiful ball gowns, or keep it casual, with jeans and T-shirts or sweats. Include suggestions in the invitation for those who may need ideas. For example, if you're having a mystery party, tell guests to wear sleuth-style trench coats, police-looking uniforms and fake badges, or seductive spywear. If the party theme is craft-related, tell the girls to dress in artists' smocks or funny aprons. For a grownup slumber party, remind them to wear their favorite pajamas or sexy lingerie. Provide accessories for the costumes to suit the theme as well, such as boas for dress-up parties, chefs' hats for cooking parties, and fuzzy socks for a spa party. Appropriate outfits help the revelers get in the mood for fun.

Refreshing Refreshments and Dazzling Drinks

Girls get hungry when they party, so serve up simple but scrumptious snacks and decadent desserts to enjoy before and after the games and activities. You can make up the treats ahead of time and freeze them, then defrost them when it's party time, to save you time, energy, and money. Or buy them in bulk at the big box stores, then add your own touches, such as mini-quiches topped with fancy garnishes, tiny taquitos with different dipping sauces, or bite-sized cream puffs filled with a variety of ice cream flavors. A decorated cake doubles as a great centerpiece, so make it match the theme, such as a teddy bear-shaped baby shower cake, a movie ticket cake for video night, or a photo cake of the birthday guest of honor. And remember, any girl "Will Party For Chocolate!" so make sure you have plenty on hand, in the form of truffles, pastries, cookies, and candy. Girls also get thirsty, so pour the wine, beer, and latest fancy cocktails, such as Cosmopolitans or Appletinis, along with alcohol-free drinks for those who don't imbibe the hard stuff, such as cranberry juice cocktail or hot apple cider. You can make the coolest blended drinks with or without alcohol! Or turn the party into a DIY cocktail-making session! Have small bottles of water available to sip on during the party games and activities, or a variety of sodas with interesting flavors, such as raspberry, lemon-lime, or egg cream. If it's a super active party, offer high-energy drinks, such as Monster, Red Bull, or Gatorade. For a spa party, try health drinks, fruit smoothies, or herbal teas. For an end-of-the-party drink, whip up your own espressos, lattes, and mochas, or let the guests make their own coffee drinks with flavored creams, sugar crystal stirrers, whipped cream, and chocolate sprinkles.

Hip Hostess

Don't forget to be a good party hostess while enjoying your own party! Make sure you greet all the guests as they arrive and chat with them for a few minutes, to make them feel comfortable and at ease. Then point out the food and drink table to orient them, indicate the bathrooms if they haven't been to your home before, and show them where to place their coats and valuables. Introduce those who don't know each other, and mention a topic they may have in common, such as a new baby, a similar job, or the same club membership. Keep circulating to ensure everyone is having a great time, and engage those who are sitting or standing alone, or need a little assistance in meeting others.

It's also important to save your energy for the party, so try to set up the decorations and food ahead of time, so you can relax and enjoy yourself at the event. To keep from stressing out before the guests arrive, hop into a relaxing warm bath with a glass of wine or cup of tea and mentally go over the details of the party to make sure you haven't forgotten anything. Review the timing of the party events, such as when you want to serve the food, play the games, and open the gifts, so your party doesn't lag, then keep to your timetable. After your bath, pamper yourself a little with a new lotion or perfume, a special nail color or lipstick, an eye-catching necklace or hair clip, and sexy underwear, just to make you feel elegant!

Framing the Fun

Smart timing is key to party success, so plan the event from beginning to end. Choose a time of day or night that's workable for you and your friends—not too early, not too late. Memorize your schedule, from greeting the guests to saying goodbye, from starting the games to wrapping them up, from serving the food to cleaning up, and you'll find everything will fall into place in a timely manner. While you need to be flexible, just observe the guests and you'll be able to tell when it's time to move on to another part of the party plans. But if they're enjoying themselves, let it continue. Be sure to give the party an ending time and don't let it run too long or guests may become bored, intoxicated, or cranky. The best way to let the lingering guests know the party is over is to begin cleaning up. They'll either help you or head on out!

Gifts and Goodies

Make sure you have some creative favors and prizes that fit your theme for the guests so they can take away a memento of a marvelous time. You might offer fancy or cartoon coffee mugs for a cappuccino party, paperback mysteries and magnifying glasses for a sleuthing party, or scrapbooking tools for a scrappers party. You can give out great gifts on a budget, such as scented candles, fancy soaps, fragrant lotions, heart-shaped candy, costume jewelry, embossed journals, decorative boxes, small plants, and personalized stationery, if you think creatively and shop wisely. And be prepared to offer gift suggestions to the guests who want to bring along something special for the guest of honor. Check to see if she's registered somewhere, or simply ask her what she needs, so you can pass along ideas for those who are stuck. Remind the guests that something in keeping with the party theme would always be welcome, such as a cookbook for a food party, a video for a night at the movies, or a calendar for a New Year's Eve party. Wrap up the gifts in festive paper or use creative wrapping, such as the Sunday Funnies, a baby blanket, a bunch of nested boxes, or a tote bag, depending on the gift and the theme.

Less Mess

For a quick and easy cleanup, take up offers from any guests who volunteer to help. Use paper products, not only because they're festive and fit the theme, but they're easy to toss or recycle at the end of the fun. Wrap up extra food and send it home with the guests—unless you plan to eat it all yourself over the next few weeks. Box the decorations and save them—you may need them again for a repeat of your hit party. Or leave the decorations up for a few days to remind you of a fun time!

Making Memories

Capture the festivities with photos and videos, and keep them in frames or scrapbooks. Send the guests home with snapshots taken at the party and printed on your computer, or e-mail them after the party as a "Thank you for coming" surprise. Or download them onto your MySpace or YouTube and send the link. Either way, they'll enjoy sharing the memories of a wonderful time.

Now that you've planned your party from start to finish, it's time to choose a theme and get that party started! In the next chapter you'll find fun, fresh, and festive ideas for wedding showers to honor your engaged friend. If anyone asks who wants to host the party, simply say, "I do!"

CHAPTER 2

Wonderful Wedding Showers

"Spend the afternoon. You can't take it with you."

~ Annie Dillard

Showers are by far the most popular parties women host. Here you'll find all kinds of wedding-themed parties to suit every style, budget, and bride, from traditional get-togethers to today's cutting-edge gatherings. Feel free to mix and match the themes, games, activities, and refreshments, and adapt them to your needs. Just use your imagination and a little creativity and your party will be fresh, fun, and fabulous for the bride, the guests, and yourself as hostess.

She's Engaged! Party

Who says the Engagement Party has to include both bride and groom (besides Miss Manners)? Here's a girls-only gathering that will help the recently engaged gal get ready for the Big Day. Celebrate the bride-to-be's good news with a She's Engaged! Party, and gather her friends together to help her plan all the wedding-to-be details. At the end of the party, she'll take home a binder filled with billions of bridal ideas.

Invitations

Make collage invitations using bridal magazine pictures, to give the guests a glimpse of the fun to come. Glue pictures of gowns, cakes, and flowers onto white cards, add party details in fancy wedding script, along with requests for materials (see next page), and mail to guests. For added fun, include a toy diamond ring or a spoonful of rice in the envelope.

What to Bring

Ask the guests to bring along a couple of the following:

○ Bridal magazines, such as *Brides, Bridal Guide, Modern Bride, The Knot, Martha Stewart's Weddings, You and Your Wedding, Bridal Best Bets*, and so on.

○ A CD with a song that could be used at the reception, such as "A Moment Like This" by Kelly Clarkson, "At Last" by Etta James, "Somewhere Over the Rainbow" by IZ, "What a Wonderful World" by Louis Armstrong, "You're Still the One" by Shania Twain, "The Chicken Dance."

○ A small bouquet of flowers, such as posies, roses, hydrangeas, or baby's breath.

○ A fancy appetizer, homemade or purchased from a gourmet store or caterer, such as crab puffs, stuffed mushrooms, chilled shrimp, or cheese spreads.

○ A nice bottle of wine, such as Chardonnay, Merlot, Pinot Noir, Sauvignon Blanc, and so on.

○ Brochures from romantic places, such as a tropical island, a European city, an exotic cruise, or Disney World.

○ Great Web sites for wedding suggestions, information, and resources, such as: *www.theknot.com, www.weddingchannel.com, www.brides.com*, or *www.herecomestheguide.com*.

As the guests arrive, have them place their contributions on the appropriate tables.

Decorations

Set up a table full of scrapbooking and craft materials, with fancy paper, glue, tape, ribbon, and scissors. Buy a large binder or scrapbook for the bride to take home at the end of the party. Set out all the items on separate tables—one for the flowers, one for the appetizers, one for the wine. Place the magazines on the craft table, and have the CDs near the CD player for easy access.

Games and Activities

Entertain the guests with a few games and activities to make your party stand out. There's nothing worse than playing the same tired shower games, so try a few of the following suggestions to personalize your party and make it pop!

"Plan Your Wedding" Book Making

Prepare the binder or scrapbook with dividers, such as "Gowns and Bridesmaids Dresses," "Flowers and Decorations," "Wine and Cocktails," "Hors d'Oeuvre and Food," "Wedding and Reception Music," and "Honeymoon Spots." Sit around the table or on the floor, spread out the magazines, and have the guests rip out their favorite wedding items—bridal gowns, flowers, food, and honeymoon destinations. Secure them to the fancy paper with glue stick or double-sided tape, and insert the pages into the binder or book, with personal comments like, "You would look so beautiful in this with your red hair," or "My husband loved this song for the first dance."

While you work on the book:

○ Have a wine tasting to help the bride determine what wine she wants to serve at her wedding.

○ Sample the appetizers and make suggestions for the reception.

○ Play selected songs from the CDs so the bride can choose the best one for the first dance, the dance with her father, and so on.

○ Help her decide what kind of flowers would be best for the bouquet, the centerpieces, the corsages, and the reception room décor.

○ Suggest popular honeymoon sites and offer the bride brochures to take home.

This engaging activity offers your guests a relaxing time and a chance to chat while they "work." And the bride-to-be will be thrilled with the cooperative, finished product, which makes a lasting memento of the party—and the wedding plans.

Engagement Etiquette Quiz

Have your guests answer these Engagement Etiquette questions and see how savvy they are about party protocol.

1. Who usually hosts an engagement party?
   A. The bride's parents.
   B. The groom's mother.
   C. The girlfriends.
   D. A marriage counselor.
2. What kinds of gifts are given at an engagement party?
   A. Wedding gifts.
   B. Honeymoon gifts.
   C. Chocolate.
   D. No gifts.
3. Does the Bride-to-Be need a ring to be considered engaged?
   A. A ring is not required to get engaged.
   B. A ring is required and must be a diamond.

    C. A ring is required and should be pierced through your navel.

    D. Only if the ring comes from a Crackerjack box.

4. When should the engagement be announced?

    A. Soon after the question is popped and accepted.

    B. At least a day before the wedding.

    C. Before the baby is born.

    D. The second after she says, "Yes."

5. Who should be told about the engagement first?

    A. The bride's parents.

    B. The groom's parents.

    C. The bride-to-be's girlfriends.

    D. The registry consultant.

6. How is the wedding announced to the public?

    A. It's spread via beauty salons.

    B. Via your favorite radio station.

    C. It's announced in the society page of the newspaper.

    D. The mothers tell everyone.

7. Whom should you not invite to the engagement party?

    A. Anyone who's NOT invited to the wedding.

    B. Ex's.

    C. Strippers.

    D. All of the above.

Answer Key: 1:A, 2:D, 3:A, 4:A, 5:A, 6:C, 7:D

Award a funny prize at the end of the game to the guest who gets the most correct answers, such as a wedding garter, a fake diamond ring, a chocolate dove, or blowup "husband" doll.

Refreshments

Enjoy the wines and appetizers that guests have brought along for tasting. Add a few appetizers of your own that are popular at weddings, such as crab-stuffed mushrooms, lettuce wraps, or chicken skewers. Pour champagne to toast the bride-to-be and down it with slices from a mini-wedding cake. Even better, ask the bakery for wedding cake samples and let the guests taste them, then vote for their favorites. Don't forget chocolate, in the form of chocolate doves, chocolate rings, or spell out the name of the bride and groom in chocolate letters.

Favors, Prizes, and Gifts

The bride-to-be gets to take home the book full of wedding tips! Also give her a countdown calendar to keep track of everything and suggestions for where to register for wedding gifts.

Send the guests home with mini scrapbooks, crafts supplies with decorate-it-yourself frames, snapshots from the party for frames, a bottle of wedding bubbles, a box of chocolates wrapped in wedding paper, a candle in the bride's colors, or a romantic video or CD.

Party Plus

Ask a wedding consultant to come to the party and offer tips, ideas, and information! Or gather the girls and attend a bridal fair together.

"Here Comes the Bride" Wedding Shower

Shower the bride with gifts, games, and goodies at this traditional yet timely shower. The rules have changed—anyone can host a bridal shower today: Best friend, big sister, coworker, mother-in-law, or mother of the bride. Make "romance" your theme, with romantic music, aphrodisiac foods, and an amorous party mood. Then ask your guests to keep the theme in mind when buying a gift or planning an outfit.

Invitations

Copy photos of the bride and groom on quality paper and use them as card invitations to the shower. For fun, copy pictures of the couple from their childhood and pose them together. Glue the pictures onto red paper cut into heart shapes. Or copy the photos onto white fabric and sew them into small heart-shaped pillows. Add plastic gold rings, tiny white toy doves, elegant white ribbon, miniature bride-and-groom figurines, and fill the envelope with heart-shaped confetti or rice.

What to Wear

Ask your guests to come dressed in romantic outfits or evening wear. You might suggest they wear old bridesmaid dresses, prom gowns, or even rent a fabulous outfit for the occasion. Encourage them to go big with the hats, and add romantic touches, such as hearts or flowers.

Decorations

Greet the guests with a balloon canopy just inside the door, using helium balloons tied to string. Hang red and pink streamers on the ceiling and along the walls. Fill the room with votive candles shaped like hearts or flowers. Set out single roses in small bud vases filled with colored rice. Tie white or pink ribbon to the candleholders and bud vases and shape them into bows. Hang paper hearts from the ceiling. Play romantic music in the background. Collect snapshots of the bride and groom throughout their childhood, mount them on fancy wedding-themed paper, and hang them on the walls. Begin with the youngest pictures at opposite ends, then have them meet with the latest photos in the middle.

Make a Romance Basket Centerpiece by filling a large basket with romantic items the bride and groom can enjoy on their honeymoon, such as bath oils and soft towels, sexy underwear and massage oil, restaurant gift certificate and movie tickets, romantic CDs and champagne. Or make a Wedding Cake Centerpiece by rolling up towels in the bride's selected colors, beginning with a washcloth, then a hand towel, then a bath towel. Secure the ends to form round "layers," and place on a fancy plate or doily. Decorate the "cake" with loops of ribbons and tiny flowers, and top with a bride-and-groom figurine or heart-shaped soaps.

Games and Activities

For the games and activities, keep the focus on romance with a side of sexiness. The more you personalize the games, such as the following Husband-to-Be quiz, the more laughs you'll get, and the more the bride-to-be will enjoy herself. Below you'll find a variety of wedding-related fun and games.

Honeymoon Night Gift Opening Game

As the bride opens her gifts, discreetly write down her comments, such as "Oooh, I've never had one of these before" or "What an amazingly cute tiny package!" or "This will look great on me" or "Do you think it will fit?" Listen for comments that can be used as double entendres for the wedding night. When she's finished with the gifts, announce to the group that whatever the bride-to-be said while opening her presents predicts what she'll say on her honeymoon night. Then read her comments aloud and watch her turn red while the rest of the group has a good laugh.

"How Well Do You Know Your Future Husband" Quiz

Sometime before the party, ask the groom-to-be a series of questions, such as "Who said 'I love you' first?" "Where did you first kiss your bride-to-be?" "What was the first meal you had together?" "What does she do that irritates you?" and "What do you like most about your future bride?" Ask him to keep all of this secret from the bride-to-be. At game time, ask her questions about the groom to see how well she knows her future mate. For added fun, have the groom show up as a surprise and give the correct answers after she's guessed.

Put the Kiss on the Groom (à la Pin the Tail on the Donkey)

Have a copy store make a blowup poster of the groom. Pin the poster on the wall, then give each guest a lipstick sticker, or pass around a real lipstick and have the guests use a cotton swab to collect the lip color and spread it on their lips. Blindfold them one at a time, spin them around, and have them try to "kiss" the groom on the lips. When it's the bride-to-be's turn, turn the poster upside down while she's being blind-folded, and see where she ends up kissing the groom.

Create a Rehearsal Bow-quet

Here's a colorful and festive stand-in for the bride's bouquet for the wedding rehearsal. Give one guest a paper plate and some scissors, and have her collect all the ribbons and bows from the shower gifts as the bride opens her present. Use the scissors to poke holes in the paper plate and to trim the ribbons that are too long. Stuff the ends of the bows and ribbons into the paper plate holes and secure them in place with tape until the plate is completely filled with colorful bows. Give the complete bow-quet to the bride.

Refreshments

Serve romantic foods, such as baked Brie, croissant sandwiches, quiche, a buffet of salads, and drinks like pink champagne with maraschino cherries, strawberry daiquiris, or fruit punch. For a favorite wedding shower drink, try a Bridalpolitan: Combine 1 part raspberry vodka with one-half part Cointreau, one part cranberry juice, and a squeeze of lime. Mix in a shaker with ice and pour into chilled martini glasses. Top with a fresh raspberry. For dessert, offer petit fours, chocolate-dipped strawberries, frosted ladyfingers, chocolate éclairs, raspberry sherbet in champagne glasses, a cake topped with flowers or rings, or a miniature wedding cake.

Favors, Prizes, and Gifts

For prizes and favors, give boxes of candy, mini bottles of wine, romance novels, romantic CDs or DVDs, heart- or flower-shaped soaps or candles, sex tip books, love lotions, silk roses, or sexy panties. Gifts for the bride-to-be are usually easy, since most brides are registered at a local department store or boutique. But you can add a personal touch related to the theme, such as sexy music, bubble bath, personalized stationery or return labels with new return address, nameplate for front door, photo album for wedding pictures, scrapbook with party photos and mementoes, books about love, marriage, and sex, an elegant frame for the wedding invitation, or a bed and breakfast gift certificate.

Party Plus

Make a Bride's Wedding Day Survival Kit. Buy a small cloth bag and have the guests fill it with the following wrapped items to help her make it through the big day: breath mints, lotion, lip balm, deodorant, perfume, bobby pins, small mirror, hand-held fan, pain reliever.

Wedding/Honeymoon Preview Shower

Prepare the future bride for her upcoming wedding with a themed party that previews her chosen wedding site or give her a party themed around her honeymoon destination. By choosing based on her choice of wedding location or honeymoon destination, the party will be personalized and unique.

Invitations

Match the invitations to the theme and give them a creative touch. For example, if the wedding will take place at a winery, choose a wine theme and make invitations by creating personalized wine bottle labels, circular wine glass IDs, or miniature bottles of wine with details attached. If the wedding is to be held outside in a garden setting, make invitations by writing party details on lengths of ribbon and tie them to silk flowers, flower seed packets, or floral garlands. If the couple plans a tropical locale for the honeymoon, send the guests postcards of the site, with party details added. If the honeymooners are leaving for a cruise, mail out brochures or small plastic boats with party details added.

What to Wear

For a wedding in the garden theme, the guests might dress for a classic garden party, à la Daisy in *The Great Gatsby* or Scarlett in *Gone with the Wind*, and come dressed in long, full skirts, bonnets, and gloves. Or have them come as green-thumbed gardeners for fun, dressed in overalls, with straw hats and gardening gloves. For a honeymoon theme, guests can dress in Hawaiian shirts, grass skirts, and leis, or wear safari gear for a Rainforest Trek, such as khaki shorts and shirts, hiking boots, and Indiana Jones hats. Better yet, have them come as tacky tourists just along for the ride, dressed in mismatched outfits (plaid and stripes), knee-high socks with athletic shoes, baseball caps, and the ubiquitous camera-around-the-neck and sunglasses accessories.

Decorations

If the wedding is to be held in a winery, buy artificial grapes and vines from the craft store and turn the room into a winery. Set out unusual bottles of wine, such as "Mad Housewife" or "Oops!" Blow up purple and green balloons, group them together in "bunches," and add them to the party décor as giant grapes. Label tables with types of wine, such as Chardonnay, Merlot, and Pinot Grigio, and use bottles surrounded by grapes as centerpieces.

If the bride-to-be is headed for a romantic honeymoon in Paris, recreate a Parisian café for the party. Play French music, such as Edith Piaf, in the background. Cover tablecloths in French Country designs and colors. Print out mini menus in French. Add baskets of silk flowers and balloons in red, white, and blue, the colors of the French flag.

Games and Activities

Here are a couple of games that will add a few laughs to the party. Feel free to borrow games from the other showers in the book, if they fit your theme and group. Most are easily interchangeable.

Meant for Each Other

Write up a number of questions to ask the guests regarding the engaged couple's relationship, and give three choices for the answer, including the correct one (check with bride-to-be for the right answers) and a funny one. For example, you might ask,

- Where did the couple meet? 1. A bar. 2. A blind date. 3. Hooters.

- What was her first reaction to him? 1. Shock and Awe. 2. Repulsion. 3. Who was that?

- What attracted her the most? 1. His piercing blue eyes. 2. His hairy chest. 3. None of your business.

- Why is she marrying him? 1. For his body. 2. For his personality. 3. For his mother.

Have the bride-to-be answer the questions while the guests check their answers against hers, to determine the winner.

Refreshments

For a Wedding Site Theme held at a winery, try a wine tasting and offer wine and cheese, grape fruit salad, and chocolate. If it's a garden party, serve garden salads and veggies, mimosas, and carrot cake. For a country club theme, offer dainty sandwiches, champagne, and a mini wedding cake. If it's a Honeymoon Theme, and the destination is Paris, set out French bread and cheeses, French pasties, French wine, and café au laits. For a romantic honeymoon cruise, serve a seafood buffet, crab cakes, and shrimp cocktail. For a tropical paradise setting, give the guests fruit salad, shish kebab, mai tais, and pineapple upside-down cake.

Favors, Prizes, and Gifts

For the Wedding Site theme, send the guests home with wine, corsages, or candles, or other decorative items related to the theme. For a Honeymoon theme, give them leis, French wine, and scented soaps. Or give the bride-to-be a gift related to the trip, such as a guidebook, map, translation dictionary, luggage tags, and so on.

Party Plus

Make it a surprise party! Don't tell the bride-to-be your plans for a girls-only engagement party. Or take her away for a spa day, treat her to a salon makeover, shop for a new honeymoon outfit, or go look for wedding gifts as a group.

Princess Bride Shower

Every woman wants to feel like a princess on her wedding day. After all, she's probably dreamed of this day most of her life. She's met her Prince

Charming and she's ready to live happily ever after, whether it's in a castle, a cottage, or a condo. So why wait any longer to place that crown on her head? Host a royal celebration with all her maids-in-waiting, spend a few enchanted hours giving her a princess makeover, and send her to her dreamy prince in a shower of fantasy fun.

Invitations

Cut out a picture of a princess dress or the bride-to-be's actual gown, then superimpose her head on the dress. Photocopy it onto card stock and cut it into a paper doll. Write party details on the back and mail to guests in envelopes filled with sparkly confetti or colored rice.

Or invite the guests with purse-shaped invitations, adding details inside, along with costume or candy jewelry, lip-gloss, or hair ribbons for added princess fun. Or buy glittery gold crowns, write the party details on the inside, and hand deliver or mail in small boxes to guests.

What to Wear

Ask the ladies-in-waiting to wear their old prom dresses or best ball gowns, including their jewels. Treat them to plastic silver crowns when they arrive. Or head to the thrift shop and buy princess accessories, such as tulle skirts, tutus, high-heeled shoes, gold crowns, jeweled tiaras, rhinestone or charm bracelets, boas, costume and candy jewelry, gaudy rings, hair accessories, fancy sunglasses, and star wands or pinwheels. Then let the guests play dress-up.

Decorations

Turn the party room into a magical castle. Roll out a red carpet to greet the guests as they arrive. Hang a banner reading, "Welcome to Castle (Last name.)" Trim the room with white lights. Place pink banners around the room with the names of all the princess guests. Fill the area with pink balloons and streamers, large tissue paper flowers, glitter, and confetti. Turn the guest of honor's chair into a throne by wrapping it with ribbon and bows. Use a pink pillow for a seat. Set the table with pink tablecloth and paper products. Create a centerpiece out of princess dolls, crowns, wands, or jewelry.

Games and Activities

In keeping with the Princess theme, gather the maids for some royal challenges, and turn them into fairy princesses with a flick of your magic wand.

Princess Makeover

Give the bride-to-be a makeover to show her some possible looks for her wedding day. Have one of the guests do her makeup, or hire a beautician to do it. Get out the curling iron and heat up a headful of curls, then arrange her hair in various styles. Take pictures as you go, so the bride-to-be can choose the look she prefers.

Kiss the Prince (the Groom)

Hang an enlarged picture of a frog on the wall. Blindfold the guests one at a time, have them place lip-shaped stickers or real kisses on the frog. The winner gets a cute little stuffed or plastic frog that may one day turn into a prince.

Your Prince Has Come

Have the groom dress up like a Prince (try the costume shop), and ask him to make a special surprise appearance. Tell him to prepare to recite a couple of lines of romantic poetry for added fun. Ask him to bring along some roses, a tiny gift of jewelry for the bride to wear at her wedding, or a box of chocolates, too.

Princess Potential

Give the guests and bride-to-be a quiz to determine their Princess Potential. If you grew up wanting to be a princess, the questions should be easy! The one with the best score wins the crown. Here are some suggested questions to get the game going.

1. What's the name of the stepsisters' cat in *Cinderella*?
2. What was Princess Diana's official title?
3. To whom should a princess curtsy?
4. How does one become a princess?
5. Who became a princess after a successful career in Hollywood?
6. Who is Princess Leia's brother?
7. What is the name of the Princess in *Enchanted*?
8. Name the Seven Dwarfs.

Answer Key: *1: Lucifer, 2: Diana, Princess of Wales, 3: Only those who have a higher ranking such as the queen and king, 4. Marry into the royal family or be the daughter of the king and queen, 5: Grace Kelly, Princess Grace of Monaco, 6: Luke Skywalker, 7: Giselle, 8: Happy, Sleepy, Grumpy, Sneezy, Bashful, Dopey, and Doc.*

Refreshments

Cut dainty sandwiches using princess cookie cutters shaped like tiaras, wands, castles, or frog-princes. Fill a teapot with pink lemonade or pink champagne and pour it into pretty punch glasses. Serve a Princess Cake by baking a cake mix in an ovenproof bowl. Turn out cake, cool, then insert a Barbie doll in the middle (one with the same hair and skin color as the bride). Frost the cake and bodice of doll with pink frosting, using a star tip. Or make it look like the bride using white frosting. The cake will look like the doll's dress.

Favors, Prizes, and Gifts

Fill pink bags or purses with princess goodies, such as lip-gloss, costume necklaces, rings, bracelets, stick-on earrings, hair clips, feather pens, heart tattoos, tiaras, wands, boas, and candy. For those who don't have a prince yet, give them stuffed, rubber, or bendable frogs.

Wacky Wedding Rehearsal

Who says the bridal shower has to be prim and proper? Shake it up a little with a Wacky Wedding Rehearsal and host a Tony 'n' Tina style mock wedding, just like the Broadway hit musical, *Tony 'n' Tina's Wedding*, full of gags, gifts, and giggles! (It's up to you whether you want to invite the Tonys, or just keep it to the Tinas.) This party should relieve any stress the bride-to-be might be feeling as the wedding plans progress. Just be prepared to laugh—not cry—at this unconventional rehearsal.

Invitations

Send out invitations that have a theme-within-a-theme, such as a Mafia slant, a Redneck flavor, or even a Spoiled Socialite feeling—whatever works for your crowd. Here are some examples to get you started.

Mafia Theme Invitation

Hey Youse,

The Godmother Wants Ya At
A Matrimony Rehearsal for Our Princess (Name here)
Includes All You Can Eat Spaghetti—Bring Your Own Chianti
Ya coming or what?

RSVP: Godmother (Your info here)

Redneck Invitation

Mr. and Mrs. Billy Bob Fudd
Request the Honor of your Presents (sic)
At the Shotgun Wedding Rehearsal
For their Precious Bridezilla
(Bride's name here)

Please Wear Something Decent
No Weapons or Dogs, Please

Spoiled Socialites Invitation

Listen, Dahling!
We're hosting a Designer Rehearsal Party
For our Best Bride-to-be (Name here)!
Bring Your Coach Bag, Tiny Doggy, and iPod.
Wear Something Fab, Glam, and Glitzy
And be ready to party for the paparazzi!
iPhone or TXT your RSVP: (Your name here)

What to Wear

Have the guests come dressed for the wedding rehearsal to match the theme—Mafia Moll, Redneck Gal, or Spoiled Socialite style. Or head for the thrift store and buy a bunch of wacky accessories to lend guests for the evening, such as fur wraps, sequined vests, feathered hats, beaded gloves, garish costume jewelry, and so on. Or buy some old bridesmaids gowns—the uglier, the better—and have the guests put them on at the party. Surprise the bride with a tacky bridal gown, rented from a costume shop or found at the thrift shop, and have her slip into it for the upcoming "rehearsal." Be sure to have your cameras ready for a hilarious group shot—and possible blackmail material.

Decorations

You'll want to make the rehearsal room as tacky as possible, so go overboard on the decorations and details, in keeping with the theme. For a Mafia Rehearsal Party, try black balloons, as if in mourning rather than in celebration, and add black crepe paper streamers, funeral flowers, and posters from *The Godfather*, *Goodfellas*, or *The Sopranos*. If it's a Redneck Rehearsal, make sure nothing matches—leftover balloons from a kid's party, weeds for flowers, etc. (Check out the Redneck Party on page 189 for more suggestions.) The Socialite's Rehearsal room should be filled with designer fun—small stuffed animals, knockoff bags, and lots of glitter and bling. Set a long table to seat everyone, and cover it with a tablecloth to match the theme—red-and-white checked, an old printed sheet, or a shiny foil cloth—with utensils to match—or not. Don't forget appropriate centerpieces: Wine bottles with melted wax dripped down the sides, buckets of ice with beer bottles, or knockoff handbags. Clear an area for the bride to walk down the aisle, roll out a red carpet, and set up a makeshift altar. Using the couple's wedding colors—or all white—create a wedding canopy by swagging crepe paper streamers across the ceiling, letting the ends drop to the floor. Set up the chairs like pews, decorated with white or colored ribbons. On posterboard, write up some wedding vows in fancy script, but change the words so they're personalized to fit the bride. Include some humor or write it in silly rhyme. For added fun, ask the guests to bring a copy of their wedding photos to the shower. Tape up the pictures around the room or set them out on the mantel, coffee table, and end tables. Add funny captions, for a laugh.

Games and Activities

Center the festivities around the bridal theme—with a twist—and you'll soon have the guests laughing in the aisles.

Walk the Plank—er, Aisle

Now the fun begins. Begin with a Practice Walk Down the Aisle—only make it a challenge. Once the bride is dressed and ready, act as Wedding Coordinator and assign the guests to various tasks—stand-ins for the nervous Groom, cocky Best Man, bitchy Maid of Honor, clueless Bridesmaid, drunk Father of the Bride, emotional Mother of the Bride, disapproving future Mother-in-Law, disobedient Flower Girl, hippy Minister/Priest/Rabbi, etc. Then start the rehearsal, encouraging everyone to ad-lib their roles. Write some humorous vows for the bride to recite, for added fun. Don't forget to videotape!

Toast the Toasted Bride

After the rehearsal, it's time for the celebratory dinner. Essentially, after a good serving of wine to loosen tongues, this is when all hell breaks loose. Have each of the "guests" roast—er, toast—the bride, with humorous speeches and anecdotes.

Predict the Bride's Future

Gather in small groups with scrapbooks and a variety of magazines, everything from *Guns and Ammo* to *Sesame Street*. Have the groups put together a page that represents the bride's future: her home, her children, her pets, her career, her car, her hobbies, and her dreams. The catch: Make sure the predictions are outrageous, such as a picture of a trailer for her home, a little devil for a child, ants for her pets, and so on.

Bride Charades

On separate sheets of paper, write down a number of typical events that might occur on the bride's wedding day, such as, "The bride getting her hair done," "The groom forgetting to come to the church on time," "The father of the bride giving her away," "The best man giving a drunken speech at the reception," "The flower girl going down the aisle," "The priest pronouncing the bride and groom, 'Man and wife,'" "The bride smashing cake into the groom's face." Fold up the papers and place them in two separate bowls. Divide the group into two teams for a game of Bride Charades. Have them take turns drawing an activity and acting it out for the other team. If you prefer, instead of teams, have the guests each take a turn acting out an event for the bride, and have her try to guess what's happening.

Gag Gift

When the speeches are finished, have the bride-to-be open her gag gifts. If the guests need ideas, suggest the following: Flannel nightgown (for frightened virgin), sex manual (to learn how), sex toy (could be anything), vibrator (in case the bride needs help), *TV Guide* (for boring honeymoon night), funny video (*Father of the Bride, Knocked Up, License to Wed*), corny or funny "romantic" music (Barry Manilow, Weird Al, gospel), pinup poster (Brad Pitt, Jack Sparrow/Johnny Depp, a wrestling star).

Refreshments

If you've given your party an additional theme, such as a Mafia Party, make it Italian, with classic spaghetti and meatballs, red wine, and cannolis for dessert. The Redneck Party requires a tuna casserole, green Jell-O, beer, and Twinkies. And at the party, serve tiny sandwiches, lots of salads, Cosmopolitans or other in-vogue cocktails, and Godiva chocolates for dessert.

Make your own bride and groom cookies out of gingerbread or sugar cookie dough, and decorate them to look like the real bride and groom. You can also use the cookies as an activity at the party and let the guests decorate them, using a little creativity and imagination.

Order a miniature wedding cake from the bakery or bake your own, using three sizes of cake pans, with the cakes stacked on top of each other and frosted elaborately with iced ribbons, flowers, and a sugar bride and groom. Or be creative with the cake and make it square, triangular, shaped in the letters of the bride's name, or her new home.

Favors, Prizes, and Gifts

Send the rehearsal revelers home with mementoes of the wacky wedding party, such as incriminating snapshots, tacky centerpieces, flashy thrift shop accessories, and sex manuals. And packs of gum go well with all three party themes!

Party Plus

Have the party in a backroom of a restaurant to make it feel more authentic—just not the one you've decided to use for the rehearsal dinner. They may not want you back after this wacky wedding party.

Check out Appendix A for more shower ideas, games, and activities.

CHAPTER 3

Bawdy Bachelorette Parties

"Love: a temporary insanity, curable by marriage."

~ Ambrose Bierce

Bachelorette parties are hotter than ever thanks to all the online sources for decadent decorations and party props, especially Girls' Night Out—and In. Luckily there are lots of ways to celebrate this "last fling at freedom." You'll find wild parties, wacky parties, and one-of-a-kind parties to help you send the bachelorette kicking, screaming—and laughing—into matrimony. Begin by deciding what kind of party fits the bride-to-be and her BFFs—Best Friends Forever. Do they like to get down, cut loose, and really have fun? Or do they prefer a titillating party with a little sexy innuendo on the side? Also consider the bride's personality—is she wild and wacky or shy and subdued? Do her hobbies include pushing the envelope, like rock-climbing, or quietly collecting stamps? Is she a high-powered exec at her job, or does her career lean toward the low-key? Take into consideration all of these points when planning her party, and it will be more personal for her—and her guests.

Bad Girl Bachelorette Bash

Revel in a risqué bachelorette bash for the bride-to-be's last night as a single gal. With the wedding looming ahead, she needs a chance to cut loose, forget about all those lost wedding invitations, wrong-size bridesmaid shoes, and overpriced buffet bids. Here are some tips to help make the blushing bride blush a little more—at her Bad Girl Bachelorette Bash.

Invitations

To set the mood for the off-color celebration, send party invitations written on colored condoms. With a permanent marker, write: "It's Sue's Bachelorette Party—and we've got you covered!" or "Protect yourself against dull parties!" and add the party details written as "Instructions for use." Or use "Rubbergrams," custom-made condom invitations that magically appear in water-filled plastic jars (from *www.rubbergrams .com*). Ask the guests to bring gifts decorated creatively with condoms. For example, you might tie a couple of condoms onto the straps of a skimpy nightgown, glue some colored condom packs onto a box of massage oils, or tie them at the top of the gift-wrapped package as a bow.

What to Wear

Ask the guests to come dressed as slutty and skanky as they wanna be, in skimpy halter-tops, net stockings, and peek-a-boo thongs. Or really spice it up and come as Hooters waitresses, sexy cheerleaders, or Playboy Bunnies. Or wear hot pants with wild or lacy tights and too-tight T-shirts stuffed with balloons or fake boobs (available at the party and costume stores). Add to the fun by providing a variety of sexy/sleazy accessories to tart up the outfits. Check thrift stores for inexpensive, over-the-top items such as sequined vests, feather wraps, stiletto heels, gaudy jewelry, even wild wigs. Dare the girls to wear their "new" outfits out on the town—if they have the nerve. Don't forget the top and bottom—big teased hair and stiletto-heeled shoes. Adorn them with corsages made from ribbed and colored condoms, tied together with ribbon.

Decorations

Decorate the party room with condoms, some blown up, others tied together to make streamers, and giant joke condoms as a centerpiece. Buy a variety of sex toys and set them around the room. Hang up posters of shirtless (or pantless) male models. Play bad girl disco music by Donna Summer or hot hip-hop by Christina Aguilera. Light candles for a sexy ambiance and drape colorful scarves over a few lamps. Check out online bachelorette sites (see Appendix C) for sexy items you can buy to spice up the place.

Games and Activities

Offer a combination of sexy stunts and romantic activities to please all the guests. And check out other game suggestions in the rest of the Bachelorette Parties, then mix and match them to suit your group.

Condom Games

1. Give all the guests a condom. The first player to blow up a condom and get it to pop wins a prize.
2. Have guests race to get a condom over a banana.
3. Challenge players to fill up a condom with jelly beans within one minute. The condom with the most jelly beans wins.
4. Play Strip Poker and use colored condoms as poker chips.
5. Set out condoms and have the guests use them to create something fun and unique for the wedding night.

Bridal Ho

Have the bride strip down to her underwear and give her a slip to put on. Then dress her up in a crepe paper bridal gown, designed for the Pamela Anderson style of bride. Offer sheets of crepe paper as well as streamers, along with tape, to help keep the outfit together. Encourage the players to make the gown as elaborate (and tacky) as possible, with lots of crepe paper bows, ruffles, and flowers. Take pictures for the groom to enjoy on his wedding night.

Bad Girl Chick Flicks

Celebrate the bride-to-be's last night with a video marathon of romantic movies featuring her favorite hunks, such as *Don Juan Demarco, Legends of the Fall,* or *The Notebook,* or sexy movies like *Basic Instinct, 9½ Weeks,* or *Cruel Intentions.* For laughs, show videos that reveal the lighter side of marriage, such as *Runaway Bride, Ex-Wives Club, Wedding Crashers,* or *Mr. and Mrs. Smith.* Then play a movie trivia game and ask questions about the films.

Refreshments

Sexy drinks are a must, with such names as "Sex on the Beach," "Blow Job," and "Screaming Orgasm." You can find lots of recipes on the Internet under "Drink recipes," but here are a few to get you started.

- Sex on the Beach: Combine 1 ounce of vodka, ¾ ounce peach Schnapps, ½ ounce cranberry juice, and ½ ounce grapefruit juice; pour over ice in a highball glass.

- Blow Job: Combine ½ ounce Baileys Irish Crème, ½ ounce Kahlua Coffee Liqueur, and ½ ounce whipped cream in a shot glass; cover mouth and knock it back.

- Screaming Orgasm: Combine 1 ounce vodka, 1½ ounces Baileys Irish Crème, and ½ ounce Kahlua coffee liqueur; pour over crushed ice and stir.

Buy naughty ice cube trays at an adult novelty store. Serve chocolate in the shape of penises or make your own with plastic candy forms. Bake a cake in the shape of a penis.

Favors, Prizes, and Gifts

Give the guests suggestive (temporary) tattoos, condom-shaped suckers, naughty chocolates, or sexy gag gifts from Spencer's Gifts. If the guests need ideas for the Bad Bride, suggest sexy (or edible) panties, chocolate body lotions, erotic novels, sex toys, a soft-porn video, or gift certificates to Frederick's of Hollywood.

Party Plus

Have a Sex Toy Party and invite a sales rep to show and tell about her products.

Or take a field trip to a sex store and explore all the options available.

Girls' Night Out Bachelorette Party

The classic and most popular bachelorette party—a night on the town with your girlfriends—never goes out of style. This is the time when girls, both single and married, can live out their fantasies for a few hours before returning to their real lives. Dress up in your sexiest outfits, hop in the limo, and head for a night of pub-hopping madness, the perfect way to entertain—and embarrass—the bride-to-be. Begin at your home for drinks, then hire a limo to drive your girl gang to the hot spots in town for dancing, drinks—and dares. Anything goes. After all, no one will remember much in the morning, so why not get a little crazy. It's time to tackle those bars and brew pubs in style.

Invitations

Make your own creative invites to prepare the girls for the upcoming night on the town. Visit a few bars you're planning to include during your Girls' Night Out and collect some logo-embossed cocktail napkins. Then write the party details on a couple of the napkins (just like you do when you take the phone numbers of cute guys). Blot a lipstick kiss at the bottom or add a fake phone number for Orlando Bloom or David Beckham, such as 555-1234 (or your own phone number), and mail the napkins to your party pals. If you're hiring a limo to drive you during your pub crawl, ask the company for some brochures. Use them as stationery/invitations by adding the party details in red marker. Include a "treasure hunt" map of the bar scene so the guests will be forewarned of the proposed stopovers. Create your own personalized invitation that looks like a scavenger hunt list. Write the party details in the form of a checklist, such as:

- ○ Come to a Girls' Night Out Party! (check)

- ○ Arrive at 8:00 P.M. (check)

- ○ Bring a sexy gift for the bachelorette! (check)

Also list the bars you'll be hitting, and leave those check boxes blank, to be filled in later.

What to Wear

Have the girls wear their hottest club outfits for their night on the town. Or ask them to dress alike, all in white T-shirts, with the name of the event on the front and back in puffy pens, fabric markers, or iron-on letters. Label the shirts with the name of the bride and the theme, such as "Becca's Last Night!" "Girls' Night Out," or "Becca's Bachelorette Bar Bash 2008!" Take along some permanent markers and let all the hot guys (and your girlfriends) graffiti the shirts. Bonus points if you can read anyone's handwriting the next day! Set out a supply of sparkling face makeup, shiny eye shadows, brilliant wet lipsticks, and mascara in shades of blue, green, or violet. Don't forget to paint your nails outrageous colors and add a few glow-in-the-dark tattoos. If you want the blushing bachelorette to feel extra special, accessorize her with a sexy garter, a giant plastic engagement ring around her neck, and a mini bridal veil. (For extra credit, decorate her veil with condoms!)

Decorations

The nice thing about hosting a night on the town is: NO CLEAN-UP! There's also very little decorating involved, but you can do a few things to add to the barroom atmosphere if you like, such as decorate the limo. Ask the driver to come half an hour early so you can fill the car with festive crepe paper and balloons. In fact, the more balloons the better, to greet the bride-to-be as she steps inside. Add a few party signs or bachelorette party props inside the limo or car, such as colored condoms, a giant rubber penis, edible underwear, or gummy penises to snack on. Attach balloons, streamers, and paper flowers to the outside of the limo, to let everyone know that something special is going on, with a sign on the back that reads, "Stop her! She's about to be married!" Ask the guests to decorate their outfits with party paraphernalia—crepe paper, ribbons, balloons, and bows. That way you can take the party decorations with you on your night out.

Games and Activities

You can begin the party fun by playing a few warm-up games over drinks before heading out. Just check out the other bachelorette parties for ideas. Then try the ones below while you're out on the town.

Sexy Scavenger Hunt

Here's a game to play while you're on your pub crawl—a scavenger hunt, with a sexy twist! First, prepare a list of scavenger hunt stunts and objects the bride-to-be must perform or find, such as:

- ○ Take a picture of the bar's urinals.

- ○ Dance with a stripper.

- ○ Kiss the first guy you see in the bar.

- ○ Get a guy's boxers or briefs.

- ○ Buy a drink for a red-haired guy.

- ○ Ask a strange guy for a condom.

- ○ Sip a drink between a guy's legs.

- ○ Get a guy to buy you a drink.

- ○ Get the phone number of the cutest guy at the bar.

- ○ Bring a sex toy and ask a guy if he knows what it is.

- ○ Flash a guy from the car.

- ○ Get some chest hairs.

- ○ Sell a condom to a guy.

- ○ Ask for a Blow Job (it's a drink!).

- ○ Get a Viagra pill.

If you take pictures of all the stunts using a digital camera, you can put the pictures together in an album when you get back to the party site.

Suck for a Buck

While you're out on the town, here's a great way to meet new guys—and embarrass the bachelorette! First, gather the following items:

○ T-shirt

○ Fabric pens or permanent markers

○ Lifesaver candies

○ 2 red-hot candies, optional

○ Nontoxic white glue, optional

1. The night before the party, lay the T-shirt on the table and write the words "Suck for a Buck" all over the shirt with the pens. Add hearts, lips, or other fun art if you like.
2. Wet the candies and stick them all over the front of the shirt. The candies will dry overnight and stick. (You can also use a nontoxic glue to secure them if you prefer.)
3. Place the two red-hot candies in a couple of strategic places on the shirt, if you get my drift.
4. Dress the bride in the shirt and have guys pay a buck to eat the candies off.
5. Charge double for the red hots!

Out of Your Comfort Zone

Instead of the usual pickup bar scene, try some place wild and new that you've never been before—and wouldn't ordinarily go—such as:

○ Strip joint—just to watch!

○ Playboy club—to check out your competition

○ Dance club—where you can rock

○ Pool hall—for a "pickup" game

○ Brew hall—to do some beer tasting

○ Gay bar—meet some fabulous new friends

○ Country western bar—to check out the cowboys

○ Sleazy bar—how low can you go?

Refreshments

If you plan to do a lot of drinking at the bars, keep the guests well fed so they don't become too intoxicated. That can ruin a fun time. Start the party with a snack bar or light meal, or hit the fast-food restaurants after every bar visit to pick up some munchies. You might even share a pizza in the limo as you ride from pub to pub. Stash some chips, crackers, cheese, nuts, and fruit aboard the limo, so you can snack between bars. Then stop by an all-night diner after your night out, and have a hearty breakfast to help sober you up. While at the bars, try some of the fun new concoctions that are popular today. Ask the bartender to whip up a "Blow Job," "Sex on the Beach," "Screaming Orgasm," "Purple Hooter," "Fucking Banana," and so on—and make the embarrassed bachelorette ask for them! Have a taste test and try to name the ingredients in each drink. Then just keep those dynamite drinks coming!

Favors, Prizes, and Gifts

When it's time for the guests to drag themselves home, give them a favor or gift to remember the evening by, since they'll probably need some help after all those "Purple Hooters" and "Screaming Orgasms." Here are some suggestions for quick, easy, and inexpensive Girls' Night Out gifts: Cocktail napkins, a set of drink coasters, personalized T-shirts, jewel tattoos, packages of Lifesavers, disposable cameras, hangover kit (aspirin, washcloth, eyeshades, tomato juice), fancy drink glass, male blowup doll, popular cocktail recipes book, bar logo T-shirt, club accessories (party purse, feather boa, dangle earrings, sexy necklace, jeweled bracelet), photo album for the blackmail pictures. . . .

Party Plus

You can use this theme for a milestone birthday party, a get-over-a-breakup party, or any special occasion where women want to cut loose and have a night on the town.

Consider staying overnight in a hotel, instead of heading home after all that partying. Then you can call room service for recovery drinks and refreshing saunas the next day.

Last Rites Bachelorette Party

Say sayonara to singlehood with a wild wake for the bride's last night and mourn the loss of her freedom! Have the guests come dressed in black, but with a twist—black panties, dyed black wedding dress from the thrift store, and so on. Play a few black-humored games, then drink—and eat—to the bride-to-be's crossing over to the "other side"—matrimony! Show them all how to put the "fun" back into "fun"erals.

Invitations

Invite the guests to mourn the loss of the bride-to-be's single status by sending out funeral notices, announcing her departure. Inscribe it with "Deceased: (Bride's name)'s Freedom. Please gather for a celebration of her single life to share stories, laughs, and alcohol." Or send them tombstone-shaped cards printed with fancy lettering to read, "Here Lies (Bride's name)'s Single Status. Gone but Not Forgotten," and add dates. Include a tissue in the envelope for those upcoming tears, a black silk rose, or a picture of the bride-to-be dressed like an angel—or fallen angel.

What to Wear

Ask the guests to wear black in honor of the occasion—and to be creative with the black outfit they choose. That means anything goes—bathing suits to bridal gowns—as long as it's black! Accessorize with veils using black netting, plastic or costume sorrow beads, and hankies "embroidered" with the bride-to-be's name using fabric pens for all the tears—of laughter. Or have them all come as angels, waiting to greet her at the pearly gates of marital heaven. Have them bring a memento of her "former" life, such as an empty beer can, some ripped panties, or fake vomit, to place at the "memorial."

Decorations

Drape the room in black—black balloons, black crepe paper, black tablecloths, and black paper products. Set up a memorial table, with pictures of the bride-to-be from her single days, along with a few items that represent her former single status. Display funeral flowers, like lilies, or make your own black silk flower corsages and wreaths. Set out tombstones featuring other brides who have lost their freedom and write funny epitaphs, such as, "Here lies Susie. Now she's wed. Became a housewife—Better Off Dead." Or "Barbie Melvin, Met her Ken. Married now—So no more men." Play funeral music, light candles, and create a casket (filled with a dummy dressed in her hottest outfit), or an altar (topped with pictures of old boyfriends) using a large empty box or a tall table.

Games and Activities

A "funeral" will be the primary activity at this party, so do it up big—the more exaggerated the better. The fun comes when the mourners share their stories of the bride-to-be's sordid past—whether they're true or not. Don't forget to have each guest place her memory object on the table as she reveals her sad tale.

Host a Wake

Pick up the guests in a hearse and have them chauffeured to the party. Ask the guests to come prepared to read personalized, humorous eulogies for the bride. Create a funeral pyre and burn in effigy objects representing singlehood, such as her Little Black Book, her thong, her old boyfriend's picture, anything the groom doesn't like. Hire a "minister" to officiate, then surprise the guests when he turns into a stripper.

The Good, the Bad, and the Married

Ask guests to take turns sharing a funny story or anecdote about the positives and negatives of married life. Some positives would be "You get to sleep with your husband instead of your teddy bear," "You don't have to pay for a massage any more," or "You can share the details of your day with your husband instead of your cat." Some negatives would be "You might never get a good night's sleep again if he snores," "From now on, you can only watch romantic movies while he's out with the guys," "Diet dinners are a thing of the past. Make sure he has his meat and potatoes."

Refreshments

Ask the girls to bring typical potluck foods for the wake, such as casseroles, salads, and desserts. Make a cake shaped like a tombstone with the bride's maiden name and soon-to-be married name.

Favors, Prizes, and Gifts

Give the mourners Memory Pictures of the bride with each mourner, weird tombstone sayings, and black silk flower bouquets. Suggest they bring along a funny gift related to the theme, such as a little black book with all the pages ripped out, a ball and chain, a housewife outfit (hairnet, slippers, and bonbons), or a maternity blouse.

CHAPTER 4

Beautiful Baby Showers

"Babies are such a nice way to start people."
~ Don Herrold

There's nothing sweeter than a shower to welcome the new baby to the family. Baby showers have changed over the years—they're a lot more fun than ever before, with all the creative themes, humorous games, and engaging activities we have today. You can mix and match the following showers to make your party as individual as the new baby you're about to greet, so pick and choose whatever matches the mother-to-be's personality, mood, or baby room. Then shower her with a good time!

Oh Baby! Big Momma Shower

Size matters, when it comes to maternity measures. There's nothing like the last month of pregnancy to make a mom-to-be feel as fat and frumpy as an overripe watermelon. Weight gain, water retention, and puffy hands and feet all conspire against her as she waits for the birth of her baby. But there's some truth to the old adage that states, "Misery loves company." So gather the gang together for a super-sized shower, where the guests come dressed just like Big Momma-to-Be. Everyone's sure to spew a few belly laughs when the gang arrives ready to pop. For this party, the "bigger" the better, so encourage the guests to go all out with tummy-busting baby bumps!

Invitations

Create an invitation that doubles as a party game. Measure out two yards of pink or blue ribbon, depending on the sex of the baby (or yellow if the gender hasn't been determined). Write the party details in permanent market along one side of the ribbon. Include a request for the guests to bring the ribbon to the party. Roll up the ribbon and place it in an envelope, along with a tiny plastic baby (available at craft, hobby, and party stores), and mail to guests in pink, blue, or yellow envelopes. For added fun, find a picture of two very pregnant women, preferably movie stars. Superimpose head shots of the mother-to-be and the specific invited guest on the picture, photocopy each one, switching in each new guest, and use it for the invitation, along with the ribbon. Use padded envelopes and include small baby items, such as ducks, pacifier candies, teddy bears, baby animals, or baby-theme ribbon.

What to Wear

To make the guest of honor feel more like the rest of the crowd, ask everyone to wear maternity clothes, stuffed with pillows, towels, teddy bears—anything creative (another game coming!). Suggest they buy inexpensive outfits at thrift stories or borrow from a pregnant friend. Big Momma will get a real lift—and laugh—when everyone at the party is in the same big boat!

Decorations

Turn the party room into a make-believe nursery. Hang up a clothesline filled with baby clothes. Set out storks, giant blocks, and baby dolls. Tie pink and blue balloons to the backs of chairs with ribbon. Cover the party table with a baby-themed tablecloth and paper products to match. Or spread a baby blanket on the table, topped with a plastic cover to protect it. Buy inexpensive bibs and use them as placemats. Serve party drinks in baby bottles with pink and blue straws. Play nursery music in the background. For a centerpiece, fill a basket with baby items, such as blocks, storks, teddy bears, rubber duckys, pacifiers, or diapers. Or display your affection—and empathy—for the mother-to-be with a centerpiece of third trimester aids and remedies. Arrange them in a large basket lined with white or printed diapers, and set the basket on the table for all to enjoy. Later you can use the centerpiece for yet another game (see below), and finally as a gift for the guest of honor to take home. Here are some items you might want to include in your basket:

- Massage oils—to practice light massage on her abdomen.

- Stretch mark ointment—helps soothe itching.

- Hemorrhoid cream—if she doesn't need it yet, she may after the birth!

- Heartburn pills or antacids—make sure they're safe for pregnant women.

- Back massager—for backache and back strain.

- Slippers—since her shoes probably won't fit anymore.

- Pillows—for added comfort while she sits or sleeps.

- Cushion—to sit on with those uncomfortable hemorrhoids.

- Breast pads—for pre-delivery leakage.

- Lip balm—for dry lips from all that Lamaze breathing.

- Puzzle books—for those breaks between contractions.

- Adult diaper—in case she can't make it to the toilet in the middle of the night, on the road, or anytime!

Buy pink and/or blue balloons and draw funny baby faces on them for a whimsical touch. Then tie matching ribbons to the ends of the balloons and float the balloons from the ceiling. Tie multiple ribbons to all the chairs, furniture, lamps, and so on. Set out diapered baby dolls or little plastic babies around the party area. Buy a couple of new maternity outfits as gifts—she'll be sick of her old ones!—and display them on the walls as decorations. Cut out pictures of pregnant movie stars and tape them to the walls so she'll have even more company. Better yet, cut the heads off some of the stars and tape or glue them on top of pictures of pregnant women, for a good laugh.

Games and Activities

Game time is Tummy Time so keep your "focal point" on the baby bump for these belly laughing activities. Just don't bust a gut!

Tape Measure Tummy

Ask the guests to pull out their invitation ribbons (if they've forgotten their ribbons, give them some more). Have the guests try to estimate the circumference of mother-to-be's tummy, using the ribbon. Pass the scissors around and have guests "cut the cord" to the estimated size. After all have cut their ribbons, let them take turns measuring them around mother's tummy to see who made the closest guess. For fun, pass out prizes for the player who overestimated and the player who underestimated the measurement.

Belly Cast

Surprise the Guest of Honor with a Belly Cast and preserve her pregnant profile for posterity. You can buy a kit for about $70 (*www .bellymasks.com*) or do it yourself with some plaster of Paris. Have mom lie down comfortably and expose her tummy. Spread some cooking oil on her tummy, then smooth on the plaster. Entertain mom with labor and delivery stories while the plaster dries, then have mom wiggle a little to release the mold and it should pop right off. Provide acrylic paints to decorate the Belly Cast, have the guests sign their names in permanent markers, draw a picture of the baby, or let Mom create her own design when the party is over.

Belly Relay Race
While the guests are wearing their stuffed maternity clothes, put them through an obstacle course and let the real pregnant mom enjoy the show as their awkward bodies try to maneuver the path. Challenges might include doing the limbo, keeping a hula hoop up, tying your shoe, doing five jumping jacks, dancing the twist, walking on a balance beam, and putting on pantyhose.

Refreshments
Use a round or oval mold to make belly shaped Jell-O, potato salad, cheese spread, or other foods. Have the bakery tint a loaf of bread pink or blue and make colorful sandwiches, or cut out footprint shapes with a cookie cutter, and spread the bread with a variety of fillings. Top them with little candy babies or bottles. Serve "Baby Cube Punch"—and make another game of it! Buy little plastic babies at the craft or party store. Fill ice cube trays with water and place a baby in each compartment. Freeze until firm. Place a Baby Cube in each glass of punch (pink or blue punch preferred)—all at the same time. When the ice melts, the baby will float to the top. The first guest to notice her baby floating yells, "My water broke!" and wins a prize. For added fun, serve the punch in baby bottles or empty baby food jars. Make a Belly Cake for a special treat and extra laughs. Buy a cake mix and follow the directions on the package to make the batter. Pour the batter into a greased, round, ovenproof bowl and bake a little longer than required (use a toothpick to see if it's done). Allow the

cake to cool, then turn it out onto a large plate. Tint frosting to match the mother's skin tone as closely as possible, and cover the cake with the frosting (Tip: Smooth it with a large, flat knife dipped in warm water). Add a raisin or cherry in the center to make the bellybutton. Include a couple of cupcakes to make breasts, if you dare. Or serve a cake in the shape of rattle, diaper, or baby bottle. Or incorporate the theme of the party into the cake, such as a teddy bear or ducky. Make sure there's lots of chocolate—it's good for baby and mother!

Favors, Prizes, and Gifts

Try these suggestions for special guest favors: Disposable camera, picture frame, photo album, baby powder-scented lotion, heart-shaped box of chocolates, clear baby bottle filled with pink or blue jelly beans, teddy bear or ducky key rings, candy birth control pills or condoms—and anything chocolate. Include a picture of each guest as her "pregnant" self, along with a decorative picture frame. For the MTB, she will probably be registered for her baby shower but you can always add a personal touch. How about disposable diapers, wrapped in pink or blue tissue and stacked like blocks. How about a list of parks, clubs, baby classes, pediatricians, and discount stores in the community contributed by the guests. Baby T-shirts with cute slogans, such as "Class of 20XX" and "Future CEO," are easy to make using your computer and iron-on transfers. Give her cute containers for her baby's "Firsts"—first tooth, first haircut, etc. Give her a day at a spa, tickets for a night out, coupons for free babysitting, a week of meals or housecleaning, a new maternity outfit or after-baby outfit, or a filled maternity suitcase or Lamaze bag. Make Mom's Emergency Apron and fill it with baby items contributed by the guests, such as a thermometer, nose syringe, rattle, bib, toys, and so on. Also consider giving her a baby-related movie, such as *Look Who's Talking*, a book on labor and delivery or baby care, bath oils and lotions, a romantic night kit with massage oil, scented candles, and sparkling cider, or a labor kit filled with a focal point, suckers, a pillow, magazines, a deck of cards, a nightgown, slippers, soothing CDs, and so on.

Party Plus

Have the party guests bring baby dolls and treat them like real babies, to give the mother-to-be a glimpse into the near future—at least for a couple of hours.

Welcome to the Family Tree Shower

Host a shower that includes as many family members as possible, from the youngest baby to the greatest great-grandmother—and even a few ghosts from families past. It's a great way to welcome the new baby to the family tree and make the new mom feel comfortable with the rest of the clan. You can invite family members from both sides of the couple, or focus on just the maternal or fraternal relatives. Add to the fun by flying in some surprise guests—distant relatives—to make it a Family Reunion as well!

Invitations

Draw or photocopy a picture of the family tree. Cut out a leaf for the new baby and write the party details on it, then stick it to the tree with double-stick tape. You can use a real leaf for added fun. Or photocopy a picture of the father- and mother-to-be as babies and glue them side-by-side at the top of the card. Below, draw an oval, and place a question mark inside, to represent the new baby. Draw lines from the father to the mother, from the father to the baby, and from the mother to the baby, to show the connection. Begin a Family Quilt by including a six-by-six inch plain piece of cotton fabric in the envelope and ask everyone to decorate the quilt square with a symbol of their family and a special message, using embroidery floss, fabric paint, or markers. Ask them to return it a couple of weeks before the party so you can put together a family quilt for the mother-to-be by party time.

What to Wear

Have the guests dress in "Family" T-shirts, with the name of the family lineage on the back, such as "Warner Family" or "Warner-Pike Family," to indicate the familial relationship. Or make T-shirts with the baby's name and her connection to each family member, such as "I'm Luke's Aunt Susan" or "Bradley's Cousin Twice Removed."

Decorations

Fill the party room with family photos of both current members and generations past, to show the mother-to-be her baby's future heritage. Have everyone bring family albums to share and set them out. Blow up pictures of the parents-to-be into poster size and tape them to the walls. If there are any family crests or heirlooms, showcase them at the party. At the table, set out place markers and draw lines on the paper tablecloth linking the relatives by their connections. Collect long-loved teddy bears from family members and arrange them in a basket as a centerpiece—with a new one for the new baby.

Games and Activities

Family oriented games are best for this familial shower, but make sure the new family member feels welcome and part of the clan. Here are some silly ways to help the relatives get acquainted and make that lasting connection.

Family Resemblance

Gather pictures of family members, and using Photoshop or a similar computer program, morph their features to show us what their "baby" would look like. Then guess who the two parts of the couple are. Be sure to do the same with the expectant couple. Substitute movie star faces if you prefer.

Beautiful Babies

Ask players to bring their baby pictures. When they arrive, tape them to sheets of construction paper, making sure no names are visible. Give guests paper and pencil and have them try to identify each baby. Reveal the answers and award a prize to the player who gets the most correct answers.

The Family Tree

Sit in a circle and have the first player state how she is related to the new baby. The second player must repeat how the first player is related—however she wants to state it, as long as it's accurate—then add her relationship. The third player does the same, and so on around the circle. For example, you might hear, "Jodie is the baby's second cousin, Kathy is engaged to the baby's mother's brother's son, and I'm the baby's maternal grandmother." When the game reaches the new mom, she must repeat all of the relationships mentioned before. By the end of the game, she'll know her baby's relationship to everyone at the party—or be totally confused!

Change the Baby

Find a baby doll, a diaper, an outfit, and a swaddle blanket. Divide into teams of four players and line them up at the table. In front of the first player, place the baby doll. Place a diaper at the second spot. Leave the third spot empty. Place a swaddle blanket at the fourth spot. On the word Go!, time the players as they 1. Remove the baby's clothes, 2. Change the diaper, 3. Put the clothes back on, and 4. Swaddle the baby— all without harming the baby in their race to be the fastest team!

Mother's Purse

Write down a list of objects that most mothers carry around in their purses. For example, you might include wet wipes or tissues, a marker, a small toy, a piece of candy, a healthy snack, a Band-Aid, a baby picture, a safety pin, a dollar in change, something that rattles, something pink or blue, something that squeaks, something that bounces, and something soft. The player with the most objects listed in her purse wins the game. Give the list to the mother-to-be so she can prepare her purse for motherhood.

Black Sheep

On index cards, write down interesting facts about family members. For example, "Uncle Bill became governor of South Carolina," "Great grandma was a silent movie star," and "Nephew Luke twice removed was a romance writer." Then make up a few stories that aren't true, such as, "Great-great uncle Bob used to be a rodeo clown" or "Aunt Jean was once a stripper." Have the new Mom guess which ones are true and which are false.

Refreshments

Have everyone bring a dish made from a favorite family recipe, along with the recipe and some of the ingredients. Ask each person to tell about the history of the dish, where it came from, how it's been passed along, and so on. Pick out some recipes from the father's heritage and add them to the mix. Or include some of the mother-to-be's family recipes to share with her husband's relatives. Serve a traditional punch from a popular family recipe and label it, such as, "Aunt Rose's Pineapple Punch." For a centerpiece cake, draw the family tree on a sheet cake using tubes of frosting, with the new baby featured prominently.

Favors, Prizes, and Gifts

Send the guests home with information about the new baby to add to their family trees, along with copies of all the recipes that were shared at the party. For gift ideas, ask guests to bring something from the family heritage, such as a blanket, photograph, or saved baby toy. Then present the mother-to-be with her Family Quilt and ask each person to explain their personalized squares.

Party Plus

Have a professional photographer come and take a Family Picture with the new mom surrounded by all her relatives. As a follow-up, host a Family Reunion Party the next day, while all the relatives are in town too.

Long-Distance Virtual Shower

It's always hard when a member of the group moves away. It's especially difficult when she's celebrating a special event, such as pregnancy or the birth of a baby. If you have a friend who's expecting and has moved away, surprise her with this long-distance shower. Gather the gang, set up the video camera, and capture the event on tape. Then mail the fun to her so she can enjoy it vicariously. Or better yet, hook up the computer with a camera for a live video feed, so she can virtually participate at the shower! This is also a great cheer-her-up party for moms who are on bed rest during pregnancy.

Invitations

Videotape yourself inviting the guests and mother-to-be to the party, make copies, and mail to guests. For example, you might hold a balloon and a baby doll, and say "Come to a Virtual Shower for Susan!" then give the party details. Begin the one for Mom-to-Be with, "Surprise, Susan! Welcome to your Virtual Shower!"

What to Wear

Ask the guests to come dressed in their favorite party outfits. Or have them wear stereotypical clothes for your geographical location— or for the Mom's new location. For example, if the party is going to be held in Florida, have everyone come as tacky tourists. If the new Mom has moved to North Dakota, wear snow gear. For New York, wear black. For Texas, wear boots and cowgirl hats. You get the idea.

Decorations

Keep the room cozy so you can videotape everyone at the party easily. In the background, tie balloons, hang up streamers, or put up posters of your city or hers, such as pictures of icebergs for Alaska, cornfields for Iowa, rain for Oregon, or the President for Washington, D.C.

Games and Activities

Make sure the games you play are visual and lively, and can be easily captured on videotape. If you play quiet games with pen and pencil, you're wasting precious party time that can't be enjoyed by the viewer. Here are some games that are sure to provide laughs for the mother-to-be—and maybe even win a couple of video awards for Best Virtual Shower!

Eat Your Peas

Here's a game that's great for videotaping—and the new Mom will be glad to miss! Buy six to eight different baby foods, remove the lids, wrap the jars in foil, and add a spoon to each jar. Give each player a paper plate and spoon. Pass around the baby foods and ask players to put a glob of each one on their plates. When all are served, have them taste the samples and guess what they are. When everyone has a list, reveal the labels to see who has the best taste buds. Mother-to-be will enjoy all the funny faces on the players as they taste the various foods!

Dirty Diaper

This is another great game that plays well on the big screen because of the funny reactions by the players. Melt a variety of chocolate bars in disposable diapers using the microwave, then fold diapers closed. Pass the diapers around and have guests try to determine the brand of candy. (NO tasting!) The winner is obviously a chocoholic, so give her a box of unmelted chocolates.

Remember the Rhyme

Get a book of classic nursery rhymes. Read the first line of a familiar rhyme, such as "Mary had a little lamb, her fleece was white as snow." Have the first player try to recite the next line from memory: ("Everywhere that Mary went, the lamb was sure to go.") Continue with each player. When a player makes a mistake or flubs a line, she's out of the game and a new rhyme is begun. The last player left wins a book of nursery rhymes.

Baby Products

Buy a variety of odd-looking baby products, or cut out product ads and glue them to construction paper. Cover or remove the product names. Pass out pencils and paper, then hold up each product and have players take turns guessing what it is and how it's used. You should get some funny answers from the more creative players. Or have the players guess the prices of all the objects—then give the collection to the mother-to-be.

Beautiful Burp Cloths

Buy a package of cloth diapers. Have guests decorate them with puffy paints, fabric markers, and so on. They might draw alphabet letters, animals, hearts and flowers, toy trucks, and so on. Remind them to include the baby's name, and sign their work. Hold up the finished products for the video camera, then send them to Mom to use as burp cloths. You can do this with white onesies, too.

Present Your Present

Have guests open their presents on camera for the mother-to-be. As they do, have them tell why they chose that gift, and offer a heartfelt comment to the soon-to-be watching mother. When the gifts are all open, put them in a box and mail them to Mom after the party.

Refreshments

Make one of the new mom's favorite recipes to let her know you miss her treats. Perhaps she's known for her Chocolate-Peanut Butter Rice Krispie Squares or her Canned Cheese on a Ritz appetizers. Or ask the guests to bring one of their favorite snacks, along with the recipe, and send the recipes to the mother-to-be. Toast her repeatedly with pink champagne or wine punch, every time someone says the word "Baby." Have the bakery create a cake in the shape of the Mom's new home state, then devour it in effigy.

Favors, Prizes, and Gifts

Give the guests notepaper to keep in touch with the guest of honor. And give them a copy of the party tape! Then mail those gifts to the new Mom.

Party Plus

If you can afford it, surprise the new mom with an in-person shower! Fly or drive to her new home and share the fun together. Or keep it easy and sign up for a Web Baby Shower (*www.webbabyshower.com*). The site includes a message board, photos, games, and pregnancy updates.

Brand New Grandmother Shower

Today's vibrant grandmother is nothing like the stereotype of the past, wrapped in a shawl, rocking in a chair, knitting booties (although booties are great!). Today's grandmother rocks, but not in a chair, and she wants to party just like she did in her party prime. Here's a baby shower wrapped around a new trend for all those young-at-heart grandmothers who want to celebrate this joyous occasion, too—the upcoming birth of their new grandbaby. Get down, granny! It's time to rock and roll!

Invitations

Photocopy a baby picture of the guest of honor grandmother-to-be on card stock paper and fold it into a card. Write "Guess who?" on the outside, under the photo. Inside, write, "Come to a Grandmother-to-Be Shower for (her name)," followed by the party details. Include three or four decorated index cards and ask the guests to write down their favorite childrearing tips, then bring them to the party. Have the guests bring pictures of their own grandchildren to show off—and use as a game.

What to Wear

Ask the guests to come dressed for High Tea, in floral or fancy outfits, with hats and gloves.

Decorations

Dress up the party room with your finest table linens, china, and silver, for an elegant tea party. For a centerpiece, gather items that a new grandmother might want to have on hand, such as a baby bath tub, lotions and shampoos, a supply of diapers, some onesies with the words "I Love Grandma" on the front, a baby blanket, and so on. As pictures of the grandchildren arrive, tape them to sheets of construction paper and stick them on the walls around the party room.

Games and Activities

Grandmotherhood is the theme of this party, so offer activities that stress this special right of passage. After all, being a grandmother should be nothing but fun and games!

Baby's First Year Book

Set up a table full of scrapbook materials with a baby theme and let the guests each create a special page for the new baby. Divide the book into categories and assign one to each guest to decorate, such as "Baby's First Bath at Grandma's," "Baby's First Food with Grandma," "Baby's Friends and Grandma," "Baby's Favorite Toys at Grandma's," "Baby's First Words to Grandma," and "Baby's First Birthday with Grandma." Assemble the pages and place them in a scrapbook for Grandmother to keep.

Grandma's Coupon Book

Pass out homemade coupons to the guests and ask them to write down a service that the new grandmother can offer the new parents, such as, "Good for one night of babysitting," "Good for running errands for new mom," "Good for cleaning the house," "Good for one gourmet meal for parents," "Good for one foot massage for new mother," "Good for one shopping spree for baby clothes." Collect them and give them to the new Grandmother.

Like Grandma, Like Baby

Pass around the collection of grandchild photos and have players guess which baby picture belongs to which grandmother. Ask them to tell what characteristics they saw in the baby that matched the grandmother, such as "This baby has grandmother's ears" or "That's definitely a (Grandmother's last name) nose," and you're sure to get a few laughs.

Hollywood Babies

Find out how hip Grandmother and the other players are. Give them a list of Hollywood stars and their baby's names—all mixed up. Have them draw lines to match the baby to the star. Whoever has the most correct matches, wins a prize. Here are some names to get you started: Kim Basinger (Ireland), Gwyneth Paltrow (Apple), Courtney Cox (Coco), Nicolas Cage (Kal-el), Julia Roberts (Phinnaeus and Hazel), Tom Cruise (Suri), Geri Halliwell (Bluebell), Jamie Oliver (Daisy Boo), Jason Lee (Pilot Inspektor), Woody Allen (Satchel).

Nursery News Headlines

Read the following headlines and see if players can guess the name of the nursery rhyme.

- Farmer's Wife Attacked by Rodents (Three Blind Mice)

- King's Men Fail to Revive Crash Victim (Humpty Dumpty)

- Violinists Give Command Performance to the King (Old King Cole)

- Wedded Pair Go Off Their Diets (Jack Sprat)

- Survey Disclosed Adequate Wool Supply (Baa Baa Black Sheep)

- Girl Frightened by Arachnid (Little Miss Muffet)

- Boy Kisses Girls, Flees (Georgie Porgie)

- Rodent Horrified as Clock Strikes (Hickory Dickory Dock)

- Woman Lacks Food, Dog Starves (Old Mother Hubbard)

- Unusual Pie Served to Royalty (Sing a Song of Sixpence)

- Lost Sheep Finds Way Home (Little Bo Peep)

- Study Contrasts Boys and Girls (Sugar and Spice)

- Lamb Stalks Owner Everywhere (Mary Had a Little Lamb)

- Sheep Stray While Shepherd Sleeps (Little Boy Blue)

- Spider Struggles up Waterspout (The Eensy Weensy Spider)

- Young Mountain Climbers Injured (Jack and Jill)

- Population Explosion (The Woman in a Shoe)

- Amateur Astrologist Bewildered (Twinkle, Twinkle Little Star)

- Arrest Made for Strange Behavior, Running Through Town (Wee Willie Winkie)

Grandmother's Advice

Write down current advice on topics related to childrearing, such as "It's okay to let a baby use a pacifier," "Baby should sleep on her back to help prevent SIDS," and "You shouldn't start solid foods until around six months." Turn them into questions for the players, such as "Is it all right for baby to have a pacifier?" "Should baby sleep on her tummy, side, or back?" "When should you start solid foods?" The person who gets the most correct answers wins a prize. The one who gets the least correct answers needs a new baby book.

Refreshments

Serve a High Tea, with small tea sandwiches, fruit or cinnamon scones, and dainty sugar cookies. For fun, review the rules and manners expected with High Tea, such as, "Never extend your pinkie finger while sipping tea," "Don't clink your spoon while stirring your tea," and "Avoid lifting the saucer with the teacup." Then enforce the rules and take off points for infractions. Offer a variety of tea flavors, along with real cream and fancy-colored sugar crystals, and serve them in unique or antique teacups. For dessert, cut a sheet cake into the letters of baby's name and frost like petit fours.

Favors, Prizes, and Gifts

Send the guests home with scrapbooking supplies to create their own books. Give them picture frames to hold photos of the new baby after it arrives. Pass out poems about grandparenting taken from the Internet. Give the Grandma-to-be a gift certificate for a portrait sitting with the new baby. (Her option: bring along the new parents.)

Party Plus

Host the party at a tea shop to make it more authentic, but still decorate the area with baby items. A High Tea is a great idea for many parties.

CHAPTER 5

Milestone Birthdays

"I don't want to get to the end of my life and find that I lived just the length of it. I want to have lived the width of it as well." ~ Diane Ackerman

The big "0" birthdays loom ahead for all of us. While many women don't like to acknowledge they're getting older, many in fact dread it, this is a great time to celebrate their lives, their achievements, their friendships. Turn that trepidation of reaching 20, fear of facing 40, shock of turning 60, or anxiety of being 80, into delight, joy, even amusement. There's so much to celebrate, so honor your friend's special day with a birthday bash. Better yet, make it a surprise to catch her off guard!

Big-Time Big-0 Birthday Party

Make it memorable for a friend turning the corner on a decade—30, 40, 50, 60, 70+, with a party that celebrates a special milestone. This is a big event that should be honored, not avoided. It's a chance—at least once a decade—to tell your friend how much you value her friendship and how much you care. So make it a party she'll never forget.

Invitations

Create a milestone invitation ripped from the headlines, to represent the importance of the guest of honor's birthday. Search the Internet to find out what happened on the day she was born, then use it as the lead for a mini-newspaper type invitation. Include the party details in the story.

What to Wear

Come dressed in an outfit that suits the decade the birthday girl was born. If it was the '40s, wear long floral dresses, hats, gloves, and black heels. For the '50s, make it poodle skirts and cashmere sweaters, oxfords and stacked hair, and so on.

Decorations

Go back to the decade for decorating ideas. If the birthday girl was born in the '60s, hang up posters of Jim Morrison and the Beatles, set out love beads and incense, and turn on music to match. For a '70s birthday, hang a disco ball, tack up posters of John Travolta in *Saturday Night Fever*, and turn up Donna Summer and the Bee Gees.

Games and Activities

Time and memory games are the best ways to celebrate a Big 0 Birthday. Take her back to the "good old days," quiz her on the "facts" of her life, and show her what the next ten years will bring her.

Retro Games

Go back in time to games that were popular when the birthday girl was growing up, such as Twister, Monopoly, Operation, or Pong. You can also find games specific to the decade, such as The '70s Game, The '80s Game, as well as decade-related Trivial Pursuit.

Decades Trivia

Make up your own Trivia Game. Do a little research using an Almanac or the Internet, write down some interesting facts, and ask the players questions, everything from popular songs of the time to movies, famous people, and infamous events.

Guess Who's Turning XX?

Search the Internet to find out which famous people were born the same year as the birthday girl. Mix them up with other famous people who weren't born the same year and have the players guess the correct ones. It's always a surprise to find out who else is also turning 40, 50, 60, and up.

What Happened the Year You Were Born?

Look up events that occurred the year of the birthday girl's birth and write them on index cards. Have her—or the guests—try to put them in chronological order.

Ten Years from Now

Have the players make up predictions for the birthday girl—ten years from now, such as "You will have traveled the world," "You will be remarried," or "You'll own your own company."

Refreshments

Serve classic dishes from the decade, such as tuna casserole for the '50s, salad bar for the '60s, and chocolate fondue for the '70s. Likewise with drinks—Cherry Cokes, martinis, and Jolt Cola.

Favors, Prizes, and Gifts

Give the guests tokens from the decade, such as Slinkies from the '50s, Beatle's CDs from the '60s, Disco beads from the '70s, and so on. For birthday gifts, suggest they bring her retro items from her childhood that will bring back memories, such as a vintage Barbie doll, a game of Chinese checkers, or a hula hoop.

Party Plus

Take the Decade Diva out to an old-fashioned diner, skating rink, bowling alley, or other favorite hangout from her childhood. (This is another theme that can be adapted to other parties.)

Biography: This Is Your Life Party

Surprise the birthday girl with a memorable review of her life from birth to present. She'll never guess what you have in store for her on this unforgettable occasion. This party takes a little preparation, gathering special guests from the past, but the payoff is worth it—she'll be in tears by the end of the party. Tears of joy, of course!

Invitations

Gather a number of pictures from the birthday girl's life, beginning with her baby picture and ending with a present-day photo. Put them together in a creative collage. Make speech bubbles for the pictures that include the party details, then photocopy the collage and mail to guests. Since it's a surprise party, include a balloon that reads: "This is a surprise so don't blow it!" Be sure to invite special "surprise" guests from her past, such as a favorite teacher, former coworker, a long-lost best friend, distant relative, and so on.

What to Wear

Ask all the "surprise" guests to come dressed the way the birthday girl might expect them. For example, the teacher might wear a typical outfit she wore in the classroom, a coworker might wear a lab coat, a best friend might dress as she did when she was a kid, and so on. Or have them break stereotype and dress in an unexpected way.

Decorations

Surprise her with a room full of festive decorations—balloons, confetti, streamers, lights, and so on. Make a special throne for the birthday girl, covered with crepe paper streamers. Put together a timeline of her life from birth to present—and perhaps some predictions for the future—and tape it to the wall. Add appropriate photos along the line. Finally, hang a drape or cloth over one of the doorways to hide the special guests until "showtime."

Games and Activities

The highlight of the party comes with the introduction of the surprise guests, so make sure you devote most of the time to a game of Guess Who.

Guess Who

The highlight of the party is the entrance of the surprise guests. Have them arrive early and keep them sequestered in an "off-limits/no entrance" room. After the birthday girl arrives, seat her in her throne and begin the story of her life. Hold a book with your notes about each person, and read them one at a time in chronological order, giving clues to the secret guest's identity, such as "Let's go back to first grade when you first moved to River Heights." Then have the secret guest speak from behind the curtain, adding additional clues, such as "Remember the time you fell off the bars and I gave you a Band-Aid?" When the birthday girl guesses who's attached to the voice, the surprise guest steps out from behind the curtain to reveal herself. Continue with the rest of the special guests. If there are some guests who cannot attend, ask them to videotape a special message, mail it to you, and then play it at the party.

Remember When . . .

Have guests write down a fond or funny memory of the birthday girl on an index card. Collect the cards, mix them up, and place them in a bowl. Read one memory at a time and have the birthday girl guess who wrote it. Then let her add to the memory with more details.

Refreshments

Ask the guests to suggest some of the birthday girl's favorite foods from the past, and serve them at the party. In keeping with the mystery guest theme, serve a "mystery meal" or "mystery dessert" that includes an offbeat ingredient that guests must try to determine, such as Pretzel Jell-O Dessert or Ritz Cracker Pie. Both are surprisingly good!

To make Pretzel Jell-O Dessert, combine 3 tablespoons sugar with ¾ cup margarine and stir until creamy. Add 2 ⅔ cups coarsely chopped pretzels. Press into a 9 by 13 pan and bake at 350 degrees for ten minutes. Stir together 1 8-ounce package of cream cheese and 1 cup sugar until creamy. Add 1 12-ounce carton of whipped topping. Spoon into pretzel crust. Dissolve 1 6-ounce package strawberry Jell-O in 2 cups boiling water. Add 1 pint frozen strawberries and stir until thawed. Let sit in refrigerator until partially set. Pour over cream cheese mixture and chill until set.

For Ritz Cracker Pie, beat 3 egg whites with ½ teaspoon crème of tartar. Slowly pour in 1 cup of sugar. Fold in 24 Ritz crackers, finely chopped, ¾ cup chopped pecans, and 1 teaspoon vanilla. Pour into greased 9-inch pie pan. Bake at 350 degrees for 25 minutes. While piecrust cools, mix 8 ounces of Cool Whip with ¼ cup brown sugar. Spread onto cool crust. Sprinkle on ¼ cup chopped pecans. Refrigerate for several hours; cut and serve. Have guests try to guess what the "secret ingredients" are in both dishes.

Favors, Prizes, and Gifts

Give the guests photos taken with the birthday girl, along with picture frames. Pass out fancy address books so everyone can keep in touch. Ask the guests to give the birthday girl a memento that's meaningful to her, such as a special song, stuffed animal, or an addition to her collection of porcelain dolls, music boxes, or beaded purses.

Party Plus

Kidnap the birthday girl and take her to a favorite place from childhood, such as a camp, amusement park, or relative's home, and host the party there.

Born to Be Wild Birthday Party

Help the birthday girl cut loose on her special day by taking her back to her wild days of high school. Let her be a daredevil teen again, experimenting with fun fashions, doing beauty makeovers, practicing the latest dances, and laughing all night long with her girlfriends. Who needs boys when you have each other—but you can still have fun talking about them, just like you did way back when!

Invitations

Make your party invitations look like "Back to High School Night" flyers to welcome the guests back to their teen years. For example, you might write, "Come celebrate (Her Name)'s 30th (cross off 30th and change to) 16th Birthday for a Back-to-Teen Night Party. Place: Elvis Presley (Paul McCartney/Justin Timberlake) High School (at your real address).

What to Wear

Ask the guests to dress as they did in high school, or come as high school stereotypes, such as cheerleaders, athletes, goths, skaters, nerds, preppies, even teachers, coaches, custodians, or principals. Have them bring your favorite tunes and junk food from the time, and come prepared to "act their age."

Decorations

Re-create the high school classroom on back-to-school night or the gym on prom night. Decorate in school colors, using banners, pompoms, and "Welcome to (Your School) High!" signs. Hang up pictures of stars and singers of the day, set out memorabilia, and play music popular at the time. Ask the guests to bring their yearbooks to share (and to use as a game). Blow up pictures of the guests from their high school days and tape them to the walls. Set out cheerleader outfits, letter jackets, and gym clothes, as well as chemistry coats, home ec aprons, and school mascot costumes. Set out textbooks, fake reports, and funny award trophies.

Games and Activities

Go back to high school for the games and activities, to see if you could still pass the exams, play the clarinet, or do the popular dance at the time.

Are You Smarter Than a High Schooler?

Ask trivia questions based on high school courses—English, Geography, Social Studies, Math—to see who remembers the most information from school days.

Yearbook Memories

Prepare a mini-yearbook ahead of time by photocopying pictures of former high school students and teachers—head cheerleader, lead jock, class president, school bad boy, PE coach. Black out the names, then see if the players can remember the names.

Makeover Marathon

Get out beauty supplies and do each others' makeup and hair, in the style of your high school years. If you need inspiration, rent movies from the times, such as *Grease, Hairspray, National Lampoon's Class Reunion, Romy & Michelle's High School Reunion,* or *Grosse Point Blank.*

High School Musical

Rent the movie *High School Musical*, and have the guests sing and dance along to the video. Provide the lyrics (you can download them from the Internet), give them a rehearsal time to practice, and "put on a show!"

Refreshments

Offer favorite junk food treats, including pizza, hamburgers, or whatever else you ate (but shouldn't have) in high school. Drink the same beer you sneaked in high school, or mix up some popular drinks of the time, such as Screwdrivers, Long Island Iced Teas, or fruity wine coolers. To make Screwdrivers, mix 2 ounces of vodka with 5 ounces of orange juice and pour over ice. To make a Long Island Iced Tea, combine ½ ounce vodka, ½ ounce gin, ½ ounce white rum, ½ ounce Cointreau, 1 ounce lemon juice, and a shot of cola, in a tall iced tea glass.

Favors, Prizes, and Gifts

Give the guests memorabilia from high school, such as pompons, banners, and book covers, as well as a mix CD of songs from high school, teen magazines, fashion accessories, beauty items, and pictures of celebrities.

Party Plus
Invite a favorite teacher to the party for a big surprise!

"Over the Hill" Party

One thing everyone says on their birthday is "I'm so old." Even if they are in their 30s or 40s. Celebrate their feelings of growing older . . .

with age comes wisdom. You're never too old—or young—to enjoy this birthday bash.

Invitations

Create a birth certificate or birth announcement to use as an invitation, using a computer or photocopy machine. Or make up your own funny obituary for the guest of honor, such as "Come mourn the loss of (birthday girl's name)'s 30th Birthday at an Over the Hill Wacky Wake." Draw a caricature of the birthday girl, or write party details on party hats or horns and include them in the envelope.

What to Wear

Ask the guests to dress like their grandmothers. Pastel cardigans, floral dresses, pantyhose, pearls, bifocals, and orthopedic shoes are the perfect attire.

Decorations

To remind her that she's moving into "old age," set out appropriate props, such as denture cleanser for false teeth, a fan for hot flashes, a magnifying glass for eyesight, granny shoes for tired feet, hair color to cover the gray, baby food for the toothless, cane or wheelchair, "help, I've fallen and can't get up" whistle, subscription to *Modern Maturity*, sex manual, iron tables, bifocals (from the thrift shop), cemetery brochures, senior citizen discounts. Hang up quotes about old people or cemetery quotes, such as "Here lies the Birthday of our Good Friend Lynn. She partied and laughed and danced to the end."

Games and Activities

Getting older is ripe with good humor, so turn the wake on its ass and laugh it up with these wacky games and funny activities. Remind her that the best—and perhaps wackiest—is yet to come.

Older Than Dirt

Hold up pictures of famous movie stars—older than the birthday girl—and have everyone guess their ages. Remind her she's still younger than those stars.

Face the Future

Display various products for old people and have players guess the name of the product and what it's for, such as anti-aging cream, adult diapers, food supplements, hemorrhoid cream, and so on. You should get some funny answers.

Advice for the Elderly

Have everyone make up a piece of advice for the elderly and share it with the group, such as "When looking for your glasses, check the top of your head first."

Read Eulogies

Ask the guests to read the humorous eulogies they have prepared in advance for the birthday girl.

Refreshments

Make soft foods, such as a Jell-O salad and macaroni and cheese. Label the foods "No fat, no cholesterol, no sugar, no flavor." Serve them in baby food jars. Set out containers of Ensure, a health drink for older people, but serve "Elixirs" instead, made from wine and fruit juice mixes. Make a cake in the shape of a casket or tombstone and write, "Here lies (her name)'s 40th Birthday."

Favors, Prizes, and Gifts

Give the birthday girl any of the props you've used at the party, including vitamins, a cane, Milk of Magnesia, and so on. Make up a T-shirt that reads, "(Her name)'s 50th—RIP."

Party Plus

Instead of a wake, turn it into a "Back to Babyhood" party, and make the invitations, decorations, food, and fun related to the babyhood theme.

Pretty in Pink Sweet Sixteen Party

Celebrate one of the younger girls in the group with a Pretty in Pink Sweet Sixteen Party, and welcome her to the world of women with food, fun, and favors. It doesn't have to be her 16th birthday—this is a great party for her bat mitzvah or her quinceañera, or any other rite of passage.

Invitations

Keep it sweet with pink party invitations to suit the theme. For ideas, try "Hearts for the Sweetheart" and use heart-shaped invitations, "Pretty Princess" with cards featuring a real or cartoon princess, "Primping and Pampering" with makeup ads included, or just "Think Pink" with everything pink. Insert a baby picture labeled "Before" and a current one that reads "After." Add tiny pink or red heart candies in the envelope.

What to Wear

Ask guests to dress all in pink, like princesses. Or have them come grungy and ready for a makeover. Offer matching accessories when they arrive, with pink heart jewelry, pink candy, pink lipsticks, pink silk flowers, pink scarves, and so on.

Decorations

Fill the room with balloons, banners, and crepe paper in shades of pink. Hang pink paper hearts from the ceiling, along with pink heart-shaped balloons. Add pink candles, pink flowers, and a pink tablecloth with pink heart-shaped candles floating in a clear bowl of water, dotted with pink flower petals. In other words, think PINK!

Games and Activities

Choose games and activities appropriate for younger girls, such as jewelry making, scrapbooking, or other crafty fun. Then let the guests chat while they create their art.

Make-and-Take Jewelry

Have the guests make their own beaded jewelry. Supply the materials, such as beads, strings, clasps, and needles, then set up a worktable, and let them create whatever they want (you can buy inexpensive beading materials from *www.OrientalTradingCompany.com* or your local craft store). Be sure to include some pink and heart-shaped beads, since pink is the theme.

Sweet Scrapbook

Let everyone make a special scrapbook page for the Sixteener, to keep as a memento, or fill with entries during the upcoming year. Supply paper, letters, stampers, stickers, and so on, then have guests create titles for every page, such as, "My 16th Birthday Party," "The Guys I Like," "My Best Friends Forever," "My Plans and Dreams," "What's Up At School," and "Awesome Vacation." Leave space for comments and snapshots.

Sixteen Memories

Ask the older guests to share memories of being sixteen, with a word of advice for the future, such as "When I was sixteen, I thought I knew everything, but I had a lot to learn, so keep learning as you grow." Have the birthday girl share sixteen of her favorite memories of childhood, such as her favorite Halloween costume, favorite birthday party, favorite adventure, and so on.

Refreshments

Serve fun foods that teenagers like, such as pizza, hot dogs, hamburgers, a salad bar, and chips and dips. For a sweet touch, think pink, with strawberries dipped in white chocolate tinted pink, pink lemonade, pink-tinted bread for sandwiches, and a pink cake with pink icing, decorated with hearts. Ask the bakery to create a cake with an image of the Sixteener on top, perhaps with "Before" and "After" photos.

Favors, Prizes, and Gifts

Pass out heart suckers, red-foiled chocolate roses, pink Beanie Babies, T-shirts with Sweet Sixteen or heart-shaped pictures of the birthday girl. Ask the guests to wrap the gifts in pink.

Party Plus

Make it a surprise party! Take the birthday girl out to dinner, get halfway there, then say you forgot your wallet and have to return to get it. In the meantime, have guests enter from a neighbor's house. When you get there, have the birthday girl wait in the car, then ask her to come in and help you search. Yell "Surprise!" For added fun, have everyone waiting, wearing T-shirts that say, "Surprise! It's (Her Name's) Birthday."

CHAPTER 6

Super Special Calendar Days

"I once wanted to become an atheist, but I gave up—they have no holidays."

~ Henny Youngman

Although you don't really need a reason to have a party, a holiday or special calendar day is the perfect excuse to gather with the girlfriends. You can host a party for one of the big holidays, such as Christmas, Halloween, or Valentine's Day, or find a less popular date to use as a theme for your event, such as Groundhog Day, Elvis Presley's Birthday, or Chocolate Day (see Appendix B for offbeat holidays to celebrate). Here are a few dates you shouldn't forget to celebrate—along with a few ideas for fun, food, and festivities. Remember your motto: Any excuse for a party!

Last Party of the Year

Celebrate the end of the old and the beginning of the new with an all-girls rockin' New Year's Eve party. What better way to start anew with good friends, fun games, and fantastic goodies. Spend the evening sharing memories of the past, and looking toward the future, with promises and predictions.

Invitations

Send out invitations that resemble newspaper headlines touting "The End of the Year Is Near." Add a subhead: "So Bring the Chips and Beer!" Note the date, time, and place of the party in the text of the article, along with other details. Tape it to the front of a real newspaper, photocopy it, then mail to guests. Fill the envelope with confetti. Other options: Write party details on party hats or horns or blowers that unroll with party details. Or use permanent markers to write the invitation on plastic champagne glasses and mail in padded boxes. Another fun idea—write party details on streamers that guests have to unroll to read. Or make invitations that look like clocks with the hands at midnight.

What to Wear

Ask the guests to come dressed as someone or something popular from the past year. When everyone arrives, have them all guess who's who or what. Or assign months to the guests and ask them to dress accordingly—a snowsuit for January, a bathing suit for August. Or dress representing a major highlight from the year—an election, a birth, a wedding—and have guests try to guess the event.

Decorations

Go all out with classic New Year's décor—balloons and streamers, paper hats, and noisemakers. Fill the balloons with confetti for a later activity. Tape news headlines from the past year to the walls, cut from magazine annuals or made on the computer. Sprinkle confetti on the tables and hang colorful streamers from the ceiling. Make a big clock out of posterboard and a bunch of smaller ones and place them on the walls, as a reminder of passing time. Add time-related phrases to each of them, such as "Time Waits for No Woman" and "There's No Time Like the Present." Create funny predictions for each guest, such as "You will marry a prince" or "You will win the lottery," and use them as place markers. Write down memorable quotes from the year—without attribution (for another game, see below).

Games and Activities

When it's "time" for games, "time" is the theme, along with predictions, resolutions, and thoughts of the future. What better "time" to share your memories of the past and hopes for the future, with the love and laughter of your friends.

12 Months in a Year

Pick out 12 major events from the lives of your friends that occurred over the year, one from each month. For example, "Rebecca had a baby," "Sue got married," and "Vicki quit her job." Write them down on index cards, mix them up, and have players put them in chronological order.

Any Excuse for a Party Day

Write down names of obscure holidays, such as Mother-in-Law Day, Groundhog Day, National Secretary Day, and have players guess the correct dates—or months. Be sure to include one from each month (see list in Appendix B).

See Your Future

Have guests write predictions for each player, such as "(Guest's name) will get pregnant" and "(Another guest's name) will buy a new house." Encourage them to be creative—even crazy, such as "Connie will learn to play the oboe" and "Gayle will give birth to triplets."

I Resolve . . .

Have players write three New Year's resolutions on index cards, such as "I will quit eating chocolate. I will find a good guy to date. I will learn how to speak French." Place them in a bowl, mix them up, then have a player draw one and read it aloud. The other players have to guess who wrote it.

"Worst Gift" Yankee Swap

Ask the guests to bring the worst/ugliest gifts they just received for Christmas—a fruitcake, a vase, a cat-embossed sweater—beautifully wrapped. Beginning with the first person to have a birthday the next year, have each player choose a gift and open it. Following players can either take the opened gift or open a new one. Ask each player to tell how she plans to use the gift.

The Tabloid Game!

Buy some supermarket tabloids and cut out the bizarre headlines, such as "George Clooney Gives Birth to Alien!" or "Oprah Buys Florida!" Take digital pictures of the guests as they arrive and tape them to a sheet of paper. Gather the group around the table, mix up the pictures, and pass them out. Spread the headlines on the table and let the guests put them together with the pictures to create personalized tabloid headlines for each other.

It's Been a Crazy Year

Buy a magazine that offers a pictorial of the year in review. Cut out the funniest, most bizarre pictures from the past year, such as the World's Biggest Pumpkin or President Faints in His Soup. Pass out to the guests and have them write a funny caption.

Refreshments

After a night of drinking and partying, serve a substantial midnight buffet to sober up the guests. You can set up a "make your own" omelet station. Mix the eggs for the guests but let them choose their own ingredients to add, such as grated cheese, bacon bits, avocado slices, chopped onion, chili peppers. For the party, have them bring their favorite beer and junk food to share. Or have them bring a food from a favorite time period or with special meaning for the New Year, such as hearty soup with black-eyed peas for good luck in the New Year (a southern custom). Serve champagne with a cherry at the bottom or strawberry/banana daiquiris with fruit skewers. For dessert, offer elegant crème brulee or cream puffs, or serve an egg custard—eggs are a symbol of beginnings and the new year. Or make a cake that looks like a round clock or a square calendar.

Favors, Prizes, and Gifts

Send the sleepyheads home with a party memory, such as an astrology book for the new year, a humorous calendar, a diet book, a coffee mug filled with aspirin tablets, funny fortune cookies, embarrassing computer-printed photos taken during the party, a clock or watch, or a bottle of champagne.

Party Plus

Make your New Year's party a black and white ball, a sleepover, a costume ball, or an all-night movie marathon.

Hot Mama Mother's Day Party

Honor the mothers in the group with an elegant afternoon affair. Just choose a theme to fit the day and mood, such as Spring Flowers, May Day, or Mother Knows Best, and take it from there. If someone isn't able to bring their mother, suggest she invite a grandmother, sister, or other close relative or friend. For a special surprise, have a long-distance mother flown in for the special occasion.

Invitations

Write your party details on a large paper flower. Or deliver mini bouquets with party details tied on. Write the word "MOTHER" down the side of a card in fancy letters and add party details or attributes of mother corresponding to each letter, such as "M-ake it a date, O-n the 10 of May, T-o come to a party, H-osted by me, and E-njoy the fun of motherhood. R-SVP!"

What to Wear

Dress up for an elegant spring garden party, in flowery frocks and light-colored dresses. Or wear stereotypical "mother" clothes, such as housecoats, stretch band pants, T-shirts, and so on. For fun, come as a mother from a particular decade—the '50s, the '70s, etc. Or suggest that the mothers and daughters dress alike in matching outfits!

Decorations

Host the party outdoors in the garden or fill the party room with flowers and plants—real or artificial. Twist crepe paper streamers to form a canopy and hang large colorful paper flowers around the yard or room. Set out family photos of the mothers and their kids. Create banners that offer the attributes of each mother, using the letters of their names, such as: "C-reative, O-pen-minded, N-ice, N-eat, I-nteresting, and E-nergetic," for "CONNIE." Play classical music in the background, or favorites from her decade.

Games and Activities

Play "get-reacquainted" games to find out how well mothers and daughters really know each other. Then spend time enriching the bond between these two special people, with a few fun activities.

How Well Do You Know Your Mother?

Ask the moms questions about their daughters and see if they can give the correct answers. For example: "What's your daughter's favorite color?" "Who was your daughter's first boyfriend?" "What did you get from your daughter for your last birthday?" Then reverse it and ask the daughters about their mothers, such as "Where were you born?" "What was your first pet's name?" "Who was your first love?"

Mother Would Never Say . . .

Have players make up phrases most mothers would never say, such as, "I used to skip school, too." "Leave all the lights on in the house." "If Susie's mother says it's okay, then it is." "Curfew is just a rough estimate so don't hurry home." "Sure, you can keep that stray dog." "Just use your sleeve."

True or False Mothers

Look up trivia about mothers in general, then ask the players if the statements are True or False. Here are a few to get you started:

○ "The oldest mother was a 65-year-old schoolteacher in India. After 50 years of marriage, she conceived naturally." (False. She conceived by artificial insemination using eggs from her 26-year-old niece and her husband's sperm.)

○ "In 1997 a woman in Iowa gave birth to septuplets—four boys and three girls—at 31 weeks, within 16 minutes, and they all survived." (True. Kenneth, Nathaniel, Brandon, Joel, Kelsey, Natalie, and Alexis.)

○ "The record for the most children is 60, born to a woman in Russia in the 1700s." (False. She had 69 children—16 pairs of twins, seven sets of triplets, four sets of quads. Sixty-seven of them survived infancy.)

○ "The average age for women giving birth the first time is 28." (False. Today it's 25.)

○ "The odds of delivering twins are one in 33." (True.) "Her odds of having three or more is one in 300." (False. It's one in 539.)

- ○ "The most popular month in which to have a baby is May." (False. It's August.)

- ○ "A mother giraffe gives birth while standing." (True. Which means he's dropped from about six feet!)

Momisms

Have players write down typical Mom statements. Then have them read part of the Momism aloud, while the other players call out the endings. The first player to finish the rest of the quote gets a point. Here are some to get you started. (Tip: These can also be used as signs on the wall for decoration.)

- ○ "Money doesn't . . . (grow on trees.)"

- ○ "Don't make that face or . . . (it will freeze like that.)"

- ○ "Always change your underwear . . . (you never know when you might be in an accident.)"

- ○ "If someone told you to jump off a cliff . . . (would you do it?)"

- ○ "Don't put that in your mouth . . . (you don't know where it's been.)"

- ○ "Close the door! . . . (Were you born in a barn?)"

- ○ "Be careful what you wish for . . . (it might come true.)"

- ○ "If I've told you once . . . (I've told you a thousand times.)"

- ○ "Eat your vegetables . . . (children are starving in China.)"

- ○ "Just wait until . . . (your father gets home.)"

- ○ "No dessert until . . . (you clean your plate.)"

- ○ "I slave over a hot stove . . . (and this is the thanks I get?)"

- ○ "I'll give you something . . . (to cry about.)"

- ○ "Because I'm your mother . . . (that's why.)"

Refreshments

Serve Mother's favorite recipes or even her mother's favorites. Or offer delicate finger foods, such as tiny sandwiches and mini-quiches, and pastries like napoleons or chocolate éclairs, with iced tea or fruit drinks on the side. If she's a Hot Mama, whip up some spicy appetizers and dips, such as pepper puffs and salsa dip. Cut slices of Mom's Apple Pie for dessert, or serve a cake with a picture of Mom on top. (They can do this at the bakery. Just take in a photo and tell them how you'd like it placed on the cake.)

Party Plus

Take the mothers out to tea, for a game of tennis, or rent a mother-daughter movie, such as *Because I Said So* or *Serial Mom*.

Haunting Halloween Party

Scare up some fun and put the "Boo!" in your Halloween Bash by creating your own hip and happening Haunted Halloween House. You can make it frightful, such as "Bride of Frankenstein's Laboratory" or "Dracula's Castle," or funny, such as "Penny's Pumpkin Patch" or "Witches and Bitches," depending on your crowd.

Invitations

Glue colorful foam letters on a sheet of gray foam cut like a tombstone, using guests' names. Place them in a large envelope, along with creepy tattoos, fake scars, plastic body parts, glow in the dark snakes, or other scary stuff, and mail to unsuspecting guests. Or write the party details on Trick or Treat bags using glow-in-the-dark markers. Place inside a large envelope, along with Halloween candies or costume accessories. Write "Open in the dark!" on the outside of the envelope, decorate with stickers, and mail to guests.

What to Wear

Ask the guests to come dressed in creative costumes. Choose a theme-within-the-theme to give the party more focus, such as Famous Murderesses and Monsterettes, The Scientific Laboratory, The Pumpkin Patch, and so on. Then give your guests an "Ex-Scream Makeover" with easy add-ons, such as wound tattoos, fake fingernails, and vampire fangs. Have plenty of "blood" on hand to enhance those pristine costumes. Hand out Dracula, Frankenstein, Werewolf, or Mummy masks. Give guests goofy glasses, wax fangs, eyeball rings, garish makeup, and colorful capes.

Decorations

Design your own fright night Haunted House. Welcome the guests with scary signs that read, "Haunted House This Way" and "Greetings from the Grave." Set up personalized tombstones and fill the front yard with giant inflatable pumpkins, monsters, mummies, and scarecrows. Stretch cobwebs over the door, complete with rubber spiders. Create themed stations in each room, such as "Witches Cottage," "Ghosts in the Graveyard," "Mad Scientist's Lab," and "Aliens from Outer Space." Make one room a "Glow-in-the-Dark Dungeon" filled with glowing teeth, eyes, footprints, wands, and so on. Cover the walls and windows with Haunted House wall hangings, and turn the party room into a Creepy Chamber, a Boo-tiful Bookcase, or a Ghoulish Graveyard. (You can find scary stuff at *www.OrientalTradingCompany.com* or *www.iparty.com*) Spook it up with a fog machine for atmosphere. Replace regular light bulbs with green light bulbs or black lights. Light candles shaped like fingers, skulls, and eyeballs. Play scary music in the background. Add creepy critters through the tomb, er, room. Sprinkle plastic spiders, rats, and snakes all around, along with bloody plastic hands and feet, skeletons, and skulls. Hang bats, crows, and vultures from the ceiling. Add black balloons decorated with skulls. Trick up the table by covering it with a "bloody" tablecloth. Serve the treats in black witch's caldrons, tombstone cups, witch's boot mugs, and skeleton hand glasses.

Games and Activities

Scare the sillies out of your guests with a few ghoulish games and icky activities.

Trick or Treat Treasure Hunt

Hide creepy items, like plastic eyeballs, gummy teeth, and slimy stuff throughout the party room. Break into teams and search for the ghoulish goodies. Even better, make them "body parts" (see below) and have the teams race to put the bodies back together.

Baffling Body Parts

Fill individual bags with creepy stuff, such as sticky spiders, brains, eyeballs, and other slimy things. Have the guests feel inside the bag and guess what "it" is. Make a scary story to go with the body parts.

Funny/Fearsome Face

Let the guests make their own masks out of plain ones, with craft supplies and Halloween goodies. Award prizes for the Funniest, Scariest, Ugliest, and so on.

Pimped Out Pumpkins

Break into teams and give each team a pumpkin. Have them carve and decorate it with craft items and creepy body parts. Award various prizes for different categories.

Horror Movie

Have players act out scenes from famous horror movies, such as *Scream*, *The Ring*, or *Invasion of the Body Snatchers*, while others guess the name of the film.

"It's Aliiiiiiiiiiive!"

Read some famous horror movie quotes and have guests try to identify the film. (These are great to post on the walls as decorations, too.) Here are some to get you started:

- "Hi, I'm Chucky. Wanna Play?" (From *Child's Play*)

- "It's alive!" (From *Frankenstein*)

- "Be afraid . . . be very afraid." (From *The Fly*)

- "You can't kill the boogeyman." (From *Halloween*)

- "We all go a little mad sometimes." (From *Psycho*)

- "Let's say this Twinkie represents the normal amount of psychokinetic energy in the New York area." (From *Ghostbusters*)

- "Yeah, but if the Pirates of the Caribbean breaks down, the pirates don't eat the tourists." (From *Jurassic Park*)

- "A census taker once tried to test me. I ate his liver with some fava beans and a nice Chianti." (From *Silence of the Lambs*)

- "Put ze candle back!" (From *Young Frankenstein*)

Refreshments

Make your own caramel apples. Insert ice cream sticks into apples, melt caramel until smooth, and dip in apples. Have bowls of sprinkles, mini chocolate chips, chopped nuts, coconut, and other decorations ready and dip the caramel-covered apples into them. Concoct a caldron of Witches' Brew. Mix red wine with cranberry juice cocktail and serve in creepy mugs with a gummy worm hanging over the side or in the ice cubes. Or freeze lime green punch in a plastic glove, remove the glove, and float the "hand" in the punch. Set the bowl over dry ice and serve the punch in glow-in-the-dark cups.

Serve Spider Cupcakes. Bake cupcakes (or buy muffins), frost them with white icing, then draw "web" on top with black or chocolate tubes of icing. Add a gummy spider in the center. Or make a pumpkin cake by baking two bundt cakes. Turn them out to cool, then set one upside down. Ice the flat side, then top it with the other cake, so flat sides are together. Frost the cake orange and add half a Twinkie to the top, frosted green, for the stem.

Favors, Prizes, and Gifts

Give the guests Halloween goody bags filled with creepy candies (vampire teeth), scary spiders (plastic), and goofy ghosts (toys). Include stage makeup, fake blood, scar tattoos, and other fun accessories.

Party Plus

Have everyone dress alike, such as ugly witches, slutty nurses, or funny scarecrows, then go out on the town in your costumes and scare up some Halloween fun.

Cookies and Cocktails Christmas Party

Host an all-girls gala Christmas Party and share goodies, gifts, and glad tidings during the holiday season. You can make it a quiet candlelit dinner, an evening of caroling, a come-and-go open house, a craft boutique, an ornament exchange, or my favorite—a cookie party! Then give your guests the best present of all: the gathering of good friends.

Invitations

For unique invitations, make them out of cookie dough. Cut out large circles from sugar cookie dough. Poke a hole near the top with a skewer to later tie with ribbon. Bake according to package directions, until lightly browned. Decorate them with icing tubes to look like ornaments, then write "Party!" in icing on the top. Run a thin red ribbon through the hole in the cookie and attach a tag with the party details. Hand-deliver to guests. The guests can put their cookies on the tree—or eat them. For extra fun, make gingerbread women that look like each guest! Here's another quick and easy invitation that doubles as an ornament—Reindeer Canes. Buy candy canes for all the guests. Twist glittery pipe cleaners around the top, under the curve, to form the reindeer's antlers. Glue wiggly eyes and a red pompom nose on the front of the cane, and attach a tree or sled-shaped card with party details included.

What to Wear

Dress up as Mrs. Claus, and ask the guests to come as Christmas characters, such as an elf, the Grinch, reindeer, snowwoman, gingerbread girl, even a Christmas tree. Or ask them to come dressed in red and green in keeping with the holiday colors, and attach bells, ribbons, or other "ornamental" accessories in a creative way. Buy or make elf hats topped with pompoms and bells, and give them to guests as they arrive.

Decorations

In addition to all the holiday decorations you've no doubt collected over the years, add a few special touches. Turn your party room into "Santa's Workshop," "Mrs. Claus's Cookie Factory," or "Penguin Party Paradise." Hang up Christmas lights around the room. Set out candles on all flat surfaces. Play holiday music—traditional songs by Bing Crosby or childhood favorites like Frosty the Snowman. "Wrap" the tables with Christmas paper instead of traditional tablecloths and tie them up like packages with big bows. Wrap the front door as well, to greet the guests as they arrive, and tape wrapped candies to the door. Arrange fresh boughs of pine to make the room smell festive, along with mistletoe and poinsettias. Hang candy canes on everything from chair backs to lampshades. Buy inexpensive stockings and write the names of guests on them, then hang them along the mantel. Bake gingerbread or sugar cookies in the shape of letters and spell out holiday greetings around the room, such as "Happy Holidays" or "Merry Christmas!" Frost the windows with spray "snow," using a doily for a stencil to make snowflakes. For a whimsical touch, hang red felt Santa legs inside the fireplace.

Games and Activities

Start with a get-acquainted game to turn strangers into friends, decorate cookies and make gingerbread girls, and wind up the party with a Christmas Surprise.

Holiday Bingo

If you're hosting a large party where some guests are not acquainted, try this mixer that's sure to get everyone on a first-name basis. Call every one of your friends ahead of time and ask them to share a few unique holiday traditions, such as "What do you do on Christmas Eve?" "Where do you shop for most of your gifts?" "What's your favorite holiday song?"

"What cookies do you bake each year?" Cut out Bingo cards, fill the empty squares with requests like, "Find someone who bakes Candy Cane cookies every year" or "Find someone who loves the Figgy Pudding song." Give everyone a card and a sheet of holiday stickers, and have them search for all the answers until someone has Bingo.

Make-and-Take Cookie Cutter Ornaments

Mix up some Baker's Clay (4 cups flour, 1 cup salt, 1¾ cups water) or use hobby clay that dries hard. Divide up the dough and tint some of it red, some green, and leave some white. Roll out the dough, cut out shapes using Christmas theme cookie cutters, and make a small hole at the top. Bake on a foil-covered cookie sheet for an hour or so, until firm. Allow to cool, insert ribbon through the holes for hanging, then decorate with acrylic paints, permanent markers, or puffy paints.

Christmas Quiz

Read up on Christmas traditions using the Internet, and jot down some facts. Turn them into questions, such as "What did Frosty the Snowman have for a face?" "What are the names of the eight reindeer?" and "How do you make eggnog?" and have the guests try to answer the questions.

Gingerbread Condo

Let the guests make their own individual gingerbread houses and decorate them with icing, candies, and cookies. You don't have to limit yourselves to gingerbread houses—use your imagination to create gingerbread stores, gingerbread cars, even a gingerbread zoo. Award a prize to the most original.

Ornament Exchange

Ask guests to bring an ornament, wrapped, then have everyone take turns opening an ornament. Or have a Decoration Exchange, Yankee Swap, Holiday Accessory Exchange, or Chocolate Exchange.

Cookie Collection

Have your guests make three dozen of their favorite holiday cookies. Set their tray of cookies on the table as the guests arrive. When all the cookies are present, give the guests a large paper or plastic plate and let them circle around the table collecting an equal amount of the different cookies to take home.

Christmas Surprise

If there's someone on your list who is ill or can't come to the party, give her a twelve-day Christmas surprise. Ask each guest to bring an assigned number of small gifts, such as candy canes, candles, books, socks, chocolates, note cards, charms, hair ribbons, makeup, magazines, ornaments, or cookies. Cut out Christmas tree or Santa shapes, and have the guests write a verse of poem on the shape, altering the details as needed. Place both in individual festive bags, number them in order, and decorate them with pens and stickers. Over the next 12 days before Christmas, sneak up to the front door of the lucky girl after dark, place the bag on the doorstep, ring the bell, and hide. She'll open the door to find your mysterious gift at her feet. Repeat each day until Christmas, then gather everyone on the doorstep for the final present.

Refreshments

Eat some of the cookies the guests have made! Make an appetizer tree with veggies and dip on the side. Buy a large cone-shaped piece of Styrofoam from the craft store, then insert toothpicks halfway into veggies. Press the veggies-on-picks into the cone, covering it completely, to make it look like a tree. Use red, white, and green veggies—cherry tomatoes, cauliflower, bell peppers, and pea pods. Make peppermint sundaes with crushed candy canes and peppermint ice cream, with extra toppings such as nuts, candies, chocolate chips, crushed cookies, chocolate sauce. Make little petit fours "presents" and ice cream "snowballs" rolled in coconut. Bake or buy a Yule log cake for a stunning, edible centerpiece.

Favors, Prizes, and Gifts

Gift the guests with the leftover Christmas cookies in a holiday box, a book of Christmas stories, holiday music, ornaments, decorations, holiday socks, DVDs such as *A Christmas Story* or *Elf*, homemade fudge, elf hats—anything holiday related—except fruitcake.

Party Plus

Many of these ideas can be used at other holidays, such as Hanukkah, Valentine's Day, Easter, and so on. Just make the appropriate adjustments.

Happy Hanukkah Party

Celebrate with friends—Jewish and non-Jewish—and have your own festive festival of lights. The date of the holiday varies from year to year, but the celebration has been going on for over two thousand years. Jewish people celebrate the victory over the Maccabees and rededication of the temple. Hanukkah lasts for eight days, to symbolize the miracle of the oil that burned for eight days. The color scheme is blue and white, the candles are bright, and the fun and games are traditional. It's time to wish your friends a Happy Hanukkah!

Invitations

Buy small menorahs, or cut them out from blue posterboard. Write party details on the nine candle lights and mail to guests. Or make a six-pointed Star of David and write party details along the outside lines. Include blue confetti stars in the envelope, along with chocolate gold coins.

What to Wear

Ask guests to come dressed in blue and white outfits, anything from casual to formal. Or ask them to wear blue jeans with white shirts, then buy Star of David or Menorah pins and pass them out to the guests as they arrive, to decorate their outfits. Or have them decorate their own white T-shirts with blue fabric paint, to make Hebrew symbols, letters, or designs. Let them dry, then ask the guests to don their newly enhanced shirts.

Decorations

Set out decorative menorahs, and ask guests to bring theirs along to share for the evening. Hang six-pointed stars cut from blue posterboard from the ceiling. Use blue and white paper products, crepe paper, balloons, and other decorations to create a festive atmosphere. Write Jewish or Yiddish phrases, such as *Nes Gadol Hayah Sham* ("A great miracle happened here") or *Shalom* ("Peace") and tape them to the walls. Play Hebrew music such as "Ma'oz Tzur."

Decorations

Let the Festival of Lights live up to its name by burning lots of candles. Set up the menorah, and light candles all around the party room. Sprinkle around chocolate gold coins. Cover the table in the traditional colors of Hanukkah—silver, blue, and white—to create a dazzling display. Choose the same colors in flowers—tulips, narcissus, and hyacinths.

Games and Activities

Enjoy some fun from ancient times—and from your childhood.

Mind Your Own Beeswax Candles

Make your own candles for your menorah. Buy candle kits from your local craft store that includes sheets of beeswax and wicks, in blue and white. Roll the beeswax sheet around the wick to the thickness needed to fit your menorah. Cut off the wick below your candle and trim the top of the wick to half an inch. Roll the candle in glitter, and decorate it with sequins, jewels, and other small items. (Tip: If the beeswax is stiff, warm it with your hands or a blow dryer.)

Dreidel Dreidel Dreidel

You may know the song, but anyone can play the game. And if you think the dreidel game is just for kids, play for cash instead of chocolate gold coins. Here's how: Buy or make a dreidel, a sort of spinning top/ die. Sit in a circle with the dreidel in the middle. Before each spin, each player puts a coin into the pot. One player spins the dreidel. The symbol that lands face up determines the number of coins that player puts in or takes out of the pot. (See below.) When a player loses all of her coins, she's out of the game. The game ends when there are no more coins in the pot. The player with the most coins at that point wins.

Key to Dreidel Symbols

- *Nun* (or nicht)—do nothing.

- *Gimel* (or gut)—take the entire pot.

- *Hey* (or halb)—take half the pot (round up if there is an odd number of coins in the pot).

- *Shin* (or schlecht)—put in the same amount that you bet.

Make a Menorah

Set out craft supplies and let the guests make their own menorahs—candleholders that contain nine candles—out of clay, wood, or a kit.

Refreshments

Make potato latkes that have been fried or baked in oil that represents the oil found in the Temple of Jerusalem. Offer a variety of toppings for the latkes, such as sour cream, chutney, butter, chives, catsup, and other condiments. Or serve a variety of doughnuts, also symbolic of the oil. Pour kosher wine, grape juice, or sparkling cider, and toast each other with a special "Chaim!" cheer. Dairy products are also traditionally served during Hanukkah, honoring the heroism of Judith, who saved her town, so set out a variety of cheeses along with Matzoh crackers. Make your own pretzels and shape them into six-pointed stars or cut out butter cookies into star shapes and let your guests munch on them throughout the party. Don't forget to sprinkle chocolate gold coins around the room too.

Favors, Prizes, and Gifts

Give the guests decorative menorahs, candles, recipes and ingredients for latkes, dreidels, and chocolate coins.

CHAPTER 7

Major Events

> "Excess on occasion is exhilarating. It prevents moderation
> from acquiring the deadening effect of a habit."
>
> ~ *W. Somerset Maugham*

When something important happens in a friend's life—a new job, home, achievement, and so on—take time out to celebrate, and show her how happy, proud, and excited you all are. You can make it a surprise party or let her know the event is coming so she can enjoy the anticipation and prepare for the celebration. Here are some of the major events you may want to celebrate with your girlfriends, everything from saying hello to waving goodbye.

"Bon Voyage" Party

When a good friend is leaving, say goodbye with a flair and give her a taste of what's to come. Wrap the party around the destination, whether it's a cruise to Alaska or a climb up the Himalayas, and wish her a bon voyage by sending her off in style. If she's moving away for good, that's all the more reason to host a festive farewell and let her know you'll miss her.

Invitations

Write your invitations on postcards or brochures that represent the vacation or relocation spot. Or use luggage tags for your party details. When including the information, use the dialect or language of the destination, such as "Aloha, Wahinis!" for Hawaii or "Howdy, Gals!" for Texas.

What to Wear

Dress according to the destination, such as kilts for Scotland, safari wear for Kenya, or Mickey Mouse ears for Disneyland. Or come as tacky tourists with loud shirts, dangling cameras, big sunglasses, and plaid suitcases. For a moving destination, choose outfits that fit the location, such as down vests for a cold weather climate or tank tops for a southern site. Or wear flight attendant or pilot clothes.

Decorations

Use maps of the vacation or relocation spot to hang on the wall, along with posters of the area. Turn the party room into the inside of an airplane, cruise ship, or hotel, or scene from the vacation destination or new homeland. Play appropriate music—country western for the southwest, Vienna Waltz for a trip to Europe. Set out items representing the destination—a British teapot, a Hawaiian lei, a Canadian maple leaf, or New York Broadway banners.

Games and Activities

Better know your geography for the upcoming games and activities—or you may find yourselves "lost."

Where Am I?

Collect brochures or postcards from various places, show them to the players, and see if they can guess the destination. Offer clues as prompts if they get stuck, such as "Everything here is BIG!" for Texas.

Traveling Nightmares

Have everyone share their worst vacation or moving experiences—lost luggage, wrong airport, no furniture for a week, and so on.

Lost in Translation

Read some simple foreign phrases aloud and see if anyone can guess the translation. For example, try, *Parlez-vous anglais?* (French for "Do you speak English?"), *Konnten Sie mir helfen?* (German for "Can you help me?") *Non importa.* (Italian for "It doesn't matter.") *No hablo español* (Spanish for "I don't speak Spanish").

Wish You Were Here

Pass out postcards from the local area to all the guests, and ask them to write a message to the guest of honor. Tell them to include their contact information at the bottom. Collect the postcards, then mail one every day after the dear departed has left, for a daily surprise in her mailbox.

Refreshments

Ask the guests to bring snacks representing the new location to share at the party. For example, if she's traveling to Mexico, have a fiesta with do-it-yourself burritos and tacos, chips, and salsa. If Boston is going to be the new home, offer Boston Clam Chowder along with seafood. Make the cake in the shape of the state or country, or make a rectangle cake and decorate it like a postcard with "Wish You Were Here!" written on top.

Favors, Prizes, and Gifts

Give the going-away girl a survival kit, complete with plug adapter, Dramamine, foreign phrase book, postcards, maps, film, snacks, travel guidebooks, magazines, and a blank journal to keep a record of her experiences. Or give her an address book with all the info filled in by the guests.

Party Plus
If you can afford it, surprise her by making a trip to her destination!

Welcome Home Housewarming Party

Moving into a new home ranks among one of the most exciting—and stressful—events in life. If there's a newcomer to the neighborhood, host a cozy housewarming party at your place, then use the opportunity to show her what a great town she's living in, with an introduction to all the cafes, crafts shops, spas, and salons in the area.

Invitations

Have an artist or friend draw a sketch of the guest of honor's new house. Photocopy it, fold it into a card, and write your party details inside. Or cut out a mailbox shape from colored tag board (folded in half so the invitation will open up along the fold line), and write the guest of honor's new address on it. Open the invitation, and write your party details inside. For fun, find a picture of a tumbledown shack and photocopy it, telling your guests it's the new home. Write your party details on the back of the picture. Or using a map, photocopy the route from each guest's house to the new home. Tie a yellow ribbon around your invitation to symbolize a welcome home.

What to Wear

Have the guests wear classic housewife outfits. Or ask them to stereotype the area in which they live—cowgirl hats and boot for Texas, rain gear for Oregon, flowered shirts for Hawaii or California.

Decorations

Tie yellow ribbons of welcome on the doors, chairs, tables, and other items inside the house, and including the trees, mailbox, and lamppost outside. Photocopy sections of a map of the community, town, city, or state to use as placemats. If your guest of honor is new to the area, hang a map on the wall with useful points of interest, such as the best grocery store, the cheapest gas station, and the most popular restaurant. If she's just relocating within the community, use the map to point out the most unusual spots of interest, using your sense of humor. For a newcomer to the area, pick up some samples from various local stores and use them as a centerpiece. Hang up local signs, such as "Historic Spot" or "Old Oak Tree."

Games and Activities

Turn your town into an entertainment center with the following fun and games.

Welcome to (Your Town)

Give your guest of honor a virtual "guided tour" of the area. Videotape various local "highlights," and jot down a few humorous notes so you can narrate while giving the "tour" during your party. Delight your guests with questionable local sites, like the city dump, while boasting about the "luxurious and prestigious neighborhood," and the local biker bar, while promising a "great nightlife."

Who's Who

Introduce everyone at the party, giving a brief description of each one's occupation, family, and so on. Then give the guest of honor a quiz on all the new information. Or give her a list with each guest's name, occupation, hobby, and other personal details, and have her guess who's who. Or ask everyone to say three surprising things about themselves.

(Your Town) Quiz

Write up some funny true-or-false questions about the area and quiz the guest of honor, such as, "The name of the local high school is Elvis Presley High—true or false?" "The population of the town is 408 (unless there's a baseball game in the city)—true or false?" "The local festival queen is called Miss Zucchini—true or false?" Make sure some of the questions are true and some are false, but have fun with it—the more ridiculous the true answers, the better.

Refreshments

Buy croissants from the local bakery, coffee from a gourmet store, and cold cuts from a good deli. Have a potluck and request that each guest bring a specific dish. For example, if it's a brunch, assign drinks (orange juice, Bloody Marys, champagne, and coffee), bread (rolls, croissants, pastries, and bagels), meat (bacon strips, ham slices, and sausage links or patties), and a fruit dish or salad, along with a dessert. Ask your guests to bring a recipe along with the food, or bring the food in a nice basket, plate, or dish to give the new homeowner. Or have your guests bring foods from the newcomer's former area, such as barbecue from Texas, fried chicken from the south, or knishes from New York. Make a cake featuring local fruits, such as a strawberry shortcake, banana cream pie, or peach cobbler.

Favors, Prizes, and Gifts

Build a Handy Girl Tree from scrap lumber, then tie on much-needed tools for the newcomer, such as a small hammer, screwdriver, tape measure, and so on. Give her a housewarming plant for her new home. Offer sample items from favorite stores, such as a salad from the grocery store deli or flowers from a favorite nursery. Ask the guests to bring a frozen meal so the newcomer will have a stock of dinners to last for a while. Give her a copy of the "Your New Town" videotape.

Party Plus
Make it a surprise party at the newcomer's home, and bring the party to her.

"You're Outta There!" Graduation Party

Whether it's high school, college, beauty school, or business school, the graduate deserves an "Outta There!" Party. Host a final farewell to school days without a lot of pomp and circumstance and make your party the top of its class. Choose a theme for the party to fit the graduate, such as "Take a Break" with a tropical setting, "You're a Star" with a theatrical background, "It's a Jungle Out There" with a rainforest theme, "Smooth Sailing" with a nautical touch, or "Show Me the Money" with a financial slant.

Invitations

Write the party details with a calligraphy pen on white parchment, then roll up and tie with ribbons using school colors. Or make a grad cap invitation from black card stock tied with a tassel and write details in silver ink. Create a fake "Final Exam" for your invitation, and ask multiple choice questions such as, "At Jennifer's Graduation Party, you want: a. lots of food, b. a disc jockey, c. a toga party, or d. all of the above." Or make personalized Report Cards with party details included. Include a kindergarten picture of the graduate, along with the senior picture, for a "Before" and "After" look.

What to Wear

Ask guests to come dressed as school stereotypes, such as a cheerleader, jock, nerd, skater, teacher, principal, or custodian. Or have them all wear grad gowns and caps, rented from a costume store or graduation supply shop.

Decorations

Tape up banners with "Class of . . ." signs in school colors. Hang grad caps from the ceiling, as if they're flying through the air. Decorate the room with school mementoes, such as saved dance tickets, dried corsages, prom programs, textbooks, old reports, beat-up binders, pictures from the yearbook. Give the guests grad caps to wear and megaphones and clappers to use at the party. Rent movies to play in the background, such as *Rock and Roll High School, National Lampoon's Animal House,* or *The Breakfast Club.* Cover the table with the newspaper want-ad section, and circle some of the weirder ads. Write famous quotes about the importance of education on scroll paper and use them as placemats. Have the school mascot serve as a centerpiece.

Games and Activities

It's back to school to test your academic skills, challenge your memory, and capture the good times.

Who's My Teacher?

Write the names of teachers on sticky labels, place them on guests as they arrive, and have players ask "Yes/No" questions to find out who they are. If the guests didn't all go to the same school, write the names of career possibilities instead, such as "Obstetrician," "Astronaut," "Beauty Queen," "Fashion Designer," and "Housewife."

Autograph Session

Give the guests autograph bears, dogs, caps, or books to sign. Ask them to make up short poems instead of just signing their signatures.

School Scrapbook

Set out scrapbooking materials and have the guests help the grad make a memory book of school life. Designate each page with a caption, such as "The Campus," "The Sorority," "The Football Game," "The Dorm," and "The Hottest Guy on Campus." Leave room for her pictures.

Refreshments

Have "school cafeteria helpers" wearing aprons and hairnets serve classic cafeteria food (only better quality) on trays. Give each dish a name card, such as "Science Experiment Surprise" or "Anthro Appetizers," "Biology Broccoli," and "Gym Jell-O." Offer popular school foods, such as pizzas, hamburgers, chips, and sodas. Serve them from lunch boxes and pour drinks from thermoses. Make a cake centerpiece that looks like the school mascot or a grad cap.

Favors, Prizes, and Gifts

Give the guests grad hats, clappers, and megaphones, scrapbooks, autograph bears, or address books, "Class of . . ." photo frames, pencils with school name or pens for future use, key chains for the "key to the future" that comes with a flashlight, compass, tool, or whistle. Give the grad job applications from fast-food restaurants, resume paper, a quality pen, a desk nameplate, a "Key" to the Corporate Restroom, or go in on a nice briefcase.

Party Plus

If you've got a bunch of grads, make it a group party for all. Invite a special guest, such as a favorite teacher or job recruiter.

Congratulations! You're Hired!

It's a special occasion when a friend lands that coveted post, so welcome her to a fun-filled "first day on the job." She'll most likely need a jumpstart when the nine-to-five grind begins! Or she may have first-day jitters that require a little advice and a lot of encouragement. Let's get this party started!

Invitations

Choose your invitations according to the type of job she's starting, to personalize it and set the stage. For example, if she's taking a medical job, make your invitations look like health forms. If she'll be working for a film studio, create a script for an invitation. And if she's going to be an administrative assistant or CEO, use "While You Were Out" messages or specially printed business cards with the party details included on them. If you want to keep it generic, you can adapt job application forms to use as invitations, make the details looks like commute books, or get brochures or other information about the place of employment and use them as invitations.

What to Wear

Have everyone come dressed as if they, too, are going to work at the new job. If the guest of honor has been hired as a waitress, wear aprons. If she's going to be working in fashion, wear a designer outfit. If she's about to teach art, come as art students in paint-spattered smocks. Or have everyone wear business suits.

Decorations

Replicate the new office, classroom, or future job site. Hang fitting signs, such as, "Quiet! Work Zone!" or make them funny, such as, "Employees Must Wash Their Hands After Every Sale!" Create a slotted wall hanging for guests to place their "time cards." Hang clocks all around the room, for the clock-watching employees. Add other details that go with the job, such as school supplies for the elementary school teacher, hair products for the salon stylist, or photographic equipment for the photographer. Play work-related movies in the background, such as *Office Space, The Devil Wears Prada, Working Girl,* or *No Reservations.*

Games and Activities

Play games that work well in an office setting, then test the players on their interview skills, for that future dream job they all covet.

Desktop Games

Buy some of the popular desktop games, such as miniature bowling, football, basketball, and sandbox that are made for bored office workers. Set them up around the room for guests to play.

Executive Darts

Hang a dartboard and let everyone try her hand at throwing darts. This game works best with a beer in the other hand.

Job Interview

Write up some questions that are often used at a job interview and put them in a hat or bowl (see examples below). Next, write up some odd jobs and put them in a hat or bowl (see below). Have players take turns picking a job from one hat and a question from another. Have them answer appropriately for the job they selected. For example, if a player picks "Clown" from the job hat and "Why were you fired?" from the interview hat, she might answer, "I was fired from my Clown job because I made the kids cry instead of laugh."

Odd Jobs: Circus Clown, Window Washer, Bank Robber, School Bus Driver, Medical Guinea Pig, Subpoena Server, Strip Club Dancer, Crime Scene Cleaner, Bird Watcher, Video Game Tester.

Interview Questions:

1. Why were you fired from your last job?
2. What were your job responsibilities?
3. What was the most rewarding part of the job?
4. What was your biggest failure at the job?
5. Why are you leaving your previous job?
6. What was your workday like?
7. What motivated you at your last job?
8. How did you handle stress on the job?
9. What kind of work environment did you have?
10. Why do you think you were successful at your job?

Job Expertise

Do a little research on the Internet, then ask a series of questions about the new job to see how prepared she is. For example, you might ask "When was the company formed?" "Who are the company's biggest competitors?" "Where is the company headquarters located?" "How many employees does the company have?" and "What kind of car does the boss drive?"

Refreshments

Serve common office or workplace foods, such as donuts and coffee, pre-made sandwiches, veggie and fruit trays, and so on. Or serve something appropriate to the job, such as Italian food for a new restaurant job, cafeteria food for a new teaching job, and health food for a new personal training job. For a centerpiece cake, make a sheet cake and decorate it with small toys appropriate to the job, and write: "You're Hired!" or "Welcome to (Name of Company)!" on the top.

Favors, Prizes, and Gifts

Buy or make your own "Pimp My Cubicle" kits for everyone attending, and include things like cute little figurines or action figures, puzzles, and other boredom busters, photos of mentors, candy, and sticky notes. Pass out stress balls to squeeze for on-the-job relief. Give them magazines to help with their careers, such as *Forbes, Wired, Women's Work, Fortune,* or *U.S. News and World Report.*

Party Plus

Surprise the new girl by taking her out to lunch her first day on the job.

"Gone Fishin'—Permanently!" Party

When the day finally comes when your friend packs up her desk drawer, turns in the key, and heads for the luxury cruise ship—or next job—help her say her final goodbyes with a great party. Choose a theme based on her favorite hobbies, such as golf, her interests, such as reading, or her goals, such as traveling, and the rest of the party will fall into place.

Invitations

Design a newspaper headline declaring the retirement day a national holiday. Include a photo of the retiree's face superimposed on the body of a goofy tourist getup or leisure outfit. Write newspaper columns listing the place, time, and date of the party, then photocopy the paper for the guests. Create a "before and after" advertisement for stress management or cosmetic surgery from a magazine, with a caption like, "Working vs. Retired." Use the same photo of the retiree in both pictures, but add lines and shadows to the "before" picture and a big fake smile to the "after" picture. Write the party details on something that relates to leisure time, such as a motorhome brochure, a hobby instruction sheet, or a golf course ad. Using a paycheck as a model, create a fake paycheck to mail to your guests. Fill in the date of the party where you would normally put the date on the check, add your guests' names in the space provided, and sign your name where the check normally requires a signature. Then write party details in the open space on the check. Write something like "Good for one evening of fun and good cheer" on the line where the amount is usually written. Use your imagination to personalize the invitation and make it humorous. Write up a fake resume for the retiree, with funny descriptions of odd jobs she's had over the years, such as "PTA Treasurer," "Brownie Leader," "Neighborhood Greeter," "Carpool Driver," and so on. Make the last entry on the resume "Guest of Honor" and write your party details underneath. Send each guest an inexpensive white sailor cap, available at party and theatrical stores, with the party details written inside. On the outside write, "Gone Fishing—Permanently," to intrigue the guests.

What to Wear

Ask your guests to come dressed as stereotypical retirees, in leisure suits, tourist outfits, fishing gear, housecoats, T-shirts, golf clothes, and beach togs. Have them dress to reflect the retiree's hobby or interest.

Decorations

Set up a retirement scene with a hammock, straw hat, sunglasses, portable radio, tropical drink, tabloid newspaper, chocolates, and travel pillow. Stuff some clothes to create a retiree lying on the hammock. Place chaise lounges, rockers, hammocks, pillows, and other comfortable seating for the guests to relax in. Hang travel posters from all over the world. Superimpose headshots of the retiree onto photos of a tacky tourist, a lazy housewife, or a woman in a rocking chair. Blow up the pictures and tape them to the walls, or turn them into cardboard cutouts and prop them around the room. Make a small hammock from fishing net to hold the guest of honor's gifts. Set out brochures from retirement communities, cruise ships, distant ports of call, airlines, and railways. If she's planning a special trip, use it as a theme for your decorations. Include items from her hobby or interest activity as props for the party. For example, if she's a golf fanatic, display golf clubs, have everyone wear golf clothes, hang golf tees from the ceiling, put up posters of famous golfers, and rent a "how-to-golf" DVD to play in the background. If she plans to paint, have the guests wear smocks or paint-spattered overalls, set up easels, make a centerpiece out of tubes of paint, and hang up prints by famous artists. Set up each table with different collections from the retiree's hobbies or interests. For example, the Scrapbooker Table could feature papers, embellishments, glue, and scissors, the Weekend Painter Table could feature art supplies, and the World Traveler might offer travel items. Create place cards to match, such as personalized golf balls, watercolor sets, travel postcards, each personalized with guests' names using permanent black markers. Cut out employment want ads, cover with clear contact paper, and use them as placemats for the guests. Circle some of the classic retiree jobs using a red marker, such as "Security Guard," "Newspaper Delivery Person," or "Fast-Food Server." Get job applications from the local stores and place them around the room or hang them on the walls, or laminate them and use them as placemats.

Games and Activities

Find out if it's time to retire, pick a hobby, or get another job, with these goofy games and activities.

Pin the Hobby on the Retiree

Blow up a picture of the retiree in her work clothes and have it mounted on posterboard. Draw or cut out pictures of some suntan lotion, a camera, a straw hat, an oversized bag, comfortable shoes, and other retiree items. Have the players take turns trying to pin the accessory onto the appropriate place on the poster. Give the decorated poster to the retiree as a memento.

Office Trivia

Ask each guest to write down a question about work, the office, the personnel, or anything related, such as "When does the water cooler get filled?" "How many sick days are employees allowed?" "What does this company really do?" Take turns asking the questions to the retiree as she tries to answer. If a player stumps her, she wins a prize.

Retiree Roast

Give the guests a chance to poke fun at the retiree. Everyone enjoys hearing funny stories about the special guest (as long as the anecdotes aren't mean-spirited). Ask them to share stores about their most embarrassing work-related movements with the retiree.

What Now?

Ask each player to write down a suggestion for a leisure-time activity. Most of your guests will probably write something funny or silly such as, "Finally learn to program the VCR," "Return your neighbor's baking supplies," or "Write that sexy romance novel—after you've had some real-life experiences," and so on.

Life After Work

Invite a tarot card reader or psychic to come and tell the retiree's future now that she's finished with work. Or have the guests themselves "predict" what the retiree will do next, by writing the predictions on cards, then reading them aloud. To make it fun, have the guests write down a prediction that begins with each letter of the retiree's name, such as "Baker," "Rapper," "Investigator," and "Entertainer," for "B-R-I-E."

Memory Book

Have each guest write down a memory of working with the retiree. Take a Polaroid picture of the guest, insert it into a scrapbook or photo album, along with the memory, for a lasting keepsake.

Refreshments

Offer classic but simple fare to illustrate the retiree's new budget, such as pork 'n' beans, Hamburger Helper, and bologna sandwiches. Serve the food on paper plates, with lots of mismatched glasses. If the retiree is planning a trip, serve food related to the destination, such as Mexican food for a trip to Mexico or Italian for a trip to Rome. If she took a bag lunch to work every day, hand your guests brown paper bags filled with surprising gourmet treats. They'll have fun opening the lunch bags and finding elegant foods. Serve champagne or sparkling cider to toast the retiree good luck. Have a bakery make a special centerpiece cake for the retiree, using work or leisure as a theme. Design it to look like the shape of a house for a retiring architect, a cash register for a clerk, or a briefcase for a businessperson. If the theme is leisure, create a cake that looks like a golf course for a golf fanatic, an open book for an aspiring writer, or a boat for a sailing enthusiast.

Favors, Prizes, and Gifts

Give the guest of honor a Retirement Suit. Put together a mismatched outfit using items from a thrift store, such as silky pajamas, a bathrobe, a jogging outfit, mismatched socks, house slippers, a straw hat, and so on. Other ideas include: Spare time fillers, such as books, tapes, puzzles, hobby supplies, mementos from work, such as a desk calendar or T-shirt, foreign-language phrase book for traveling, retirement guide, hammock or pillows, sports equipment, bottle of wine, subscription to *AARP* magazine, blank book for writing a novel or journal, leisure suit, sweatshirt, or other casual articles of clothing, photo album with pictures of coworkers, gag gifts, such as fake gold watches, chocolate watches, funny business cards, job souvenirs, office supplies, calendar filled with boredom busters, deck of cards, retirement, leisure, or hobby magazines, badminton or croquet set, humorous book about retirement, inexpensive pen sets, fancy lunch bag or box, address book, and photo album. Give antacids to those who are still working.

Party Plus

Host the party at a fancy hotel, on a rented yacht, at a nearby resort, in a cabin, or other creative venue, tied to the theme or interests of the retiree. Set up a reproduction of the retiree's office or workspace. Have a retirement expert come and speak to the group and offer tips for retiring. Have each guest bring a craft project or other task that needs doing, and offer it to the retiree to complete, since she has "time on her hands."

CHAPTER 8

Singles Only Parties

"Ever notice that Soup for One is eight aisles away from Party Mix?"

~ *Elayne Boosler*

Celebrate singlehood and invite your friends who are still mate-free for a good old, all gal gathering. Currently there are 96 million unmarried people in the nation, so you and your pals are certainly not alone. Come cheer each other on, with one of these great themes for those who like their independence and autonomy. Who needs a man with friends like yours! You go, girl!

Valentine's Day Sucks

Who invented this holiday, anyway—the greeting card companies? No doubt. While guys usually dread this day, girls fantasize about it, hoping for something romantic. Unfortunately, they're often disappointed when the day doesn't meet their expectations. Luckily, today you can find sarcastic cards as well as mushy cards, so you're not alone if you don't favor this super-sweet holiday. Here are some ways to enjoy Valentine's Day in spite of the sentiment.

Invitations

Buy several anti–Valentine's Day cards to use as invitations, or make your own, using the "Roses are red" formula, with sassy, silly homemade Valentines. Cut hearts from pink, purple, red, and white construction paper, add lace, glitter, and stickers, or make them from leftover candy wrappers, magazine ads, and cut-up pieces of Valentine cards. Then write a poem to invite your guests, such as,

"Roses are red, Violets are blue, Men are pigs, So kiss them 'Adieu!'"

Or "Roses are dead, Love is a lie, Jim is a jerk, Let's roast the guy!"

What to Wear

Have the guests dress up in their fanciest outfits, sluttiest clothes, or come like slobs and just be comfortable. Or tell them all to wear their PJs, slippers, and robes—as long as they're comfy and not sexy. Or have T-shirts made with the bad guy's face, circled in red with a line through it, and pass them out to guests.

Decorations

To give the party room a feeling of romance gone wrong, hang up sheets of pink or red crepe paper all over the walls, then add "Valentine's Day Sucks" graffiti using large black markers. Set up a small table in the center of the room and cover it with a white cloth and add negative phrases with markers, such as "Men are Pigs" or "Love Hurts." Cut out hearts from pink, red, violet, and white construction paper, then cut them in half, creating a jagged line. Sprinkle them over the table. Make more hearts from black construction paper, with all the evil boyfriends' names written on them in glitter pens. Play lady-killer music, such as Shania Twain's "Whose Bed Have Your Boots Been Under." Set out bowls of potpourris for a sweet aroma, light scented candles around the room, and set the table with your best dishes and champagne glasses. Place a black or chocolate rose at each setting.

Games and Activities

It's time to ridicule all those sappy sentiments that circulate during Valentine's Day, so get your goofy game on and kick the "man" out of romance!

Venus vs. Mars

Write down some fun questions about men to ask the group, and enjoy the hilarious answers you get. For example, you might ask, "Why do men call each other by stupid names like Jerk-Off and Pea-Brain?" "Why do men fight over the bill?" "Why don't men like to shop?" "Why does a man only have three bathroom products?" "Why don't men like cats?" "Why don't men worry about how they look?" "Why do men act like children?" "Why don't men put the toilet seat down?"

Romance Rules!

Find out how romantic you are by asking questions, such as, "Where's the best place to make love?" "What's your idea of the perfect date?" "Name an aphrodisiac food." Vote on the best answers. Or reverse it with a game of Romance Rules—Not! and ask the opposite of such questions, such as, "Where's the worst place to make love?" and so on.

Anti-Valentines

Hand out heart-shaped paper, along with colorful markers, and have everyone write an anti-love poem to an ex. Get them started with, "Roses are red . . ." Read the poems aloud when everyone is finished. For added fun, mix them up and guess who wrote which poem!

Chick Flicks

Put on a nonstop marathon of chick flicks featuring strong women, such as *Thelma and Louise, Fried Green Tomatoes, Ms. Potter,* or *The Spirit of Diana.*

Refreshments

Offer the guests popcorn and candy during the movies, then treat yourselves to a nice dinner—steak, lobster, the works. Or just eat junk food all night! Save room for decadent desserts, such as chocolate brownies or hot fudge sundaes.

Favors, Prizes, and Gifts

Send the girls home with gourmet chocolates, sexy underwear, a romance novel, or a joke book about men.

Party Plus

Host the party at a bar or dance club and flirt your pants off all night to help get over the broken heart.

"Get Over It" Party

We all have bad days now and then. Could be triggered at work, by a man, or simply be the blues. Turn her mood around with a "Get Over It" party that will lift her spirits. Choose a theme based on her hobby or interest to personalize it and make it even more special, to show her that life has plenty of exciting things to do and see, in spite of feeling temporarily down and out.

Invitations

Cheer her up by reminding her of the things she loves to do. If she likes to backpack in the jungle, make passport invitations or send guests a compass with party details attached to the back. If she's into golf or tennis, write party details on golf or tennis balls, and mail them in small boxes.

What to Wear

Have everyone wear "Get Over It (her name)!" T-shirts with her picture ironed on. Or ask the guests to dress for the selected theme. For example, if she likes to camp, set up camping equipment, even a tent, and ask guests to dress outdoorsy. Or have them come as green-thumbed gardeners! For a favorite vacation spot, guests can dress in Hawaiian shirts, grass skirts, and leis, safari gear for a Rainforest Trek. If it's a hobby-related party, ask guests to come in tennis outfits, golf attire, or anything that relates to the theme and reminds her of the joys in life.

Decorations

Whatever she's into—scrapbooking, cooking, jewelry making—decorate with related supplies. For example, if she loves to scrap, set out scrapbooking materials, cooking utensils if she likes to cook, or costume jewelry if she's into bling, along with posters offering silly sayings, such as "Scrapbooking 101: Be prepared to spend your paycheck on paper, glue, and ribbons." If she's a gourmet cook, write up simple instructions, such as "How to Make a Peanut Butter and Jelly Sandwich: Step 1. Buy white bread (if you can still find it!). Step 2. Taste-test peanut butter (to make sure it's good and chunky). Step 3. Throw out jelly and substitute chocolate (much better!)." Hang up pictures of people she admires, places she wants to visit, and things she wants to do.

Games and Activities

Get her back into a good mood with a few laughs, a few memories, and a whole bunch of fun.

You're Special! Quiz

Ask the guests questions about the guest of honor, such as her hobbies and interests, her job, and exciting things that have happened in her life. For example, you might ask: "When's her birthday?" "What time does she leave for work in the morning?" "Has she ever met any movie stars?" "What's her favorite song?" "Name three plants she has in her yard." After each player answers a question, have the honored guest give her answer to see if she's right. Award a chocolate when a guest has a correct answer. Whoever has the most chocolates wins a prize—more chocolate!

Favorite Memory

Ask the guests to share a favorite memory about the guest of honor and videotape the responses. Give her the tape to keep, to remind her of how much she's loved. Or have guests go around and tell what they admire about her the most. Have someone write down the statements, then print it out on the computer in a fancy font on nice paper to keep.

Refreshments

Make all her favorite foods—her favorite salad, her favorite sandwiches, her favorite dessert. Or make the refreshments match the hobby or interest, such as gourmet food for the gourmet cook or lots of salad for the gardener. If she's a sports nut, offer sports drinks, power bars, Hero sandwiches, ball-decorated cupcakes. For the scrapbooker, make a patchwork cake.

Favors, Prizes, and Gifts

Give the guests gifts that would cheer up anyone, such as a book of humor, a box of candy, some fun underwear, new beauty products, a great CD, a comedy DVD, or a funny picture of the guest of honor and friends.

Party Plus

Make it a surprise party! Or take her away for a spa day, treat her to a salon makeover, shop for a new outfit to cheer her up. Or go to a comedy club for a good laugh and lift for low spirits.

Men-Are-Pigs Breakup Party

Help your broken-hearted friend through her depression with a Men-Are-Pigs Breakup Party—and watch her recover faster than she can eat a carton of ice cream (although that's a good idea too). Besides, a party is a lot cheaper than therapy. This one works perfectly for the girl who's been dumped by her boyfriend or a new ex-wife going through a divorce.

Invitations

Have fun with the invites and superimpose the bad guy's head on a pig's body, a "Wanted" poster, or other embarrassing picture. Draw a red circle around the picture with a line through it. Write party details at the bottom. Or use a copy of the divorce papers, altered with party details.

What to Wear

Dress to kill and wear your hottest outfits to show how steamy you still are. Or make T-shirts with the creep's face doctored by adding a mustache, warts, big ears, and so on.

Decorations

Hang posters of the pigman with embarrassing alterations and accessories, such as his face on a female lingerie model's body, in a pigsty, with a box of Viagra, and so on. Set out male voodoo dolls filled with pins. Hang a banner that reads, "Wedding dress for sale; worn once by mistake" or "You go, girl!" If you can find anything of his, such as an old shirt, a CD, or a letter, bring it to the party and doctor it— cover the shirt with fake blood, break the CD into pieces, and burn the letter in an ashtray. If she's ready to get rid of her wedding gown, write funny slogans on it with permanent marker and hang it, in effigy, from the ceiling.

Games and Activities

Men: Can't live with them, can't kill them, so make the best of them with some silly antics and activities. No one says you can't laugh at them!

Picture This

Photocopy a picture of the idiot for all the guests. Pass out black markers and have them "decorate" the picture any way they like—draw a unibrow, put his hair in pigtails, add a clown nose, shoot an arrow through his head, and so on. The best picture wins a prize.

Penis Piñata

Order a penis piñata from the Internet or make one yourself, then hang it up and let the ex have at it with a baseball bat. Make sure the piñata is stuffed with chocolate—or gummy penises.

Rated Ex Movies

Watch videos that feature dumped wives and girlfriends who overcome their breakups, such as *Under the Tuscan Sun, First Wives' Club, War of the Roses, Waiting to Exhale,* and *Le Divorce.* Eat gourmet chocolate and ice cream while you watch.

Sob Stories

Ask the guests to take turns sharing their breakup stories. Pass a box of chocolates to the speaker while she tells her sob story. The most devastating breakup wins a prize.

Burn It

To help your friend get over the breakup, make it payback time. Have her take something of the ex's and set it on fire over an ashtray, pan, or garbage can. (Be careful you don't burn the house down. That would just make things worse!) Try old letters, underwear, and a favorite picture of the two of them. If burning isn't an option—his CDs would give off toxic gases, his socks would smell up the place, and his favorite chair is too big—donate it to the thrift shop or local prison—or just stuff it into the garbage . . . after dousing it with Lysol.

Voodoo Magic

Go online and order an inexpensive Voodoo doll from a Voodoo shop—or make your own by tying some old socks (preferably his) into the shape of a head, body, arms, and legs. Add a face with a black marker and write the name of the "victim" across the front. Pass around the voodoo doll and give everyone a pin. Have them place a curse on it as they take turns jabbing the doll with the pin. Give the ex a knife . . .

Men Are a Joke

Tell jokes about men. One easy way is to change "blonde jokes" into "men jokes" by substituting the word "men" for "blonde." But here are some men jokes to get you laughing:

- "My husband and I split up because we were incompatible. I'm a Virgo and he was an asshole."

- "We divorced over religious reasons. He thought he was God and I didn't."

- "Half of all marriages end in divorce. That's the good news. The bad news: The other half end in death."

- "Ninety percent of men kiss their wives goodbye when they leave the house. Fifty percent of men kiss their houses goodbye when they leave their wives."

- "What should you do if you see your husband rolling around on the ground in pain? Shoot him again."

- "If you saw your ex-husband or his lawyer drowning in the river, would you go to lunch or a movie?"

Refreshments

Drinks are a must, so make them fun. Mix up some margaritas, Cosmos, Mojitos, Appletinis, or a favorite with exes—a Dirty Bastard. Fill a glass with ice and pour in 1½ ounces vodka, ½ ounce blackberry brandy, and fill the rest with cranberry juice. Squeeze in a little lime and mix well. Give the guests "Peppermint Peckers" (available online at Plumparty.com or Bachelorette.com) to munch on. Serve an obscene cake—two round balls and a teeny tiny rectangular penis. Fill in with chocolate and devour.

Favors, Prizes, and Gifts

Let the girls have their own voodoo dolls to take home and use when necessary. Give them their own packages of Peppermint Peckers. And chocolate.

Party Plus

Check out the Bachelorette Party chapter (page 31) where you'll find ideas for a "Free At Last" night on the town.

BFF Party—Best Friends Forever

Once in a while it's just nice to celebrate special friendships, whether you host a party for just one friend or the whole gang of BFFs. It's a chance to show your friends how much they mean to you, and to thank them for all they do. It's those BFFs that get you through the hard times, the good times, and the wild times, so pay it back—or forward—with a fun-filled Friends Forever fête!

Invitations

Find a picture of you and your best friend—or the whole group. Photocopy it to make personalized invitations, then write party details around the outside edges. Label the girls in the pictures with nicknames or personality characteristics, such as "The Sweet One," "The Funny One," "The Good Listener," and so on.

What to Wear

Choose a theme for the party and dress appropriately. For example, if it's a "Day at the Mall Party," wear something fashionable. If it's a "Mani & Pedi Party," put on comfortable clothes. If you're hosting the party at your home, you can wear anything from funky PJs to faded prom dresses. Better yet, wear the same thing the BFF usually wears!

Decorations

Decorate in your BFF's favorite colors. Fill the room with crepe paper streamers and balloons, along with anything else that matches the colors—stuffed animals, candles, scarves, pictures, and paper products. Turn one of her best photos into a giant poster and hang it on the wall. Have everyone sign it with a special message. Play her favorite music in the background.

Games and Activities

Friends love to find out more about each other, so try the following games and activities that help you explore your friendships.

What We Love About You

Have the girls all tell the BFF what they love about her, such as "I love you because you're really kind," or "I love you because you always share your chocolate." Go around several times until you've exhausted the topic—then start giving funny answers, like "I love you because you watch Jerry Springer."

Who Knows Her Best

Ask some bizarre questions about the BFF and see who can answer them the best. Questions might include, "What animal would she like to be?" "Why would she make a good astronaut?" "What food would she never eat?" "Why does she take so long to get dressed?" "If she had to choose between (hot guy) and (another hot guy), who would she choose and why?"

Complete Makeover

Although you love her just the way she is, give her a makeover anyway. Put a bunch of makeover tasks in a hat, such as "New Hairstyle," "Fancy Manicure," "Creative Pedicure," "Leg Wax," "Eyebrow Redesign," "Makeup Makeover," "Foot Massage," and so on. Have everyone draw a task from the hat, then perform it on the BFF—all at once, if possible!

Refreshments

Serve do-it-yourself mini pizzas—and make a special one for the BFF with all her favorite toppings. Or give her a slice of each of yours! Decorate cupcakes with the BFF's name and each guest's name, such as "Lilly & Stefanie = BFFs 4EVER." Have her serve each one to each friend. Or make a cake with a picture of her face featured on top.

Party Plus

Take her out for a day of her choosing—to the park, horseback riding, a tennis tournament, dance lessons—it's up to her!

CHAPTER 9

Smart and Crafty Parties

"I am thankful for the mess to clean after a party because it means I have been surrounded by friends."

~ Nancie J. Carmody

Many smart and crafty girls enjoy gathering with friends for an afternoon or evening of handwork, whether it's crafts and chats, stitching and bitching, scrapping and sharing, or book talk and treats. It's more fun to work with friends around than by yourself, so arrange a Smart and Crafty Party for a few hours of productive fun. Here are some suggestions for those at-home girls-only get-togethers who like to keep their minds—and hands—active.

Cool Crafts Party

For those crafty women in your life, gather for a few hours of creative fun. Choose a theme, such as Jewelry Making, Scrapbooking, Furniture Decorating, or Stained Glass Crafting, then simply provide a variety of art materials and inspired craft kits, set up some tables, and let the artists put their imaginations and creativity to work. Everything from the invitations to the party favors are sure to be priceless!

Invitations

Write the party details on white paper using an invisible pen, (available at craft stores) or use a white crayon. Include a companion pen or colorful marker in the envelope, along with a note directing the guests to "Color the paper with the enclosed pen for a fun surprise!"

The details will magically appear. Or make a collage invitation, using magazine pictures, scrapbook materials, or photos.

What to Wear

Ask guests to bring a plain white T-shirt for a craft activity (or you can provide them).

Suggest they wear comfortable, old clothes. For fun, provide old shirts, smocks, or aprons for the guests to wear during the party. Turn the shirts into "Painter's Smocks" by adding color splashes, using acrylic paints, permanent markers, or fabric paints.

Decorations

Set up craft tables and cover them with colorful plastic tablecloths, then set out a variety of arts and crafts supplies, such as paints, crayons, markers, clay, wood, stencils, glitter, glitter pens, neon pens, glow in the dark pens, fabric pens, sequins, jewels, ribbon, glue, tape, stapler, scissors, string, and construction paper. Set up different Craft Centers, then let the guests choose whatever they want to do. You might include a Jewelry Store, Tennis Shoe Makeover, T-shirt Shop, or Picture Frame Place, then let them go to work. Frame or display the finished products and give everyone an award, such as "Most Creative!" "Funniest!" "Best Use of Materials!" "Most Colorful!" and "Strangest!" For a festive display, add multicolored balloons, crepe paper streamers, and a sign that reads: "Gallery Grand Opening!"

Games and Activities

Working on your crafts is the main activity at this party, but you can expand it with a few new suggestions for crafts they haven't tried before. If you want to turn a craft into a game, set a timer to see who can complete a project first!

Photo Frames

Give the guests frame-making kits and have them make their own picture or art frames, decorated with paint, antiquing rubs, jewels, glitter, ribbons, stickers, and so on. Take digital pictures of each guest, print them from the computer, insert them into the frames, and send them home as favors. Better yet, choose a theme for the frame, such as "Our Craft Party," and decorate accordingly.

T-Shirt Art

Have the girls decorate the white T-shirts, using fabric paints, permanent markers, buttons, ribbons, decals, rivets, and fabric jewels. Allow the shirts to dry, then have the guests pose for pictures or model their new creations. You can also do this with hats, aprons, and carry-bags. For added fun, provide iron-on letters or T-shirt transfers for special photos and let the crafters personalize their shirts even more.

Greeting Cards

Give the artists colorful paper, pens, and decorations, and let them create personalized birthday and holiday cards to give to the guest of honor, as well as other special friends. Include suggestions for other fun holidays, such as "National Chocolate Day," "Goof-Off Day," and "No Good Reason to Send a Card Day."

Refreshments

Offer easy snacks to eat while they work. Serve colorful party drinks. Bake cupcakes and let the guests decorate their own, using tinted frosting and colorful candies. Or do the same with sugar cookies and turn them into a work of edible art.

Favors, Prizes, and Gifts

Pass out mini craft kits so the guests can be creative at home. Buy some small paint buckets, write the names of the girls on the buckets with puffy paints, and fill the buckets with glue sticks, scissors, tape, markers, paints, brushes, and other craft items.

Party Plus

Take a class at an arts and crafts store or ceramics shop together, and turn it into a party.

Book Lovers' Literary Party

If you belong to a book group—or want to form one—here's a way to make your favorite characters—and your party—come to life. Choose a book to serve as a theme, such as a historical romance novel by Jane Austen, a biography about Princess Diana, a mystery by Sue Grafton, or a literary work like *Jane Eyre*, and design the party around it. It's time to "book" a date!

Invitations

Create invitations that look like miniature books by folding two pages together in half. Write the name of the party on the front cover, such as "Book Lovers' Party" or "Literary Luncheon," or combine it with the title, such as "P is for Party" or "The DaVinci Party." Fill in the party details inside as text, written in the tone of the featured book. For the back page, write up a blurb "About the Author/Hostess" and include an RSVP. Include a prop to go with the book, such as cotton hankies for a tearjerker, magnifying glasses for a mystery, or an appropriate bookmark.

What to Wear

Ask the guests to dress as a famous author, like Dorothy Parker or Anne Rice, or come as a character in the book you're currently discussing.

When they arrive, stick the name of a famous female character or writer on each guest's back, such as "Bridget Jones" or "Charlotte Brontë."

Decorations

Gather old posters from your local bookstore or make your own using your computer and the Internet. Set out books around the room, stacked or upright and propped open. You can find some cool literary novelties online at *www.literaryluminaries.biz*, such as coffee mugs, posters, book bags, bookmarks, and notecards, featuring the caricature images of Virginia Woolf, Jane Austen, Louisa May Alcott, Charlotte Brontë, Elizabeth Barrett Browning, Emily Dickinson, Sylvia Plath, and Mary Wollstonecraft Shelley. Or match the décor to the mood of the book, with candles, low lights, and masks for a mystery, hearts, chocolates, and printed tissues for a romance.

Games and Activities

Check your L.Q.—Literary Quotient—with a few bookworm challenges.

I Am What I Write

Write the names of characters or writers on stickers and adhere them to the backs of the guests as they arrive. At game time, have each person take a turn asking questions to the group to find out who she is. Tell her she can only ask yes or no questions, such as "Am I dead?" If she gets stuck, have players take turns giving her clues.

Literary Quotations

Write down famous quotes from well-known books and have the players guess the title and author. Here are some to get you started:

○ "Life and death appeared to me ideal bounds, which I should first break through, and pour a torrent of light into our dark world." (Mary Shelley, *Frankenstein*)

○ "... what loneliness is more lonely than distrust?" (George Eliot, *Middlemarch*)

○ "One is not born a woman. One is made one." (Simone de Beauvoir, *The Second Sex*)

○ "Marriage, fun? Fiddle-dee-dee. Fun for men you mean." (Margaret Mitchell, *Gone with the Wind*)

○ "No, I think I'll just go down and have some pudding and wait for it all to turn up. .... It always does in the end." (J. K. Rowling, *Harry Potter and the Order of the Phoenix*)

○ "It is a truth universally acknowledged, that a single man in possession of a good fortune, must be in want of a wife." (Jane Austen, *Pride and Prejudice*)

Act One

Act out a scene from a famous novel, such as *The Da Vinci Code*, and see if others can guess the title and characters. Make it a game of charades by having the players divide into teams, write down the titles of books, then draw them from a hat and pantomime them for their teammates.

On the Other Hand

For a thought-provoking critique of the book, have one player make a positive statement about the book, such as "I thought the characters were well developed," then have the next player make a negative statement, such as "The writer used too many adverbs." Go around the group, then vote whether the book was good or not so good.

Refreshments

Choose food related to the book or the genre. For a mystery novel evening, serve "Name Your Poison" drinks (alcoholic) and "Mystery Bars" (chocolate layered bars). For a romance novel evening, serve "Love Potion Number 9" (pink champagne) and "Piece of My Heart" heart-shaped cookies. For a fantasy novel, make a "Magic Elixir" (mixed drink) and serve it with "Disappearing Delights" (yummy cookies that seem to disappear quickly!). Make a cake in the shape of a closed book with the title written on top using a tube of icing. Stick a bookmark into the side at the top.

Favors, Prizes, and Gifts

Give each guest a paperback book, a bookmark, reading glasses, a book store gift certificate, or something from the Literary Luminaries Web site.

Party Plus

Go to a local book signing in your community and buy signed copies of the book.

Romance Writers' Party

Bring out the sexy siren inside, and take turns writing a romance, scene by sexy scene, until your throbbing heart pulses with . . . well, you get the idea . . . Pass out the pens and paper and watch the steam rise and the would-be writers pour their hearts out on the page.

Invitations

Using a steamy romance novel as a guide, create a card with a hot hunk on the cover. Title the card "Romance Writers' Party" or "A Night With (Fill in Hot Guy's Name)." Write the party details like a book blurb, such as "Come help ripped rogue, Brad Clooney, rescue the love of his life, Scarlett Monroe, from the evil Dash Spade . . ." Plant sticker kisses on the envelope and mail to guests.

What to Wear

Ask the heroines to come dressed as their favorite female protagonists, such as Jane from *Becoming Jane* in a long skirt and ruffly blouse, Kinsey Milhone from the Sue Grafton mystery series in a trench coat and basic black dress, or even Pippi Longstocking with pigtails and striped tights with holes in the knees and sneakers.

Decorations

Choose a setting for your romance writing party, such as a tropical island, a rain-forested jungle, or a regency castle, and recreate it in the party room. Hang posters of hot guys on the walls for inspiration. Set out romance novels and buy extras from the thrift store, then rip off the covers and use them as placemats, coasters, and so on. Decorate with aromatic candles, hearts, even lacy underwear. Play romantic music in the background.

Games and Activities

Have fun with fiction as you write your own hot scenes and hilarious scenarios.

Write a Raunchy Romance

Choose a volunteer to do the typing on a laptop computer, then sit in a circle and begin the story, with a prompt like, "Raven haired, voluptuous Scarlett Monroe had no idea when she accepted ambitious yet arrogant Dash Spade's proposal that he planned to take her to the steamy, bug-infested jungles of Timbuktu . . ." Have each player add an overwritten sentence or sexy scene until the throbbing story comes to a climax, er, conclusion. Encourage the writers to make the story as flowery, erotic, and ludicrous as they want.

"Kiss me, you fool!"

Read a few lines from a famous love scene, such as "Frankly, my dear . . ." and have players guess the name of the book, and who's speaking to whom.

Dark and Stormy Night

Share some of the winners from the "It was a Dark and Stormy Night . . ." contest. Go to *www.bulwer-lytton.com* for some great—and hilarious—examples.

Rewrite!

Get out some favorites books, such as *Gone with the Wind*, and have the group rewrite the ending to let poor Scarlett catch her Rhett Butler, marry the twins, or start her own fashion business.

Refreshments

Serve food featured in a favorite romance novel. Or offer the guests aphrodisiac foods, such as nutmeg, oysters, figs, coffee, garlic, and of course chocolate. Pour romantic blended drinks, such as daiquiris and mai tais, with little umbrellas in them or serve champagne. Make a cake shaped like an open book, using two rectangle cakes placed side by side and decorated with icing. Use a strip of licorice as a bookmark.

Favors, Prizes, and Gifts

Give them romance novels, bookmarks, writing utensils, and blank journals so they can continue in their free time or start their own.

Party Plus

Hire a male model to come pose for inspiration while you write your story!

Nancy Drew, Girl Detective Party

Many of us girls grew up with Nancy Drew. Why not host a Detective Party and have your guests/sleuths solve a puzzling mystery—without the help of Ned Nickerson. You can give the party a Nancy Drew theme, or choose a specific book from the series, such as *The Secret of the Old Clock* or *The Witch Tree Symbol*, and use that as a basis for your party—everything from the clues and clothing to the snacks and sleuthing supplies.

Invitations

Make Top Secret Dossiers by folding a 6-inch by 9-inch manila envelope in half and writing the party details inside the fold. Decorate the envelope, inside and out, with stickers or stamp imprints featuring magnifying glasses, flashlights, puzzle pieces, and so on. Add clues to the inside pocket of the folder, then seal the envelope and mail to your sleuths, with "Top Secret: For Your Eyes Only" written on the outside. Include a mini-magnifying glass, skeleton key, or tiny flashlight inside the pocket for added mystery. Or buy Nancy Drew stationery to use for the invitation at *www.chroniclebooks.com* or *www.amazon.com*.

What to Wear

Ask the sleuths to come dressed as Nancy Drew during any period of her adventures, from the 1930s to the present. If they need ideas, suggest a trench coat, cloche hat, thick heels, flowery frocks, or even a disguise. For those who dare, go for Nancy's titian (red) hair, using a wig or spray-on color! Don't forget the sleuthing accessories—a flashlight, magnifying glass, compass, skeleton key, binoculars, and so on.

Decorations

Choose an era and decorate to suit. Nancy's favorite color is blue, so be sure to have blue balloons, paper products, and other blue decorations. Put together a detective kit with all the necessary tools listed below. Type up quotes from the books and print them out to make signs for the walls. Set out Nancy Drew books around the room. If you can find an old trunk, use it to hide supplies. Check the thrift shop for Nancy Drew–style fashions and hang them up around the room. If you're using a particular book, such as *The Secret of the Old Clock*, set out an old clock and other objects mentioned in the story. Create a Nancy Drew Detective Kit and put it on display. Include such tools as:

- Flashlight (to see in dark passageways when the lights go out).

- Magnifying glass (to study mysterious footprints of nefarious characters).

- Compass (to find your way out of the labyrinthine tunnels).

- Fingerprint powder (or face powder) and clear tape (to lift suspicious fingerprints).

- Notebook and pencil (to jot down important clues).

- First aid kit (in case someone is bitten by a poisonous snake).

- Pocket knife (to cut through rope bonds).

- Small tool set (to free yourself from inside a locked trunk).

- Change of clothes (in case you get your outfit dirty or need a disguise).

- Morse Code decoder (in case you have to tap out a secret message to your chums).

- Lipstick (to write SOS in case you're kidnapped).

Games and Activities

The investigation of a baffling mystery is clue to this party. The game is afoot!

Sleuth Hunt

Write up clues, Nancy Drew style, and have the group solve a mystery. For example, you might hide the party favors, then write clues to their location. Your first clue could be, "Where would Nancy Drew look for a handwriting clue?" (In the notebook lying on the party table!) Give each sleuth a different accessory—a flashlight (to be used to search in a dark closet), a magnifying glass (to read a clue written in fine print), a compass (to indicate a certain direction to find a clue), and so on. When they reach the "scene of the crime," there lies the body, er, favors!

Drew's Clues

Pick up a copy of my book, *The Official Nancy Drew Handbook*, (available from Quirk Books or *www.amazon.com*) for tips on how to be a girl sleuth like Nancy Drew. Teach the rest of the detectives the skills explained in the book, such as, "How to use lipstick to write SOS backward when you're bound and gagged," "How to lift suspicious fingerprints with face powder," "How to pack the perfect handbag for all contingencies," and "How to disguise yourself and go undercover to follow criminals or your cheating boyfriend."

Nancy Drew Fanatic

Ask questions about Nancy Drew's many adventures, such as "Who was Nancy's first best friend?" (Helen Corning), "What's the name of Nancy's first mystery?" (*The Secret of the Old Clock*), and "Who really wrote the Nancy Drew books?" (Mildred Wirt Benson, then Harriet Stratemeyer).

Nancy Drew at the Movies

Rent or buy some Nancy Drew videos, such as the originals featuring Bonita Granville, the TV series with Pamela Sue Martin, or the current one with Emma Roberts, and watch the shows together while munching on Hannah Gruen's refreshments.

Refreshments

Offer foods mentioned in Nancy Drew stories, such as Hannah Gruen's Lemon Bars, dark chocolate layer cake with walnuts, blondies, fruit cup, chocolate nut sundaes, butterfly pie, strawberry shortcake, and so on. You can find recipes for Nancy Drew's favorite foods in *The Nancy Drew Cookbook*. (Just be sure it hasn't been drugged by a suspicious villain!) Make a batch of taffy and have an old-fashioned taffy pull with your sleuth friends. Have a bakery decorate a chocolate cake with a copy of a Nancy Drew book cover on top.

Favors, Prizes, and Gifts

Any of the sleuthing items mentioned in the list above would work, plus a Nancy Drew tote bag or T-shirt (*www.cafepress.com*), a copy of a Nancy Drew book, books about Nancy Drew, and *The Official Nancy Drew Handbook*.

Party Plus

For more ideas and information about Nancy Drew, check out my Web site, *www.NancyDrewForever.com* and another great Web site by Jenn Fisher at *www.NancyDrewSleuth.com*.

Crop Shop Scrapbooking Party

Scrapbooking is scorching hot! Probably because it's a fun activity, it preserves your precious memories, and it's great to gather with girlfriends and work on your various projects. The scrapbooking fad doesn't appear to be disappearing anytime soon. So ask your friends to bring some special pictures or mementoes for a themed scrapbook, some scraps to share, and get to work on saving those special vacations, holidays, events—and parties!

Invitations

Scrap an invitation. Buy blank cards and cover the front and insides with festive party paper, featuring balloons, snacks, or scrapbooking tools. Type up the details on the computer using a fancy font, print them, cut them out with scalloped scissors, and glue them to the card in a creative way. Add decorative ribbon, paper clips, stickers, and a snapshot of the group invited to the party.

What to Wear

Things can get messy at a scrapbook party so wear old clothes, smocks, aprons, or casual outfits that can be easily washed. They may want to bring slippers or socks, sweaters, pillows to sit on, and other comfort items. For fun, ask them to "scrap" their outfits and come creatively dressed!

Decorations

Scrapbooking supplies will serve as your decorations, but to make the party room more festive, add samples of your scrapbooking work, such as your own memory albums, picture frames, notecards, embellished books, or creative signs you've made using scrap techniques. Set a separate table for food (so the food scraps don't get on the paper scraps!) and lay out patterned scrap paper to serve as placemats and table décor. Scrap nameplates they can keep, using heavy card stock and fancy lettering, with embellishments added. Play music in the background, softly, for lulls in the conversation.

Games and Activities

Cut and paste, scrap, and swap your way to a fun time at your scrap-happy Scrapbooking Party.

Make Memories

Obviously the primary purpose of a Scrapbooking Party is creating scrapbooks, so just display the materials and let the guests pick and choose what they want to use and how they're going to create their books. Good materials and tools to have on hand include: paper cutters, scalloped scissors, double-sided tape, glue sticks, narrow ribbon, stickers, brads, colored paper clips, rubber stamps and ink pads, stick-on lettering, scrapbook paper, and albums.

Pass the Paper

If there's someone you want to surprise with a special gift, pass out sheets of scrapbook paper and ask everyone to create one page for the lucky girl. Let them choose any theme for the page they want—friendship, a fun time, a look at the future. Then present the scrapbook to her at a special event and watch the tears roll.

Swap the Scraps

Ask everyone to bring one thing to swap, such as a tag—enough for every guest. These should be made ahead of time—all the same—then exchanged at the party, so each guest goes home with a bunch of new—and different—tags. Or make it part of the activity and have guests make duplicate copies of a tag, enough for each guest, then swap them. You can also have a rubber stamp swap, a scalloped scissors swap, a paper swap, a ribbon swap, an embellishment swap, and so on.

Refreshments

Finger foods are best, so the guests can pop in a few bites and get back to work. Ask them to eat at a separate table so you don't spill food or drink on the pages. End the party with a Crop Cake, made from a rectangular cake and decorated to look like the open pages of a scrapbook. Write a special greeting in icing, such as "Scrapbook Stars!" or "Make Memories!" Outline the pages with licorice strips and use a variety of small candies to embellish the pages.

Favors, Gifts, and Prizes

Give your scrappers a small box containing a variety of scrapbooking supplies, materials, or equipment, or give them an album for their next project.

Party Plus

Many scrapbooking stores host their own scrapbooking parties and events, so you can join in on one of those. Or invite a scrapbooking hostess to your home to teach the group new scrapping techniques and tricks.

Knit Wits Stitch Party

Stitchery is back and it's booming, everything from knitting and crocheting to embroidery and needlepoint. Even quilting bees are all the rage. So gather your needles and yarn, and stitch up a Knit Wits Stitch Party. Bitching is optional!

Invitations

Write your party details on a piece of fabric with fabric pens or puffy pens to get your stitching party started. You can make it look like needlepoint by writing the words in tiny dots. Add embellishments, such as decals, iron-on letters, beads, ribbon, and so on.

What to Wear

Suggest the guests wear something handmade, knitted, or embellished with embroidery or stitchery. This is the time to show off your handiwork!

Decorations

Set out lengths of colorful fabric, skeins of yarn, and other materials and tools needed for your party. Place nameplates at the table: Write the guests' names in glue, then top the glue with colorful yarn. Hang up any craftwork you've completed to inspire the girls. Add a few stitchery books, such as *Stitch and Bitch*, here and there for reference.

Games and Activities

You'll be in stitches after a few hours of sewing, knitting, and chatting.

Knit One, Purl Two

You'll spend most of the party working with your needles and thread, yarn, floss, and other materials. If someone is new to the group, have guests each take a few minutes to teach her how to get started.

Bitchy Topics

While you work, bring up a topic for all to discuss, such as something controversial, a piece of gossip from the tabloids, a new TV show that needs reviewing—anything that will interest and entertain the girls while their fingers fly. Or turn it into a problem-solving session and ask if anyone has a concern to share with the group. Then go about brainstorming solutions while you wave those needles.

Quilting Bee

Take turns creating quilts for each other, based on a theme, such as a new baby, special hobby, or milestone birthday. Design the quilt together, pass out squares for guests to create, then patch the whole quilt together at the end.

Refreshments

Finger foods for busy fingers are best. Have a veggie and fruit tray, mini-sandwiches, and small candies or cookies to consume while working on those sweaters, shawls, and stitch pictures. You can pour some wine, but avoid too much alcohol or someone may end up with a muumuu instead of a muffler.

Favors, Prizes, and Gifts

Send them home with stitchery supplies, books on how to create accessories, and include a small bottle of hand lotion to repair those worn fingers.

Party Plus

Host the party at a knitting store or have an instructor come and teach the girls a few new tricky stitches.

Handy Girl Party

If you have a friend who's handy around the house or garden, a girl who's more comfortable at Home Depot than the mall, here's the party for her! Bring on the tools, create a game plan, and before you know it, you'll have built yourself a blowout of a party—just for handy girls!

Invitations

Make invitations by writing party details on hardware store signs or sales sheets. Write something like, "Gayle the Tool Gal Is Turning 30! Help the Amateur Green Thumb/Household Handy Girl Construct the Next Exciting Chapter in Her Life With the Gayle Depot Party! Bring a gift card of any amount from the hardware store. You can do it! We can help!'" Or write the party details on the back of a hardware store gift card and mail to guests.

What to Wear

Put on your gardening gloves or tool belts and come as gardeners or handypersons. When guests arrive, give them all work aprons (you can order them inexpensively on the Internet in bulk), then dye them Home Depot orange or other applicable color. Personalize them by ironing on T-shirt transfers with the name of the guest of honor, such as "Gayle's Depot!"

Decorations

Drape backyard tables in orange plastic tablecloths, and add other orange paper products. Decorate with Home Depot gift cards and other items with the store logo. Make up posters with the game instructions (see below) and create a Wienie Wagon for serving the food. Put up sale signs and hardware department signs, such as "Tools," "Electrical," "Plumbing," "Flooring," and so on.

Games and Activities

It's "Hammer" Time! Test the guests' skills and see who "nails" the prize! Just don't "screw" up!

Nail the Nail

Set a block of wood on a sturdy table. Have each player pound a nail into the wood in only three hits. The deepest nail wins—a new hammer.

Size Matters

Set out two stakes or small flags at a distance of 30 feet (or whatever you like, such as the guest of honor's age). Have the players estimate the length, then measure it. The closest to the answer wins—a tape measure.

Pick a Plant

Buy six or eight small potted flowers and write the names on posterboard. Set the plants in a row and have the guests match the names to the flowers. The one with the most correct answers wins—a plant of her choice.

What Color Is Brown?

Select 10 shades of brown paint swatches from the hardware store, such as "saddle brown," "antique brown," "cinnamon," "latte," and "oak." Glue them to posterboard, then write the names around the board— but not next to the correct colors. Have the players try to identify the various shades. The winner gets a new paintbrush.

Guess the Gizmo

Pick up some inexpensive, strange-looking gadgets at the hardware store. Tape them to posterboard and have the players guess what they are or what they're used for. The winner gets to keep all the gadgets.

Build a Birdhouse

Give everyone a kids' wood crafting kit, such as a birdhouse, herb garden, or airplane. Have them race to see who can complete the project first. Let them all keep their crafts—finished or unfinished.

Refreshments

Serve hot dogs and hamburgers, chips, and soda or beer from a Wienie Wagon made from cardboard.

Prizes, Favors, and Gifts

Give the handy girl Home Depot or other hardware store gift cards she can use on those never-ending projects. Let the guests keep their special aprons. If you have enough potted flowers, give them to the guests as they leave, along with some flower-decorated household tools.

CHAPTER 10

Around the World Parties

"When preparing to travel, lay out all your clothes and all your money.
Then take half the clothes and twice the money."

~ *Susan Heller*

Take your friends on a trip around the world, without leaving home! There are so many wonderful places to enjoy, even if you don't have a plane ticket or hotel room. Try one of these mini-vacations and enjoy a new culture in good company. Grab your coat, your camera, and your compass—All aboard!

Geocaching/Letterboxing Treasure Hunt

Geocaching is a treasure hunting game where players use a GPS (Global Positioning Satellite) unit to hide and seek hidden "caches" or treasure boxes. Letterboxing is a similar hunt for a bottle that contains a notebook and rubber stamp, using maps, clues, and a compass to find the hidden treasure.

Adventure parties like these are all the rage these days, thanks to new technology, clever clues, and creative twists on a popular theme. In the past, miners and explorers would hide a cache (pronounced "cash") with food and emergency items to rediscover later when needed. Today they're filled with toys, trinkets, and tchotchkas, as well as pens, logbooks, and other fun discoveries. Teams use inexpensive GPS units—electronic global positioning satellite—to hunt for and find hidden caches set up locally. This half treasure hunt/half mystery game is easier than it sounds. Just key in the "waypoint"—longitude and latitude—to find the coordinates, head on over, then find the cache, hidden somewhere within six to twenty feet.

Invitations

Photocopy a local map, mark the party location, including coordinates, then write party details on the back. To whet their senses of adventure, include a toy compass and a clue to the first cache inside the envelope, then mail to guests.

What to Wear

Divide up the teams ahead of time and ask each guest to come dressed in preselected team colors. Or have everyone wear camouflage or sport clothes. Don't forget athletic shoes—there's some walking involved.

Decorations

Decorate the starting point—your home, a picnic table at the park—with maps, arrows, street signs, and compasses. Set out some of the tiny trinkets teams will be searching for such as action figures, tiny stuffed animals, stickers, costume jewelry, magnets, key chains, and other small fun items.

Games and Activities

Can you find the hidden treasure? Getting there is half the fun, with this geocaching game.

The Hunt Is On!

The Setup

You'll need at least two GPS units for two teams, more if you divide up into more teams. Ask the guests if they have a device—many people are buying them because the prices are reasonable (as low as $100) and they're fun to use. You can also rent a couple from the electronics, camping, or boat stores, if you prefer. To prepare the hunt, choose a starting point—your home, a park, café, or local landmark. Choose five to ten sites for the hunt, depending on how long you want the party to last, and write down the coordinates of each, using your GPS unit. Fill a small container, such as a plastic lidded bowl, small covered box, or lidded can, with enough of the same trinkets for each team. For example, if there are two teams, place two action figures in the bowl. Then insert the coordinates for the next cache. Hide the container at the first site— not too easy, not too hard to find. Repeat for each site, leaving different trinkets behind, along with new coordinates to the next sites.

On Your Mark . . .

At game time, gather the guests and divide into teams. Have them name their teams, such as "Trezure Seekers," "Gold Diggers," or "GeePers Creepers." Give each team a "cheat sheet" that lists the coordinates, along with a "give-up" sheet that indicates where the hunt ends—at your home, a restaurant, etc. Tell the teams they must find each site using the GPS unit, retrieve a trinket from the cache, replace the container where they found it, and continue to the next waypoint. Include a puzzling clue for fun, such as, "Look up high, perhaps a tree, holds the cache for all to see." Each trinket is worth a point. If they can't find a cache, they can use the "spoiler" sheet to move on to to the next site, but they will lose a point since they won't be retrieving a trinket. The team who arrives back to the end site with the most trinkets wins the game. Note: Watch out for "GeoMuggles"—random onlookers who might spot you finding the cache. Be subtle. Remember, this is supposed to be a treasure hunt with hidden loot. You don't want GeoMuggles to crash the cache!

Refreshments

Geocaching teams are likely to get thirsty on the hunt, so provide them each with a bottle of water or a sports bottle with a sports drink. For fun, hide some candy (packaged to prevent bug raids) in a couple of the caches to discover to help keep their energy up. When the teams arrive at the end point to count up trinkets and decide on winners, they're apt to be ravenous, so provide a buffet deli lunch or bake DIY pizzas. If they've been out in hot weather, welcome them with refreshing drinks and cold cut platters, or make a hearty soup with warm French bread for the cold weather hunts. Serve food to match the terrain—gourmet entrees for city treks, veggies and salads for hunts in the park. Offer beer, wine, and/or soda, along with sports drinks if the weather's warm, and hot chocolate or lattes if it's cold outside. If you're celebrating a special occasion, make or order a cake shaped like a treasure chest and top it with all the trinkets from the hunt. Or serve cupcakes decorated like compasses.

Favors, Prizes, and Gifts

If money is no object, give them all their own GPS units. Have extra trinkets and give them a handful to take home. Hand out maps of local historic areas, along with recommendations for attractions. Give them inflatable globes, compasses, or a subscription to *www.Googleearth .com*.

Party Plus

If you don't want to create your own hunt, you can go online and find hunts already set up and waiting for you in your local area. Try *www .geocaching.com* for information and a list of hunts. Instead of using GPS units, send the group on a tour of your town, or a historic section of another town, and offer interesting information about each place. Have them take pictures of each cache, using a camera phone, a digital camera, or Polaroid camera, instead of taking a trinket. Or try Letterboxing, a combination of treasure hunting and riddle solving, with clues online leading to hidden letterboxes containing a logbook, inkpad, and rubber stamp (*www.letterboxing.org* or *www.altasquest .com*).

Spicy Spanish Fiesta

Spice up the señoras and señoritas at a fiery fiesta that's hot-hot-hot! Then add sizzle with a South of the Border spirit using dazzling colors, fiery lights, and lots of salsa in the songs and snacks. It's time to mambo, Hot Mama!

Invitations

Send a bouquet of festive paper flower invitations. Buy large paper flowers from the flower mart or import store, or make your own using sheets of colorful tissue paper, cut into flower petals, and tied together with floral tape. Write the party details on the petals, or on a card attached to the bouquet. Hand-deliver to guests like a flower messenger.

What to Wear

Ask the guests to don their serapes, sombreros, and sandals, and dress in brightly colored clothing. Suggest full skirts, halter tops, and peasant blouses, or Latin-designed shirts and cool shorts.

Decorations

Set up a South of the Border stage. Cover the patio, backyard, or party room with lots of red, white, and green balloons, streamers, and paper lanterns—colors of the Mexican flag. Hang festive banners that read: "Olé!", "Hot, Hot, Hot!", "Salsa!", and other Mexican party phrases. String up white or colorful lights around the party area, or buy salsa lights shaped like hot chili peppers and place them around the serving table. Hang piñatas from the ceiling or trees, filled with candy or party favors. Put up flags from Latin American countries. Set out bouquets of bright paper flowers. Pin up posters of hot Latin pop stars, such as Ricky Martin or Enrique Iglesias. Hang travel posters featuring tropical beaches and popular tourist destinations. Distribute brochures with information on cruise ship tours, beach resorts, and travel packages. Set the table with a Mexican designed paper tablecloth, and matching paper plates, cups, and other decorations. Make a centerpiece out of a cactus plant, paper flowers, or maracas. Turn sombreros upside-down and use them as serving bowls for tortilla chips. Set out red, green, and white lighted candles around the room. Play Latin and Salsa music, such as Elvis Crespo, Los Tucanes, Paulino Rubio, and others.

Games and Activities

Dance, dance, dance—and sing your heart out—for a party full of fiery fun.

Time to Mambo, Mama!

If anyone knows how to do the Mambo or other Latin dance, have her teach the others. Otherwise, hire a dance teacher to lead the guests in the Macarena, Tango, Lambada, and so on.

Create a Dance Craze

Divide into couples and have them make up a new dance to a popular Latin song, such as "Mambo #5," "Shake Your Bon Bon," "The Mexican Hat Dance," or "Samba De Janeiro." Award a prize for the Most Authentic Dance, Most Creative Dance, and Weirdest Dance.

Sing Sing Señoras

Sing along to your favorite tunes, such as "Un Dos Tres," "Maria," "I Like It Like That," "Hot, Hot, Hot," "La Bamba," "Guantanamera," and so on. Let the guests use a microphone to sing along one at a time, karaoke style, and videotape them as they perform. Play back the tape for laughs. Or have small groups lip-sync to a popular song, and create a dance to go along with it. Tell them to name their group, something like "Lip-Syncers Loca," "La Salsa Señoritas," "'N Lip-Sync," "Samba Serenaders," or "Latino Lovers." Have them practice in separate rooms with a cassette player, then together at show time. Award a prize for Best Lip-Sync Act.

Play "Habla Español"

Give the group paper and pencil. Read some Spanish phrases and ask the player to write down the translations—only make them funny. For example, *No me molesta!* ("It doesn't matter") could be interpreted as "Don't touch me!" Award a prize for the most entertaining "translation."

Refreshments

Spice up the snacks by laying out a Gourmet Burrito Bar and let the guests make their own fiery burritos. Include bowls of refried and black beans, chopped tomatoes, shredded cheeses, chili peppers, chopped olives, shredded chicken, beef, or pork, sour cream, guacamole, salsa, and extra hot chilies for the fire-eaters. Serve chips in upside-down sombreros with sides of salsa or melted cheese dips. Pour Mexican beer, such as Dos Equis, Corona, and so on, with a slice of lime. Make margaritas in the blender, using storebought mix. Dip the glass rims in salt and serve with a slice of lime. Serve Tequila Slammers! Pour 1½ ounces tequila and ½ ounce lemon lime soda in a shot glass, cover with a napkin, and hold it tightly. Slam the shot glass onto the table (not your good table!) and remove the napkin. As the drink begins to fizz, slam it down your throat. End the meal with cool, refreshing bowls of flan, a Mexican custard topped with caramel.

Favors, Prizes, and Gifts

Say adios, amigos, with paper flower bouquets. Pass out posters or travel books to Mexico and South America. Give your guests margarita mix and a pair of margarita glasses. Buy small items from the Mexican import store, such as maracas, piñatas, or figurines, and pass them out to your guests.

Party Plus

Host the party at a Mexican restaurant or Salsa club, then go dancing after the meal.

Club Med Luau

A traditional luau is a celebration of food and fun that's perfect for you and your girlfriends. When you throw a little Club Med into the mix, you get a fantasy trip to the islands, a tropical dance party, and a Hawaiian feast, all in one! Aloha and welcome to hot and steamy Club Med Luau!

Invitations

Say Aloha and welcome to the wahinis with floral shirt-shaped invitations. Or send them picture postcards of beach scenes. Begin with "Wish you were here . . . and you WILL be!" then add party details. Mail invitations in colorful padded envelopes and include inexpensive plastic flower leis, mini fans, plastic sunglasses, or silk flower bracelets to get your guests in the "hang loose" mood. Or leave messages on guests' answering machines, and play the ukulele as you talk. If you can afford it, have a florist deliver real flower leis or fragrant corsages, with party details attached. Send small packets of macadamia nuts with party details written on small pieces of paper and glued to the back. Little paper drink umbrellas make fun invitations, with the party details written on the umbrellas themselves.

What to Wear

No shoes, no hose—no way! Beachwear only at your luau, so ask the wahinis to dress as Hula dancers, bathing beauties, or tacky tourists in Hawaiian shirts, muumuus, or sarongs. When they arrive, greet them with silk or plastic flower leis, bracelets, and anklets. Have a supply of grass skirts, floral hair clips, coconut bras, beachcomber and other tropical hats to use as accessories. If it's a pool party, have them come in swimsuits, with shorts, tank tops, cover-ups, or other beachwear on top. Pass out thongs—the foot kind, not the panty kind! The rubber ones are inexpensive, colorful, and can be personalized with permanent felt-tip pens and other decorations (see next section). Dot the guests' noses with florescent zinc oxide as they arrive.

Decorations

Transform your yard, pool area, or party room into a tropical paradise. Set out Tiki torches, colorful lanterns, or string holiday lights along the fence or around the tree trunks. Place pink flamingos around the party area, or inflatable palm trees, parrots, and tropical fish. Swag fishnet on the tables and fences, and attach sea creatures and a life preserver to the netting. Toss beach balls around the yard. Glow sticks at night add a festive feeling to the tropical mood. Fill the area with tropical flowers—real or fake. String a floral garland up the trees and around the fence. Borrow or buy inexpensive beach chairs and cover them with bright beach towels. Buy posters featuring tropical scenes and hang them on the walls. Hang pictures of the cast from *Hawaii Five-O* or *Magnum P.I.*, or posters of the Beach Boys and Don Ho. Play luau music in the background, such as Don Ho, IZ, "Elvis Sings Blue Hawaii," steel drum music, and so on. Buy some stuffed toy parrots and place them strategically around the room, so they're overlooking the party. Make fake palm trees out of large sheets of brown and green construction paper or crepe paper, and tape them to the walls or fence. You can buy or rent fake trees from the local party store if you prefer. Drape floral leis around the food, and hang some from the trees. Use paper lanterns to light up the area. Set out tribal masks, hang lots of wind chimes, and light flower-shaped candles floating in bowls of water. Fill a kiddy pool with water and fill it with floating candles, flowers, or fish. Or fill it with sand and toss in some sand toys to make a sandcastle. Cover the table with straw mats, wrap the sides with grass skirts, and set it with floral paper products. Add silk flowers, leis, seashells, and scented candles. Use Hawaiian fabrics to cover the table and throw over the chairs and benches. Use tropical shirt can insulators, fancy hurricane glasses, or cups shaped like coconuts and pineapples, and seashell bowls. Beachcomber hats make great serving bowls. Set out fishbowls, some filled with real fish, others filled with snacks. Serve the guests drinks in carved-out coconuts or pineapples, or buy plastic tropical-style glasses for the fancy drinks. Make starfish placemats for the guests, and mark each place with a personalized coconut, decorated into a funny face with a black felt-tip pen. Drape green crepe paper around the table and fringe it to look like a grass skirt. Don't forget the tropical swizzle sticks, umbrella toothpicks, bamboo sticks, and pink flamingoes.

Games and Activities

Get into some island fun with these tropical games and activities that will make you sweat!

Limbo Ladies and Hula Hoopers

It's not a luau without a Limbo contest, so set up the Limbo Pole and see how low you girls can go. Have a hula hoop contest to see who can swivel their hips the longest. Then have guests make up tricks with the hula hoops.

Singing Hos

Have lip-sync contest to Don Ho hits. Or sing karaoke to favorite Hawaiian songs while the audience shakes maracas. Include favorite island songs like, "Iko Iko," "Kokomo," "Copacabana," "Don't Worry Be Happy," "Blue Hawaii," "Red Red Wine," and "Aloha Oe."

Coconut Head

Make funny faces out of coconuts using permanent markers, wiggly eyes, plastic glasses, straw hair, and other accessories. Award a prize for the one that looks the most like its creator.

Beach Wear

Let the guests accessorize their own straw hats or flip-flops using crafts items, such as fabric markers, paint, shells, buttons, ribbon, plastic flowers, small toys, and so on.

Uke It Up

Get out the ukuleles and guitars and have the guests perform songs from the tropics. Rent some steel drums and let the girls take turns keeping the beat to the music.

A Three-Hour Tour?

Play a game of Gilligan's Island Trivia, such as "How long was the tour?" "Who played the rich guy?" "What was his character's name?" and so on.

Refreshments

The best part of a Luau is the food, so make sure you have lots of tropical treats at the table. Make a big fruit salad and serve it in a carved-out watermelon bowl. Serve easy-to-eat kebabs made from cut-up ham, pineapple chunks, cheese cubes, and cherries. Carve out Pineapple Boats and fill them with cut-up pineapple, cherries, raisins, and coconut. Fill coconut bowls with macadamia nuts and set them around the room. Serve Laulau—authentic roasted pig! Or just keep it simple and roast a side of pork. Barbecue salmon, mahi mahi, or red snapper, and top with cut-up fruit. Make teriyaki chicken wings or Jerk chicken. Offer tropical side dishes such as coconut rice, fresh fruit, and poi—a starch made from taro root. Wash it all down with fancy drinks such as Rum Runners, Banana Boats, piña coladas, mai tais, and other coconut and pineapple drinks. For a nonalcoholic drink, pour Hawaiian punch or use drink mixes without the alcohol. Serve drinks in carved out coconuts, pineapples, oranges, or tropical style glasses. Place fruit garnishes in the drinks, along with small umbrellas, swizzle sticks, and cherry kebabs. End the luau with a Sand Pail Cake. Tear up an angel food cake and put the pieces into a new large sand pail. Pour in chocolate or banana pudding and mix well. Top with crushed vanilla wafers to look like sand. Insert a small shovel to serve. Or make a Seascape Cake that doubles as a centerpiece. Cover half a rectangular cake with blue tinted frosting to look like the sea, cover the other half with white frosting, and sprinkle on brown sugar to look like sand. Set toy Hawaiian dancers and candles (Tiki torches) on the "sand," and tiny plastic fish or sharks in the "water."

Favors, Prizes, and Gifts

Say Aloha with your hands and heart by giving the guests sand pails filled with tropical candy, shell necklaces, sunglasses, leis, and suntan lotion. Let them keep their beachcomber hats and decorated flip-flops. Give the guests flower orchids for their hair. Cover them with shell necklaces and bracelets. Pass out perfumes, soaps, or lotions in tropical fragrances. Give them packages or small cans of macadamia nuts.

Party Plus

Hire a professional Hula dancer to teach the wahinis how to shake it, or a musician to teach the ukulele.

Texas Hold 'Em Poker Party

Texas Poker is all the rage—maybe because it's so much fun. Tell the good ol' gals to put on their cowgirl boots and hats and stomp on over to your Poker Party, to learn the game of Texas Hold 'Em. They'll go home richer, at least in memories, if not money! And remember, everything's bigger at a Texas party!

Invitations

Make your own playing card invitations using the computer, and add party details to the back. Start with, "Do you know when to hold'em and when to fold'em?" Or print out Texas icons or maps and write your party details on them. Include a sheet with the rules to Texas Hold 'Em so they can review before they come to the party. When counting the number of guests, think about how many you can fit at your table and whether you'll need more tables.

What to Wear

Ten gallon hats, big hair, and boot-scootin' boots are recommended. Square dance costumes would be fun, or keep it casual with well-worn jeans and plaid shirts. Include a bandana in the invitation and ask the guests to use it creatively when they dress up.

Decorations

Turn the room into a mini-Texas. Hang up the Texas flag and decorate with the flag colors. Add posters of famous Texans, set out stuffed armadillos, horses, and cows, and cut out cacti from green posterboard, filled with toothpick needles. Include any western gear or wear you have, such as saddles, cowboy hats, even a bale of hay. Use western-themed paper products or the colors of the Texas flag, include bandana placemats, and place a yellow rose of Texas at each table.

Games and Activities

Deal yourselves into an exciting game of cards. You'll all come up winners in the end!

Texas Hold 'Em

The Setup

Get some poker chips—around thirty to forty per player. Make up a sheet identifying the denominations of the chips as follows: white chips = $1, red chips = $5, blue chips = $10. You can also include green chips for $25 and black chips for $100 if you really like high stakes—or make up whatever value you'd like! Buy one or two decks of cards for each table. Find some that fit your group's personality, with cartoon characters, arty pictures, or even naked guys or male models for fun. Also buy "Dealer Buttons" or make them yourself using stickers, to keep track of the dealer. Keep the buy-in low so this remains a fun evening, not stressful. Remember, the point of the party is to have a good time with friends, not to win your next car payment.

How to Play

Deal each player two cards and turn five cards up on the board. The object is for players to make the best five-card hand using any combination of the seven cards in four betting rounds. The first two have a limit of $2, the last two $4, but you can change the amount to suit the group. Choose a dealer to wear the Dealer Button. (Change dealers each hand, moving clockwise.) The two players to her left determine the amount for the ante or pot before the cards are dealt (called "posting the blinds"). The first "blind"—the player to the left of the dealer—puts up half the minimum bet, while the second "blind" puts up the full amount. Dealer deals two cards to each player, face down (called "hole cards"). No other players put any money in the pot at the beginning of the hand. Players place their bets, beginning with the player to the left of the dealer. Players can call, raise, or fold when it's their time to bet. After the first round, the dealer discards the top card of the deck (called "burning the card"), then deals the next three cards face up (called "flop cards"). They can be used by all the players. Players then get another round for another $2, and may use any of the face up cards or their own to form the best five-card poker hand. During the betting, players can do nothing ("check"), increase the bet ("raise"), or choose to sit out ("fold") when it's their turn. The dealer then turns a fourth card face up (called a "turn"). The minimum bet is doubled ($4) and play begins to the left of the dealer. For the final play, the dealer turns the fifth card face up (called the "river") and final betting takes place with another $4 bet. Now it's time for the "showdown." Players may use any combination of their two hole cards and five board cards to form the highest five-card hand. That determines the winner. For the next round, increase the blinds.

Refreshments

Host a barbeque, of course. Make it a chuck wagon using a small tent. Include ribs, chicken, and beef brisket, or make sandwiches with lots of BBQ sauce on the side. Don't forget Texas-sized oven fries, corn on the cob, potato salad, and baked beans. Serve Texas Lone Star beer for those dry throats. Make a cake that looks like a playing card for dessert.

Favors, Prizes, and Gifts

Give the poker players a bandana, costume cowboy hats, festive playing cards, and the rules to the game to take home.

Party Plus

Make it a Bunco party instead of Texas Hold 'Em. You can find boxed Bunco games at the toy or game store.

Viva Las Vegas Night!

Who needs Vegas when you can host a Casino Night right in your own home. You can rent the equipment or make your own. Just remember to play for fun, not fortune, and you'll all go home winners! And what happens at Vegas Night, stays at Vegas Night!

Invitations

Send the guests invitations that look like funny money, using your computer. Include the party details, along with a lead line that reads, "Good for One Night of Gambling at (your House) Casino." On the envelope, intrigue them with the words, "Do you feel lucky, Punk?" Include a few chocolate poker chips to get them started.

What to Wear

Since this is Virtual Vegas, ask the guests to dress up for the party. Or go for comfort and tell them to wear their jeans and plain T-shirts. When they arrive, attach stick-on rhinestones to glam up the shirts for a night of glitter.

Decorations

Turn your party room into a casino. You can rent casino equipment from the local party store, or make much of it yourself using posterboard, markers, and imagination. Line the room with twinkling lights and hang up a disco ball. Sprinkle fake money, chips, and cards around the room. Cover tables in green felt. Give the guests small plastic buckets personalized with their names to hold their winnings. Pass out visors, arm garters, nametags, and gambling-related pins or stickers to add to their outfits.

Games and Activities

Are you and your friends game for a night of gambling and girl fun? Roll the dice and place your bets!

Play Poker

Write up the rules for different variations of poker—Five Card Draw, Seven Card Stud, etc.—then set up the games ready to play at one of the felt-covered tables. Post a sign with a reminder of the best poker hands in order:

○ Royal Flush=A, K, Q, J, 10, all of the same suit

○ Straight Flush=Any five card sequence in the same suit, such as 8, 9, 10, J, Q of hearts

○ Four of a Kind=All four cards of the same kind, such as all kings

○ Full House=Three of a kind combined with a pair, such as A, A, A, 5, 5

○ Straight=Five cards in sequence, but not the same suit

○ Three of a Kind=Three cards of the same kind

Roulette

Rent a roulette wheel, or make your own out of posterboard, shaped in a circle. Divide the wheel into 37 slices and number them from 0 to 36. Then use your chips to place one of the following bets:

- Straight Up=Bet on one number, which pays 35 to 1.

- Split Bet=Bet on two numbers, which pays 17 to 1.

- Street Bet=Place your chip on the vertical line between the outside and inside betting areas, which pays 11 to 1.

- Corner Bet=Place your chip touching four corners of the numbers you're betting, which pays 8 to 1.

Have the players roll a dice onto the board to see if they win—or lose.

Craps

Write up the rules of craps, then set up the dice at another table, ready to play. The basics are simple. Place your bets before a shooter rolls the dice. If the shooter rolls a 7 or 11, you win. If the shooter rolls a 2, 3, or 12, you lose. If the shooter rolls any other number, that number becomes the "point number" and the shooter must roll that number again before a 7 is rolled. Then you win even money for your bet. But if a 7 is rolled before the point number, you lose.

Left, Right, Pot, or Hold

This hot new game is all the rage, and doesn't require a lot of skill. Have players bring three one-dollar bills to the party. Write down the rules on posterboard, then have players sit in a circle. The first player rolls three dice onto a tray that has a lip (so the dice won't roll off). If "1" comes up, she must pass one dollar to the player on the left. If "2" comes up, she must pass one dollar to the player on the right. If "3" comes up, she must put a dollar in the pot. If 4, 5, or 6 come up, she gets to keep the money until her next play. Continue circling around the room, until only one person has all the money!

Refreshments

Serve fancy cocktails with umbrellas and colorful stirrers. Set up a buffet of snacks for guests to nibble on between games. Ask everyone to bring a dish for a full-on all-you-can-eat buffet, Vegas-style. Make a rectangular cake decorated like a dollar bill or a circular cake decorated like a quarter for the slot machines.

Favors, Prizes, and Gifts

Aside from their winnings, send them home with a handful of dice, mini-gambling games, a deck of cards, their visors, and a book on how to beat the house, like *The Badass Girl's Guide to Poker*.

Party Plus

Find a local legal casino and play cards with the professionals. Or place your bets on your favorite card games, from "War" to "Rummy."

CHAPTER 11

Dress-Up Parties

"I don't understand how a woman can leave the house without fixing herself up a little. You never know, maybe that's the day she has a date with destiny. And it's best to be as pretty as possible for destiny." ~ Coco Chanel

What girl doesn't like to dress up once in a while—whether it's a glamorous gown or a crazy costume. Here are suggestions for dress-up parties where your girlfriends can do it up big, everything from heels to hair.

"Get a Clue" Party

Remember when Mrs. Peacock got caught holding a candlestick in the conservatory? Bring back your favorite childhood mystery game with a "Get a Clue" Party. Just pull out your magnifying glasses, don your trench coats, and put your heads together to solve an intriguing—and entertaining—mystery, based on the board game, Clue!

Invitations

Make mysterious invitations by cutting out letters from magazines or using your computer to create a Ransom Note with a fancy font. Add specific details from the board game, such as pictures of the weapons, names of the rooms, and so on (see page 172 for examples). Assign each guest a suspect role, either someone from the Clue game, or a new suspect you've created for the game set perhaps at Clueless High School, Clueless Corporation, Clueless Hospital, or other site.

What to Wear

After you assign the guests their roles, make costume suggestions for each one. For example, if you set the game at Clueless High School, the characters and costumes might include:

○ Cafeteria Lady White, dressed in white, with an apron and hairnet

○ Custodian Green, in a green T-shirt and overalls, sporting a janitor's cap

○ Coach Mustard, wearing a yellow sports logo shirt, baseball cap, and a stopwatch

○ PE Teacher Peacock, dressed in a blue logo T-shirt, short shorts, and a whistle

○ Principal Plum, in a purple shirt, with glasses and a purple pen

○ Secretary Scarlett, sporting a red blouse or dress, necklace with a red stone, and red nail polish

If you have more guests than you have roles, ask the rest to come dressed as detectives or as characters from Clueless High.

Decorations

Cordon off areas in the house or party room and label them like the board game: The Library, Study, Conservatory, Kitchen, Dining Room, Lounge, Billiards Room, Ballroom, Hall. Or create rooms from your theme, such as a Clueless High School Cafeteria, Principal's Office, Detention Hall, P.E. Locker Room, Science Lab, Gymnasium, Custodial Closet, and Swimming Pool. Lay out the "body" using a taped body outline and place the weapons on a table in the center of the room. You can use the traditional weapons from the game—a knife, candlestick, revolver, rope, lead pipe, and wrench, or use weapons that relate to your Clue theme, such as high school–related objects:

- Bunsen burner (use a cigarette lighter) for Coach Mustard

- Whistle (big plastic one) for P.E. Teacher Peacock

- Cafeteria knife (a plastic knife) for the Cafeteria Lady White

- A ruler (a large heavy one) for Principal Plum

- A P.A. mic (a toy microphone) for Secretary Scarlett

- Meat Loaf Surprise (a play dough mixture) for Custodian Green

Games and Activities

Unraveling clues and solving the crime are your jobs as detectives, so put on your game face and see if you can guess whodunit!

High School Clue

Set Up the Crime

First decide who's the victim, such as the Crabby School Bus Driver, Smart Aleck Student, Pompous Jock, Slutty Cheerleader, Weird Science Teacher, Dorky Vice Principal, Slacker Crossing Guard, Zealous Narc, and so on. Select enough black cards from a deck of cards to equal the number of players, then replace one of the black cards with a red card, and mix them up. Pass out the cards. The girl who gets the red card is the murderer. Tell her to keep this secret. Have each player make up three reasons why they could be guilty and include the motive, the weapon, and the opportunity. For example, the Cafeteria Lady might be guilty because 1. She's sick and tired of cooking mounds of mashed potatoes (motive), 2. She's always packing a sharp knife (weapon), and she has a lot of free time while the potatoes are boiling (opportunity). Then write down an alibi that prevents her from being the murderer—if she's innocent—such as "I was having an affair with the Principal at the time of the murder." Make up one or two clues that help prove your guilt or innocence, such as flirting with the principal in front of the others, then write them on sticky notes and hide them in plain sight in the room.

The Accusations Fly

Give each suspect the weapon that goes with her character. Start introducing yourselves in character, state how you knew the victim, and why you're innocent. If you're the murderer, you can stretch the truth but you cannot lie. Have the other guests and detectives ask questions— except they cannot ask directly, "Are you the murderer?" At the end of a timed session, have detectives try to guess whodunit, along with motive, weapon, and opportunity, based on what they've garnered from the statements of the suspects. If no one guesses correctly, continue the game until someone identifies the guilty party.

Refreshments

Serve colorful foods that represent each character and give them a creative name. For example, you might prepare Plum's Plum Jam 'n' Toast, Peacock's Blue Hurricane Blast, Mustard's Mustard Green Salad, Green's Green Beans, White's Mashed Potatoes, and Scarlett's Strawberry Dessert.

Favors, Prizes, and Gifts

Send everyone home with a Clue board game, a murder mystery novel, a copy of *Murder By Death* or *Clue* DVDs, a magnifying glass, or a flashlight.

Party Plus

Buy an already prepared mystery game instead of writing your own—although it won't be as much fun! Or order one of my scripted "Library Mysteries" at *www.pennywarner.com.*

Fashionista Party

For those who love sparkly jewels and glitzy gems, have a Fashionista Party with all the bling and accessories, then shake up the closet a little and get a fashion makeover. Invite your girlfriends over to help one another with fashion tips, clothing swaps, and DIY jewelry.

Invitations

Cut out bizarre fashions from a trendy magazine or catalog, create a collage, and photocopy it for all the guests. If possible, add the heads of each of the guests to the fashions. Write party details inside, as if they're fashion blurbs, such as, "Head for the runway—You'll be wearing the latest prêt a porter this year!" Ask the guests to bring a "what was I thinking" outfit they haven't worn in a long time to exchange.

What to Wear

Have the guests come in casual—even sloppy—clothes and bring along something fancy to change into. Or for fun, have them dress in black and white outfits—but with a twist on the elegance of monochrome. They can wear anything, including a bathing suit, pajamas, a tuxedo jacket with boxer shorts, exercise wear, even a black and white striped jailhouse jumpsuit—as long as it's black and white.

Decorations

Decorate the party room in a black and white color scheme, with balloons, paper products, and fashion posters or pictures. Hang up some of your own "what was I thinking" outfits to get the party started on the right foot. Set out a full-length mirror and a "catwalk" or red carpet for modeling the new fashions. Have decorated department store bags handy to take the clothes home in.

Games and Activities

Accessorize the fun with cool clothes, designer duds, and lots of bling!

Clothing Swap

Have everyone lay out their clothing on chairs, couches, and tables, or hang them along the mantel or windowsill. Take turns trying on the outfits, model them for the others, and ask for comments on how they look. If an ensemble works out for you, it's yours to keep! (Donate leftover clothes to the thrift shops.)

DIY Bling Bling

A girl can never have too many diamonds, so host a jewelry jam and make your own bling to go. Provide a variety of beads and the supplies to create necklaces and bracelets, then let the girls go to work creating their own designs.

Designer Line

Create fashions using swap clothes or clothes from a thrift shop using each other as models. When the outfits are finished, model the outfits on the catwalk, with each designer narrating their creations. Videotape the event, then give out awards for "Best Use of Color," "Most Creative Combination of Clothes," "Sluttiest," and so on.

Refreshments

Serve black and white snacks when the group gets hungry, such as caviar on crackers, olives and sour cream dip, licorice whips, and white chocolate for dessert. Or give them model food—salads, low-cal drinks, and sugar-free candy.

Favors, Prizes, and Gifts

The models get to keep their new outfits and the jewelry they've made. Include small bottles of perfume or makeup to finish them off.

Party Plus

Make it a "Swap Anything Party" and include CDs, housewares, decorator items, jewelry—anything that's new or like new and no longer wanted.

Red Hat Ladies Tea Party

> "When I am an old woman, I shall wear purple,
> With a red hat thatdoesn't go and doesn't suit me."
>
> ~ Jenny Joseph

The Red Hat Society was founded by Sue Ellen Cooper in 1998, specifically for women over fifty. Her idea was to provide social contacts and fun events for women who have decided not to go quietly into the older years. Today there are about 1.5 million Red Hatters in forty thousand chapters in the United States. This "dis-organization" is not a sorority or service club, according to the Red Hat Web site (*www.redhatsociety.com*). It's strictly to "encourage silliness, creativity, and friends in middle age and beyond." Celebrate the official Red Hat Society Day on April 25, or any time you're in the mood for red, purple, and fancy hats.

Invitations

The leader of a local chapter, called the Queen, is usually the one to host an event, so she's in charge of invitations. If that's you, make miniature red hats out of felt or card stock, and write party details on the back. Glue on a festive purple feather, and mail to guests. Add a teabag to the envelope to steam up the invitation a little.

What to Wear

Red hats, obviously, are de rigueur, along with purple attire. Use your imagination when putting your outfit together. Remember, part of the requirements of Red Hatters are creativity, silliness, and fun. By the way, if anyone is under fifty, they are to wear pink hats and lavender attire, until they reach the requisite age.

Decorations

Dress the room in shades of red and purple, using balloons, crepe paper streamers, fabric and ribbons, and lots of hats, placed on tables, lamps, mantels, and the back of chairs. Write out the poem by Jenny Joseph (called "Warning," see *www.redhatsociety.com*) on posterboard, and hang it on the wall. Find other "attitude" poems about women and include them (see my quotations at the beginning of each chapter for suggestions). Finish the room with red, pink, and purple flowers and candles.

Games and Activities

Entertain the girls in red with a hat trick or two!

Primp Your Hat

Have a Red Hat Decorating Day, with lots of accessories to add to the hats, such as ribbon, buttons, decals, appliqués, pins, and so on. Just provide the materials and equipment and let the Red Hatters use their creativity. For fun, provide some unusual hats to decorate, such as straw hats, sailor caps, pirate hats, baseball caps, and so on.

Red Hat Scrap

Many Red Hatters also enjoy scrapbooking. There's even a book out on the topic called *Designer Scrapbooks the Red Hat Society Way*. Set up scrapbooking tables with lots of red and purple papers and accessories, and share some time making memories. (See Scrapbooking Party for ideas.)

Red Hat Boutique

Gather together to make crafty gifts and sell at a holiday boutique. You can make it general crafts or give it a specific theme, such as Christmas, Spring, or Halloween. You might make mini-scrapbooks, holiday decorations, embellished clothing, homemade jewelry, or even hats! Spend the profits on your next event!

Red Hat Funvention

Host your own regional Red Hat Funvention! Spend a couple of nights at a hotel with the Red Hatters, and enjoy an evening of pampering, cocktails, PJ breakfast buffet, fashion show, shopping, speakers, swimming, and socializing. Have a contest for best hat, best outfit, best scrapbook, and so on. Don't forget to include a traditional High Tea.

Red Hat Café

Society members also like to cook—and eat—so gather for a gourmet meal, prepared by the group, using favorite recipes, or ones from *The Red Hat Society Cookbook*. Choose a theme for your café day, such as Mexican, Southern, or American Classics, and tailor the meal to that. Eat what you make!

Refreshments

Host a High Tea (see page 210), and serve dainty desserts and tea sandwiches. Tint the bread pink or lavender, for fun. Include a platter of red and purple grapes, red bell peppers and eggplant dip, strawberries dipped in white chocolate that's been tinted lavender, and strawberry ice cream. Make a cake in the shape of a hat and frost it red. Add purple icing decorations and a large feather on top.

Favors, Prizes, and Gifts

Give the gals anything that will embellish their hats, as a memento of the afternoon or evening. Buy inexpensive red or purple scarves, jewelry, or socks to go with their outfits.

Party Plus

Have a Sweet Potato Queens Tea Party, based on the Sweet Potato Queens (*www.sweetpotatoqueens.com*) and wear matching costumes and accessories in green, beauty queen style, with tiaras, boots, sunglasses for added flair. Or make it a YaYa Sisterhood Party (*www.sisterhoodcircle.com*) and celebrate your sisters with food, fun, and friendship.

Sports Jersey Party

Who says you have to be a guy to enjoy sports? If your friends are into sports, put together a sports party to match a televised event, such as the Super Bowl, the Olympics, a tennis match, or World Series playoff game. It doesn't matter if your favorite football team is playing in the championship game or sitting this one out—you can still root for a good time! And you barely have to lift a finger—except to control the remote! Just set up a stadium right in your own TV room and host a day of cheers, jeers, and beers. Men at the party? Totally optional!

Invitations

Create your own invitations using mini-sports balls, baseball cards, or copies of the sports page. Or write the information on the back of your favorite team's pennants. Place in a large puffy envelope and fill it with peanuts still in the shell! Mail to fans.

What to Wear

Ask your guests to wear their favorite team's colors. Or have them come in costumes related to football, such as a player, a cheerleader, a referee, or a crazed fan. As hostess, you might want to come dressed as a food and drink vendor.

Decorations

Turn the party room into a sports arena or ballpark, with banners, posters, team colors, and sports equipment. Hang posters of the team or star players on the walls. Cut out footballs or other balls from brown construction paper and hang them from the ceiling. Buy paper products in your favorite team's colors and decorate the room with crepe paper streamers to match. Arrange your furniture and chairs in a half circle around the TV to simulate a stadium. Mark out your party room floor with field yard lines using tape or rope, set up a few homemade goalposts, and cover the walls with sports banners. Use programs for placemats and ball-shaped platters for serving food. Give the crowd foam "We're Number One" fingers. Have several inflatable balls to kick and toss around at the party. Serve snacks and drinks on a table that looks like a gridiron. Cover it with a white paper tablecloth, draw on yard lines with felt-tip pen, and tape drinking straw goalposts to either end. Add stickers, banners, or football cards to feature the teams. Make a centerpiece of footballs, helmets, and pennants—or whatever matches the sport. Or add a touch of whimsy with some Ace bandages, Ben-Gay, crushed beer cans, and Gatorade.

Games and Activities

The game on TV is just the beginning of the fun, with these sports-related challenges and activities.

Place Your Bets!

Keep the action going when the game goes to commercial. Have everyone bring pennies or dollar bills and place bets on the winning scores. You can bet on the score at each quarter, bet which players will earn the most points, and bet which team will win the game. For added fun, place penny bets on everything that you could possibly bet on, such as:

○ Who will win the coin toss?

○ Which beer commercial will be next?

○ Which coach is easiest to lip-read?

○ Who will swear first?

○ Who will spit first?

○ Who's going to be injured first?

○ Who will have the dirtiest uniform?

Sports Scores

Quiz the fans on sports trivia during the commercial breaks. Ask questions according to the level of the group's expertise. If the sports fans are rookies, keep the questions simple, such as "What's the name of the Florida football team?" or "Who's the cutest guy on the New York

Jets?" or make them challenging for the armchair cheerleaders, with questions about past Super Bowl winners and record-breaking stats.

Halftime!

Take a break at halftime and go outside for a game of tag football or other physical sport. Or practice some cheerleading routines to get your energy flowing again. Or just get up and dance to the halftime music.

Refreshments

Feed the hungry fans famous ballpark food. Offer the crowd traditional ballpark franks, chili and corn bread, soft pretzels, peanuts, and beer. For fun, make a giant sub sandwich. Cut several loaves of French bread in half lengthwise, and fill with favorite meats, cheeses, and condiments. Lay the loaves end to end, cut the ends off all but the last two end loaves, then slice up the giant sandwich and stick long toothpicks in each section. Let the guests serve themselves a slice when they get hungry. Dress like a vendor to serve the food. Serve a cake shaped like a ball, or make cupcake balls.

Favors, Prizes, and Gifts

Send the fans home with sports memorabilia, pennants, kick balls, and other sports related items. Give them tickets to an upcoming game—professional, amateur, college, or high school. Buy T-shirts with the team logo and personalize them with fans' names on the back. Hand out sports almanacs or fact books. Give the fans some football cards to take home.

Party Plus
Get the girls together and go out to a ballgame!

Snooze You Lose Slumber(less) Party

You're never too old for a sleepover with the girls, so put on your nightie, baby dolls, or flannels and try to stay awake during your all-nighter. This is a party where you can really let your hair down—and do it up again—so get going on those makeovers, margaritas, and man-talk!

Invitations

For creative invitations related to the theme, send toothbrushes personalized for each guest with a permanent felt-tip pen. Attach a note that looks like a sleeping bag, and insert the party details inside.

What to Wear

Ask the girls to wear their PJs, a robe, and slippers, and bring a sleeping bag and pillow. Or suggest a type of nightwear, such as your oldest pajamas, your flannels, your baby dolls, your sexiest negligees, or funniest nightwear.

Decorations

Hang stars from the ceiling, posters of constellations or nighttime views, and a glow-in-the-dark moon for an outdoor under-the-stars atmosphere. For extra fun, set up a tent in the living room—or host the party in the backyard for a sleepover camp. If you plan to show movies during the party, set up a "concession stand" filled with popcorn, candy, and other treats.

Games and Activities

Remember the fun you had at your teen sleepovers? Well, you're never too old for some slumber party games and tricks.

Slumber Party Fun

Enjoy some typical slumber party fun such as:

- Have a pillow fight
- Play box games
- Tell ghost stories
- Make snacks
- Learn new dances
- Watch scary movies
- Go on a scavenger hunt
- Sing karaoke
- Do makeovers
- Play Twister
- Do puzzles

Let's Make a Deal

Find three boxes. Inside one of the boxes place a cool prize, such as a CD, a DVD, or a box of chocolates. In the other two boxes, place funny objects, such as giant underwear or a book on erotica. The first player gets to choose one box and keep the contents. Repeat for all the players, replacing objects in the boxes and mixing them up.

Truth or Dare

Play a grown up version of Truth or Dare. Write up a bunch of questions and a bunch of dares—or have the players write them—on individual index cards. Place them in two separate piles, one with the Truth questions and one with the Dare statements, face down. Have the players choose a card from the Truth pile and answer it, truthfully. If she refuses, have her take a Dare card and follow the instructions. Here are some suggestions for cards:

Truth Cards:
- What is your best physical characteristic?
- If you won a million dollars, how much would you give to charity and which charity?
- Which movie star would you like to kiss?
- Where would you like to kiss someone?
- What did you look like on your worst day?
- What secret did you accidentally spill?
- Which movies stars do the other women look like?
- What kind of plastic surgery would you have?
- Which player tells the worst jokes?
- What would you change your name to?
- Would you tell someone if she had bad breath?
- What kind of animals do the other players remind you of?
- If you had 1 hour to live, what would you do?
- What's your favorite age and why?
- What's your biggest fear?
- What is your worst habit?
- What have you borrowed and not returned?

- How much do you weigh?

- Which movie star do you look like the most?

- What do you like the most about guys?

- When is the last time you cried and why?

- Who is the most important person in the world to you?

Dare Cards:
- Do the moonwalk.

- Imitate your favorite animal.

- Demonstrate a karate move, even if you don't know one.

- Put on lipstick without a mirror, with your eyes closed.

- Make the player next to you laugh in 30 seconds.

- Move a piece of fruit across the room with your nose.

- Try to juggle three objects.

- Yodel Happy Birthday to You.

- Try to touch your nose with your tongue.

- Try to wiggle your ears.

- Draw a face on your tummy and make it "talk."

- Snort like a pig.

- Pick up a pen with your lips.

- Have an argument with yourself.

○ Give your Academy Award acceptance speech.

○ Give fashion show comments on the other players' clothes.

○ Try out for a role in your favorite movie.

○ Kiss both of your feet—with your shoes and socks off.

○ Eat a piece of food from the floor.

Give It a Twist: Instead of doing one dare, pick two cards and do both tasks at the SAME time.

Refreshments

Serve pizza, old-fashioned ice cream sodas, and s'mores when guests get the midnight munchies. Offer bowls or bags of popcorn along with a variety of toppings, such as cinnamon and sugar, melted butter, pizza seasoning, Parmesan cheese, shredded Cheddar cheese, or Mexican seasonings. In the morning, serve whipped cream and fruit on waffles.

Favors, Prizes, and Gifts

Give the guests a book on dream interpretations, a travel toothbrush and toothpaste, and other overnight amenities. Pass out fuzzy socks, sleep shirts, or nightlights to take home.

Party Plus

Have a Hotel Slumber Party, and let the staff clean up the mess in the morning. While you're there, enjoy room service, the pool, the workout room, and an all-you-can-eat breakfast buffet. Or host a Naughty Nightie Party and have a salesperson share all her sexy sleepwear with the group.

Redneck Party

Check your neck—you may be a redneck and not even know it. Put on your Daisy Dukes and head for the trailer park for some tacky goodies and games. Thanks to comedians like Jeff Foxworthy, TV shows like *Git-R-Done*, and cookbooks by Ruby Ann, White Trash Parties are more fun than a mouth full of tobacco. Invite Bubba-Sue and Beulah-Jean to dress in their tackiest outfits and come as their favorite rednecks, for a down-home, backwoods time.

Invitations

If you can't invite your friends simply by shouting over the back fence, here are some other suggestions for gathering the group. Create your own *Enquirer* newspaper by cutting and pasting the party details onto a real issue, then photocopy and mail to guests. Write your invitation on the back of a redneck recipe for "Roadkill Stew" or "Spam Surprise." (Check out Ruby Ann's *Trailer Park Cookbook* for more ideas.) Make a Confederate flag from red, white, and blue paper, decorate it with online clip art, such as a bent beer car, old truck, bubba teeth, woman smoking, professional wrestlers, Jerry Springer, and so on. Add a few extras to the invitation, such as "Come celebrate Becky-Sue's grajiation from Tammy Faye's School of Cosmatology and Taxadermy," "No shirts, no shoes, no problem!" "No animals—except dogs, of course," "If you're bringin' a date (or your sister), make sure you get her back to school on Monday." Include some of Jeff Foxworthy's "You know you're a redneck . . ." quotes, or make up your own. When you address the envelopes, add "Bubba" or "Couzin" to the names, or hyphenate their first and middle names, such as "Becca-Sue" or "Bradley-Ed." Include a pair of bubba teeth with the invitation, and add: "Teeth, optional."

What to Wear

Tell your redneck guests to come in redneck wear, and threaten them with a penalty if they don't. Give them a list of suggestions to help them plan their "outfits," such as: Pigtails with bent wire clothes hangers to make them stick out. Really big hair and lots of hairspray and dark roots. Freckles, blue eye shadow, fake lashes. Daisy Dukes cutoffs, tube tops, mini skirts, robe, black bra showing. Platform shoes, house slippers, barefoot, flip-flops. Stuffed T-shirt to look pregnant, with a fake cigarette and a beer as accessories. Other accessories: Beer cap earrings, hair rollers, fake tattoos, airbrushed press-on nails, black eye, jewelry that says "SEXY!", blacked out teeth (using theatrical makeup or black gum), outfits made from American or Confederate flags, and a baby carrier for holding beer. More ideas: Overalls with a mechanics logo tacked on, can of Skol, biker leathers, Harley Davidson shirt, NASCAR shirts and hats, beer logo shirts, flannel shirts with sleeves ripped off, long johns, duct tape repairs, mullets made from thrift store wigs, beer gut showing.

Decorations

Trash up the place with a few creative touches to welcome the trailer park partiers. Make a sign for the front yard out of plywood that reads: "Billy Bob's Mobile Home Park and Bait Shop" and surround it with Christmas lights. Stick pink flamingoes, pinwheels, gnomes, and tacky lawn ornaments in the yard. Tack up clotheslines and hang outrageous articles, such as a huge bra, grandpa undies, torn clothes, rags, dirty underwear, and a fake baby (baby doll). Park a beat-up truck on the lawn or put it up on jacks. Sprinkle the yard with empty beer cans, KFC buckets, broken lawn furniture, kids' toys, old appliances, lit-up Santa and reindeer, old work boots, tires, tools, etc. Make a wind chime out of empty beer or soda cans. Hang hubcaps along the fence. Inside: Use

Enquirer headlines for placemats, old printed sheets for tablecloths, tin pie pans for plates, paper towel napkins, then set fly swatters at each place. Decorate the walls with posters from NASCAR, country-western singers, beer signs, velvet Elvis portraits, WWF, Jerry Springer, and Kid Rock. Hang Christmas lights around the room, some drooping, some burned out. Create your own banners, such as: "Leopard Prints—Not Just for Church Anymore," "Beer—More than just breakfast," "The shitter is that way . . . (with an arrow)." Make personalized Mug Shots: Take pictures of guests with digital camera, print them out on preprinted paper with "(Your Town) Police Department" on top, arrest date, serial number, etc. Give each one an AKA, such as Becca "The Bee-otch" Melvin. Cover the furniture with plastic or kid-printed sheets. Play videos on the TV—*Jerry Springer* episodes, wrestling, *Cops*, NASCAR, Wild Turkey Hunting, *Git-R-Done*, Jeff Foxworthy comedy, or *The Blue Collar Comedy Tour*. Decorate the bathroom with fuzzy toilet accessories. Set the toilet paper nearby. Hang towels with slogans, written in permanent felt pen, such as "For your face, not your butt." Set out tall prayer candles and other tacky candles, fake flowers, and trashy magazines. Cover the windows with aluminum foil, ripped here and there, and hang beach towels and sheets on other windows. Make your own vending machine out of a cardboard box. Dispense "live bait, beer, and chaw." Music suggestions: Lynyrd Skynyrd, Gretchen Wilson, Charlie Daniels, Allen Jackson, *Redneck Wonderland*, *Redneck Hooterville*, *The Only Redneck Album You Will Ever Need*, *Redneck Country*, *Blood, Sweat, and Beers*, bluegrass, old time country-western. Place settings should include styrofoam carryout trays, plastic fork and knife packages, jelly and jam glasses for drinks, salt and pepper packages, napkins from various fast-food restaurants, and beer huggies. Make a birthday cake centerpiece by setting up beer cans and topping them with large tapered candles. On posterboard, copy silly sayings from "You know you're a redneck if . . ."

Games and Activities

Lucky for you and your friends, games at a Redneck Party are no-brainers. Sometimes literally . . .

Who Cut the Cheese?

Set out an array of foiled-covered jars and spray cans of spreadable cheeses, along with some Saltines, Wheat Thins, and Triscuits. Have a taste test with the cheeses to determine which one tastes the most like . . . cheese.

Redneck Short Attention Span Games

1. Nearly Beer

   Have a beer tasting and let the players guess which one is the cheapest.

2. Arm in Arm

   Challenge each other to an arm-wrestling contest. For added fun, place paper plates of whipped cream in the landing spots . . .

3. You're a Ding Dong

   Have a Ding-Dong, Twinkie, or Cherry Pie (packaged) eating contest.

4. Drink Up

   Play beer-drinking games, such as "Take a swig every time you say the words 'Yo Mama!'"

5. T-Shirt Contest

   Have a T-shirt Contest—with a twist. Fold and soak shirts, and freeze them overnight. Hand them out to the guests and see who can get the shirt on first.

6. Spam Contest

   Have a "Carve the Spam" contest and tell the contestants to make a hood ornament in less than three minutes.

7. Underwear Frisbee

   Nail some big nails onto the fence and have players take turns tossing giant undies onto the hooks.

8. Redneck Horseshoes

   Play with plastic toilet seats.

9. Chicken!

   Have a contest tossing rubber chickens.

10. Boob Tube

    Show redneck comedy videos, such as Jeff Foxworthy, *The Blue Collar Comedy Tour, Joe Dirt, and Git-R-Done*.

11. Redneck Music

    Dance to Redneck music and sing to redneck karaoke, such as "Redneck Woman/Here for the Party."

12. Girl Fight!

    Have a pretend "girl fight" with pillows. (No nails allowed!)

13. Are You Being Funny?

    Make up your own "You know you're a redneck if . . ." punchlines.

Refreshments

Have the guests create a new redneck dish with interesting ingredients like Jell-O, hot dogs, Cool Whip, Spam, Cheetos, and so on. Serve sliders or have the party catered by KFC. Offer tater tots, pork rinds, potato chips and onion dips, Jiffy Pop right out of the container. Make stew and called it Squirrel Stew or Roadkill Stew. Don't forget the Spam, Vienna sausages, beef jerky, and Slim Jims. Serve baked beans heated, but out of the can. Spray cheese and Ritz crackers or Saltines make great snacks. Moon pies are a must, along with white bread sandwiches with peanut butter and mashed banana, grilled, Elvis style. Also consider making Green Jell-O with hot dogs, tuna casserole, pigs feet, pigs in a blanket, Chili Frito Pie (small bag of Fritos cut open with dollops of chili, cheese, and sour cream), macaroni and cheese with sliced hot dogs on top, Rice Krispie Squares, Chex mix, sardine dip. For drinks, have a keg of beer, wine coolers with Boone's Farm wines, boxed wine, Jell-O shooters, RC Cola. Build a wedding or anniversary cake by piling up Ding Dongs and Twinkies. Place Barbie on top of a cake, but give her a makeover—cut up her clothes, blacken her teeth, give her a mini cigarette and mini bottle of booze, darken her roots with mascara, or cut her hair into a mullet.

Favors, Gifts, and Prizes

Keep it redneck and send the guests back to their trailers with a Whoopee Cushion, toilet brush sets, redneck teeth, beer cozies, anything with a flamingo, NASCAR items, Lynyrd Skynyrd's Greatest Hits, rat traps, flea powder, duct tape, zebra print lacy panties, deer thermometer, WWF wrestling T-shirts, Chia Pets, cheesy car air fresheners, fuzzy dice, fly swatters. Include books like *White Trash Etiquette* by Dr. Verne Edstrom, *Git-R-Done* by Larry the Cable Guy, *I Had the Right to Remain Silent but Didn't Have the Ability* by Ron "Tater Salad" White, *The Redneck Grill, Extreme Mobile Home Makeover, Games Rednecks Play*, and *Hick Is Chic*, by Jeff Foxworthy, or a *Blue Collar Comedy Tour* DVD.

Party Plus

Try this theme when you want to host a special birthday or anniversary party, a country-western or square dance party, a surprise party, or a summer barbecue. Host a Beverly Hillbillies White Trash Party and dress up tacky-style for a good time in La-La Land. Or make it a Trailer Trash Bunco Party and play Bunco in your tacky attire. Or instead of dressing tacky, wear outfits actually made from real trash, such as supermarket bags, rags, cereal packets, garbage bags, foil, puzzle pieces, tickets, or a prom dress made out of colored condoms.

CHAPTER 12

Fun with Food Parties

"Life is uncertain. Eat dessert first."

~ *Ernestine Ulmer*

There's nothing more crowd pleasing than a food-themed festival! All you need is a theme to use as an excuse for serving up your favorite snacks, meal, drinks, and desserts. As long as there's something good to eat, your party is guaranteed to be a success. You can have the event catered, ask the guests to bring potluck, or create the refreshments right there at the party with a cooks-in-the-kitchen theme. Remember, "food is life"—and the life of the party—so spice it up, mix it up, and serve it up!

Oktoberfest Party

Time to tap the keg on an Oktoberfest Party! Traditionally, Oktoberfest is celebrated the last two weeks in September, but any time you're in the mood for brew and brats will do. Potato soup, sausages, hot salads, dumplings, and beer—the food and drink of an Oktoberfest party—is just what the stomach ordered. Parteigeist!

Invitations

Photocopy some German beer labels and write your party details on the back. Or use small German flags for festive invitations. For fun, include some German words, such as *bis bald* (see you soon), *bitte* (please come), and *guten appetit* (enjoy the meal).

What to Wear

Ask the frauleins to dress in traditional German outfits, with puffy white blouses, colorful dirndl skirts, lederhosen, and white aprons. Or have them wear T-shirts with beer logos!

Decorations

Set up a tent in your yard with large tables and benches for your guests. Add blue and white streamers, balloons, and tablecloths, the official colors of Bavaria for a colorful, festive look. Or decorate in the colors of the German flag. Set out a variety of German beers, mini flags, and write German phrases to hang on the walls or fences. Add travel posters of Germany, brochures, and postcards around the party area. Place flowers on the tables as centerpieces, especially blue and white ones or Bavarian favorites, such as Lobelia and geraniums. Rent or buy large beer mugs or ceramic steins. Play traditional German music, polkas, or beer drinking songs in the background.

Games and Activities

All those beer-drinking games you learned in college are perfect for an Oktoberfest, so start with those, and the rest of the party will be a blitzkrieg!

Sing Along

Buy some German beer-drinking CDs and write down the words to some of the fun songs on posterboard. Then have the guests sing along, while waving their beer steins to and fro.

Kazoo Band and Polka!

Give your guests kazoos to play along with the music. Get up and dance the polka. Make sure your polka CD includes the infamous Chicken Dance!

Beer Stein Races

Divide into teams and have them line up. Fill two steins to the brim with beer (or water), and have the first two players from each team race across the yard and back, trying not to spill. The team with the most beer in the stein after everyone has had a turn wins the race and gets to drink the leftovers.

Beer Tasting

Buy small real or plastic glasses, six for each guest. On a white paper placemat, draw six circles, and give each player a pencil or fine-tip marker. Pour six different beers into the six cups (making sure the bottles or cans are wrapped so no one can see the labels), and have the guests taste the beers in unison, one beer at a time. Ask them to write down what kind of beer they think they're drinking—give them a variety of choices—then reveal the answer. The players with the most correct answers win.

Sprechen Sie Deutsch?

Have the guests try to translate from the German. Here are a few phrases to get you started.

Guten tag (good day), *naturlich* (of course), *alles gute zum geburtstag* (happy birthday), *was is das?* (what's that?), *est ist kostlich* (that's delicious), *mehr bier, bitte* (more beer, please).

Refreshments

Beer is the main ingredient at this party. Purchase a keg or two of German beer, or select a variety of bottled German labels for your party. Cook up traditional German food, including German sausages, bratwurst, hot German potato salad, sauerkraut, sweet and sour cabbage. Top it off with Black Forest Cake and some German pastries.

Favors, Prizes, and Gifts

Give the frauleins a six-pack of German beer, some festive flowers, a box of German chocolates, or some German pastries to take home.

Party Plus

Host the party at a German restaurant or beer hall.

Java Jitters Party

Coffee parties offer friends a chance to gather and enjoy each other's company along with a hot cup of a favorite java drink. So brew up some caffeine for a "latte" fun, then munch on mocha cookies and espresso desserts. For the noncoffee or caffeine drinkers, substitute hot chocolate, tea, decaf, or coffee-flavored drinks.

Invitations

Write your party details on coffee filters, then slip them in the envelopes with a few fragrant coffee beans. Or buy inexpensive coffee mugs, write the party details on the mug using permanent markers, and hand deliver or mail in padded boxes to guests.

What to Wear

Ask the guests to come in various shades of brown to match the coffee and décor.

Decorations

String up brown crepe paper streamers and fill the ceiling with brown balloons. Set out bags of coffees from various countries, hang coffee posters on the wall, and place coffee mugs around the room or on the table. Make the centerpiece an espresso maker, a plastic bag of coffee beans in a wicker basket, or a display of colored sugars on a stick.

Games and Activities

Everything you ever knew about coffee will come into play with these games and activities.

Java Tasting

Try a variety of coffees from different countries, such as Colombian, Guatemalan, Jamaican, Kenyan, and Sumatran, and see if the guests can match them to their labels and locations. Offer sips rather than full cups, so your guests aren't bouncing off the walls too early in the game!

Amateur Barista

Have the guests take turns making up their own flavored coffee drinks (see suggestions in Refreshments). Award a prize for the best one.

Coffee Bee

Write down facts about coffee and turn it into a Coffee Bee, testing the guests on their java savvy. Here are some little known tidbits you might want to use as a basis for True/False questions:

- Cowboy Coffee is made by putting ground coffee into a clean sock and immersing it in water over a campfire. (True)

- Testing positive for caffeine is prohibited on the International Olympic Committee list (more than 12 micrograms or 5 cups). (True)

- Turkish brides must provide their new husbands with coffee or there's "grounds for divorce." (False; bridegrooms must provide it for their new wives.)

- Italians drink their espresso with sugar, Germans with hot chocolate, Mexicans with cinnamon, Belgians with chocolate, Moroccans with peppercorns, Ethiopians with a pinch of salt,

Middle Eastern with cardamom, Austrians with whipped cream, and Egyptians just plain. (True)

○ Espresso has twice the caffeine of regular coffee. (False; it has one-third the caffeine.)

○ Coffee beans are really beans. (False; they're berries.)

○ The three biggest coffee drinkers in the world are Americans, French, and Germans, together consuming 65 percent of the world's coffee. (True)

Coffee Color

Set out paint samples from Home Depot or any hardware store in shades of brown and have players give them coffee names, such as mocha, latte, cappuccino, espresso, café au lait, iced coffee. If players match with the same color assignment, they get a point. The player with the most points wins.

Refreshments

Serve bite-sized desserts, such as biscotti, ladyfingers, sweet biscuits, scones, cookies, slices of coffee cake, and mini-muffins. Ice cream or whipped cream is great with coffee too. Try a variety of coffee flavors from different cultures, such as Mexican, Spanish, French, African, and Cuban. Add flavors to the coffees, such as chocolate, Irish cream, orange, cinnamon, Grand Marnier, Kahlua, mint, almond, or raspberry flavoring. Make blended drinks using coffee such as mocha smoothies or coffee ice cream shakes. Serve the coffee drinks with colored sugar stirrers on a stick and flavored creams.

Favors, Prizes, and Gifts
Give the guests personalized coffee mugs, exotic coffees, coffee flavorings and sugars, coffee flavored candies, coffee scented candles, and gift certificates to Starbucks or Dunkin' Donuts.

Party Plus
Go to a coffee bar and try a variety of coffees there. Or have a cooking party using coffee as an ingredient in a dessert.

Chocoholic Orgy
Believe it or not, chocolate is good for you. Dark chocolate contains antioxidants (they help prevent heart disease and cancer) as well as serotonins (to make you feel good). So host an all-out chocolate marathon filled with chocolate goodies, drinks, and desserts. Then eat it, drink it, spread it, lick it to your heart's content!

Invitations
Write your party details on the inside of chocolate bar wrappers (or wrap them around bars of chocolate à la Willy Wonka) and mail them to guests in padded envelopes filled with chocolate sprinkles and Hershey kisses. Or make the invitations, ransom note style, using candy wrappers. For example, you could write, "Hey MAMBA! It's a WHOPPER of a Chocoholic Party that's full of SNICKERS. Come TWIX 7:00 and 7:30 P.M. for a NUTRAGEOUS time. HUGS and KISSES, (Your Name)." Or give your guests a chocolate rose with the party details attached.

What to Wear
Ask everyone to wear chocolate-colored clothes.

Decorations

Dress the party room in chocolate colors, using balloons and streamers. Set out candy bars, hang them from the ceiling, and make a collage out of wrappers for the table. Set up a chocolate fountain as a dazzling centerpiece. Place chocolate-scented candles and soaps around the room. Make place markers out of chocolate bars.

Games and Activities

Explore all the possibilities chocolate has to offer with a few fun activities. Just don't forget to sample it along the way!

Chocolate Factory

Make your own chocolates using quality baking or melting chocolate and candy forms, or make truffles using a favorite recipe.

Chocolate and Wine

Surprisingly, chocolate and wine go perfectly together, so have a chocolate and wine tasting, by pairing various chocolates—bittersweet, dark, milk, and white—with a variety of wines, such as Merlot, Cabernet, Pinot Noir, and so on.

Chocolate Bouquets

If you can keep from eating all the chocolate, make chocolate bouquets from chocolate bars. Give each guest six or eight different bars, and the same amount of stiff floral wire. Insert the wire into the ends of each candy bar. Gather the bouquet together and wrap it with green floral tape, then with green cellophane. Tie it off with a ribbon and place in a vase.

Chocolate Movies

Watch movies that feature chocolate, such as *Like Water for Chocolate, Chocolat,* or *Willy Wonka and the Chocolate Factory.*

Refreshments

Overdose on chocolate! Make a chocolate and strawberry pizza, chocolate fondue, chocolate-dipped pretzels, truffles and bonbons, and a variety of chocolate bars, such as plain, with nuts, fruit, mints, caramels, and toffee. Pour hot chocolates or mochas, and serve chocolate layer cake with chocolate ice cream covered in chocolate sauce for "dessert."

Favors, Prizes, and Gifts

If they haven't had enough chocolate, send them packing with personalized chocolate bars (*www.babybar.com*), homemade fudge, mini-boxes of chocolates, chocolate soaps, chocolate sauces, and chocolate recipes.

Party Plus
Head for a restaurant and just order dessert.

"Look Who's Cooking" Party

Here's a party to please any palate, even if some of your friends aren't master chefs. Just divide up the meal, set the table, and enjoy a gastronomic gathering. It's a good idea to pair up cooks with noncooks, so you have a little experience to balance the clueless in each couple. Have samples available for snacking as you cook, so the chefs don't eat all the goodies before the meal is complete!

Invitations

Create invitations that look like menus, with a preview of the meal to come. Fold a sheet of card stock, write the name of the party on the outside along with the "(Your Name) Café," then fill in the party details inside. Or buy inexpensive chef hats at the restaurant supply store and write the party details inside the rim, with their names personalized on the outside in fabric pens, and mail to guests.

What to Wear

Ask the chefs to wear their favorite aprons, or provide matching ones for the guests, along with paper or cloth chef hats. (You can get them online inexpensively and use them as an activity later.)

Decorations

The party takes place in the kitchen and dining area, so focus your decorations there. Set out kitchen gadgets as a table centerpiece, such as whisks, ladles, and so on, in a fancy bowl lined with a festive napkin. Use your best linens and dishes for the meal, or buy fun paper products to match the theme, featuring wine, cheese, chocolate, or other foods. Cut out pictures of famous chefs, such as Emeril and Anthony Bourdain, and hang them on the walls for inspiration, along with photographs of mouthwatering foods. Dangle a few kitchen utensils from the light fixture or ceiling for atmosphere. Set out fresh kitchen towels featuring food at each prep station for the chefs to use—one per person. Play music that fits the style of food, such as Andrea Bocelli for Italian food, Edith Piaf for French food, and a Mariachi band for Mexican food.

Games and Activities

It all started with your Easy-Bake Oven when you were a girl playing house. Now it's time to turn your talents loose in the kitchen, and whip up some more food and fun.

Make a Meal

Before the party begins, divide the group into pairs and assign each pair one part of a four- or five-course meal, including the appetizer, entrée, salad, soup, and dessert. (Add more courses if you have more chefs and can fit them into your kitchen.) Prepare the recipes on large index cards, and gather all the ingredients (or ask the guests to bring their assigned meal ingredients). Set up stations in the kitchen for each pair, with the recipe and ingredients, and equipment at hand. When the guests arrive, give them their assignments—partner and meal—and show them their station. Over wine and conversation, prepare the meal. When each course is ready, sit down and enjoy at the table.

Iron Chef Contest

Like the television show, host an Iron Chef Contest between two teams, racing to complete a tasty dish with the same ingredients. Then vote on the best meal.

Accessorized Aprons

Before you start cooking, have everyone sit down at the table with their aprons. Set out decorating supplies, such as puffy paints, fabric pens, appliqués, beads, and so on, and let the chefs personalize their aprons to fit their personalities.

Refreshments

The meal you all prepare is the focus of the party. You can use your own favorite recipes, try something new out of *Bon Appétit* or *Cooks* magazine, or ask the guests to send you their favorite recipes ahead of time. You might also have some extra snacks on hand to munch on while you cook. And don't forget the wine. As a bonus, pair a different wine with each course.

Favors, Prizes, and Gifts

After a full meal, send the chefs home with copies of all the recipes, some of the leftovers, and a copy of a cooking magazine or book. Let them keep their personalized aprons and hats, too.

Party Plus
Give the party a theme, such as Italian Night or French Cuisine, and make it a regular event. Or focus on one course, such as Appetizers Only or Just Desserts.

Marvelous Martini Party

Shaken or stirred, martinis are back in style. Today you can mix your own flavored martinis—everything from watermelon to chocolate—by adding interesting ingredients, everything from melon juice to chocolate sauce. So turn on the latest Bond film, sip your elegant drink, and wait for 007 to appear.

Invitations

Write party details on plastic martini glasses and send them in padded boxes with an olive included. Or send a picture of your favorite James Bond with a speech bubble inviting the Bond Girls to a secret mission.

Decorations

Go back to the '50s and make your Martini Party an elegant affair. You could use a black and silver color scheme for the decorations, or go with a retro '50s look, with icons from the past. You can find cool bar signs, neon signs, cocktail napkins, and paper plates, to give the party room a cozy, classic feel. Play James Bond movies in the background or jazz music, such as Django Reinhardt or Cab Calloway. Set the table with martini glasses filled with black and white jellybeans, olives, nuts, or chocolate, for snacking. Include a few cocktail shakers as a centerpiece, filled with flowers.

Games and Activities

Martini mixes provide the entertainment at this mixer, so let the shaking begin.

Martini Mixology

Prepare a variety of different flavored martinis ahead of time, such as an Appletini, pomegranatini, strawberritini, in separate containers. Give players martini glasses and pour a small amount of the first mix in each of their glasses. Have them taste the martini and write down what flavor it is. Continue through all the flavors, then reveal the answers to see who makes the best Martini Mixologist.

Flavored Martinis

Next experiment with different flavors of martinis. You can find recipes online for a variety of flavors, including Appletinis, Cosmopolitan, Dry Martini, Gimlet, Manhattan, Melon Martini, Rob Roy, Vodka Martini, and Woman Warrior (vodka, blue Curaçao, and freshly squeezed lime, shaken, with ice). Go to *www.drinkalizer.com* for a great list of martini drinks and recipes.

Refreshments

Start the party with a Dirty Martini mix. Pour 2 ounces of gin, 1 tablespoon dry vermouth, 2 tablespoons of olive juice into a cocktail shaker and shake well (unless the guest prefers stirred). Pour into a chilled martini glass and garnish with 2 olives. (Makes 1 serving.)

Serve fancy appetizers with the martinis so your guests don't fall into their glasses, so to speak. Martinis go especially well with caviar and smoked salmon, as well as gourmet cheeses and crackers. Also serve some nonalcoholic drinks when you've all had enough. You can mix fruit juices, iced tea, and seltzer to make fake but tasty "martinis." For dessert, shake up some Chocolate Martinis. Melt an ounce of gourmet dark chocolate on a plate in the microwave. Dip the rim of a martini glass into melted chocolate and place in the freezer for a few minutes to harden the chocolate. Pour 3 ounces of vanilla vodka, 3 ounces of Godiva chocolate liqueur, 2 ounces of crème de cacao, and a dash of half-and-half into a cocktail shaker, along with a handful of ice, and shake well. Strain into the chilled, chocolate-rimmed glasses.

Favors, Prizes, and Gifts

Martini supplies would be the perfect gift to send with the guests—ingredients for a specific martini recipe, glasses, and/or a shaker. Decorated cocktail napkins would be a fun favor, as well as a cocktail recipe book.

Party Plus

Go to a Martini Bar and taste-test a variety of flavored drinks, while you check out the room for any James Bond types.

Mother/Daughter High Tea Party

High Tea, a longtime custom in Britain, has reached the American shores and taken the country by storm. Give your friends and family a chance to sip and socialize at a dainty tea and crumpets party, complete with gloves and hats. A High Tea makes a wonderful way to celebrate; mothers and daughters party and share herbal teas, decadent desserts, and a relaxing afternoon together.

Invitations

Send out creative teabag invitations to your mother-daughter guests. Buy a box of herbal teabags and remove the tag from each bag. Cut out same-size replacements from white paper and write the party details inside the fold, with the words "Your Presence Is Requested . . ."

or "The Queen Demands Your Appearance at a Mother/Daughter High Tea . . ." on the outside. Reattach to the teabags, slip into envelopes along with a sprinkling of aromatic tea, and mail to guests.

What to Wear

Dress up for High Tea! Ask the women and girls to come in elegant tea party dresses, complete with gloves, hats, heels, and hose. When they arrive, present each one with a plastic tiara and some costume jewelry or decorative brooch. You might even suggest they dress up as queens and princesses!

Decorations

Set up Ye Olde Tea Shoppe in your party room. Create a regal reception area, using a pink and white color scheme. Drape matching paper streamers from the ceiling and tie bunches of pink and white balloons to the backs of the chairs or float them on the ceiling. Set your fanciest table with a white lace tablecloth, best china and silver, and of course, a fancy teapot and cups. If you don't have enough cups for everyone, borrow from neighbors or ask the guests to bring their own. Or buy inexpensive teacups for everyone and send them home as party favors! Play classical music in the background, light some pink and white candles for atmosphere, and set a big bouquet of pink and white flowers as a centerpiece. Give the guests matching pink and white corsages to wear with their outfits.

Games and Activities

An elegant afternoon of tea and cookies provides its own entertainment, along with a few mother-daughter activities.

Serve a Proper High Tea

Steep some tea or boil water for fruity herbal teas and serve in your fancy teapot. Offer milk, cream, even whipped cream if you have it. Set out bowls of sugar, honey, and artificial sweeteners, along with sandwiches and cookies. (See Refreshments for suggestions.) Teach everyone how to behave at a proper tea, using their best manners.

Decorate Sugar Cookies

Roll and cut out sugar cookies, and bake according to package directions. Set out bowls of tinted frosting, tubes of colored icing, and cups of decorative candies, and let the "ladies" create their own cookies.

Paint Your Own Teacups

Buy some plain white teacups and let the guests paint them with glass paint (available from the craft store). Suggest simple designs, such as hearts or dots, or use stencils or rubber stamps. Allow to dry and hand them out as gifts at the end of the party.

Pretty Pictures Frames

Make picture frames from cardboard, decorate them with fancy foil wrapping paper, stickers, glitter, decals, and so on. Take Polaroid or computer snapshots of the mother-daughter pairs—a copy for each one—and give them to the guests for their frames.

Mother-Daughter Makeovers

Do each other's makeup! Ask guests to bring their own makeup, then let the daughters make over the mothers, and vice versa! Provide lots of mirrors to check out the handiwork. Then have a fashion show and model some fancy clothes to go with the makeup.

How Well Do You Know Your Mother/Daughter?

Write down questions for the pairs to answer about each other, such as "What time does she usually get up?" "What is her favorite TV show?" "What does she wear to bed?" "What is her favorite free-time activity?" Read the questions, have the pairs answer them on paper, then read the answers aloud to see which mother-daughter team knows one another best.

Refreshments

Along with the tea service, make finger sandwiches cut into strips, spread with a variety of fillings. For fun, have the bakery tint a loaf of bread pink, and make the sandwiches on pink bread. Serve plates of raspberry scones, petits fours, the sugar cookies you made, and other breads and sweets to go with the teas. And don't forget chocolate!

Favors, Prizes, and Gifts

Give the moms and girls teacups, homemade and decorated or storebought, along with some herbal teas. Present each pair with matching scarves or pins. Insert snapshots into the decorated frames for a longtime memory of the event.

Party Plus
Go to a teashop and have your party there.

Wine and Cheese Tasting Party

As if you need an excuse to drink wine, here's one anyway. Host a Wine and Cheese Tasting Party, where you have to guess what kind of wine you're drinking, then vote on the best of the lot. By the time the party is over, no one will care which one is the best—just that it was the best time they've ever had!

Invitations

Create fun invitations by making your own wine labels, using the computer, a fancy font, and some clip art of grapes or wine bottles. Write the name of the party and add the details. Ask the guests to bring an assigned bottle of red and/or white wine, such as a Cabernet, Merlot, Chianti, and Pinot Noir, Chardonnay, Pinot Grigio, Sauvignon Blanc, and Riesling. Have them wrap the bottles in plain brown paper bags to obscure the labels for a game later.

What to Wear

Ask them to dress in wine colors. Or get iron-on decals of wine bottles or glasses for T-shirts, have the guests wear white shirts, and iron on the decals when they arrive. Or give them a pin featuring a bunch of grapes, a scarf with a wine design, or socks that feature wine glasses and bottles.

Decorations

Cover your tasting table with a paper tablecloth in a wine design (so you don't have to worry about spills on your good tablecloth). Decorate the table with plastic grapes, wine glass decorations, and other wine related décor. Add wine-colored candles, and sprinkle the table with wine bottle labels.

Games and Activities

Test your wine-drinking acumen with a few sips from your favorite bottles—and learn some new wine terms.

Wine and Cheese Tasting
The Preparation
Set out glasses for each guest, with identification labels so everyone knows which glass is hers. Write up a numbered list, with spaces for

each bottle. Include a ratings system from 1 to 10 next to each bottle, 10 being "Superb," 1 being "Swill." Add a space for guests to estimate the price of the wine, and include other aspects of the wine to judge, such as appearance, aroma, flavor, and so on, if you like.

The Tasting

Pour the first glass of wine, preferably white if you're serving both red and white wines, but don't peek at the label. Ask the guests to taste the wine, try to guess what kind it is, and give it a rating. Offer a variety of cheeses and snacks with the wine. (See Refreshments below for suggestions.)

Wine Characters

Quiz the guests on their wine acumen, using the following terms. Have them take turns giving definitions—real or made up.

- Attractive (easy to drink)

- Big (full-bodied)

- Flabby (lacking acidity)

- Robust (intense)

- Supple (well-balanced with tannins and fruit)

- Green (like unripe fruit)

- Heady (high in alcohol)

- Barnyardy (smells like farm animals)

Cheese Tasting

Serve a different cheese with each pouring of wine, and have the tasters rate the cheeses, much like the wines. Have them guess what kind of cheese it is, how much it costs, and whether it goes well with the wine.

Refreshments

To balance the intake of wine, offer a variety of cheeses along with French bread or crackers. For the white wines, serve Swiss, Gouda, or Baked Brie. For red wine, try Gruyere, Muenster, or Blue Cheese. Serve cheesecake for dessert, with a nice dessert wine, such as Muscat. Other good appetizers include goat cheese, shrimp cocktail, olive oil dip and bread, hummus, and pâté.

Favors, Prizes, and Gifts

Give the tasters a bottle of wine to take home, along with a hunk of cheese and a box of gourmet crackers. Let them keep their wine decorated T-shirts and other wine accessories. Give them a book on wines.

Party Plus

Take the tasters to a wine bar or tasting room and learn about the different wines as you sample them.

CHAPTER 13

Music and Dance Parties

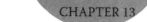

> "We're fools whether we dance or not, so we might as well dance."
>
> ~ *Japanese Proverb*

Dancing frees the spirit and soothes the soul. Besides that, it's great exercise and just plain fun. When it's time to kick up your heels and crunk, conga, cha cha, or just shake it, turn on the CD player or iTunes, crank up the music, and cut loose on the dance floor! You don't have to be inhibited when you're with your girlfriends. After all, they're probably the ones who taught you to dance in the first place, way back when.

Boot Stompin' Boogie Night

Put on your boots and scoot on over for a night of country-western music and two-steppin'! You cowgals can whoop and holler 'til the cows come home—or the police are called.

Invitations

Create a WANTED poster to use as the invitation to your party. Print up pictures of your friends on parchment paper, label the paper with "Wanted: Preferably Alive and Kickin'!" and the party details, then roll it up and tie it with a bandanna. Include a mini-cowgirl hat, a plastic horse, or photo of your favorite country-western singer, and mail to guests.

What to Wear

Country-western wear is required, anything from square-dance outfits to denim and flannel. Ask the guests to wear boots if they have them, and to use the bandanna you included in the invitation in a creative way. When they arrive, provide them with inexpensive cowgirl hats from the party or costume store, and pin on sheriff badges. Optional: Toy guns and holsters.

Decorations

The main event is dancing to a boot-scootin' beat, so make sure you have room enough for everyone to kick up their boots. Add a couple of bales of hay, some fake (or real) cacti, and toy horses, cows, and other farm animals around the room. If you have any horseback-riding equipment, set it out, including rope for lassoing. Set out guitars and other appropriate musical instruments. Hang up posters of your favorite CW stars and play classic country CDs in the background, such as Patsy Cline, Johnny Cash, and Hank Williams Jr. Set the table with western theme paper products, and make a centerpiece using small cacti, cans of pork and beans, and a bottle of whiskey.

Games and Activities

Be creative with your dance steps, learn a few new ones, then dance 'til you drop!

Hip-to-Be Square Dance

Hire a professional "caller" to entertain you with authentic square dancing. While you're at it, you might as well hire a professional dance instructor to teach you how to do-si-do. Or if you're game, put on a square dance record and have the group comedian do the calls.

Line Dancing

Surely someone in the crowd knows how to line dance, so have her teach the others. If not, make up your own dance, or ask the square dance caller to teach you. You can also rent a DVD that teaches line dancing, and learn it that way.

Country-Western Whispers

The CW circuit is filled with intriguing bits of gossip, scandal, and romantic entanglements. Do a little searching on the Net and find out the dirt, then turn it into a True/False quiz for your guests. For example: "Renee Zellweger was married to Keith Urban for only four months." (False: It was Kenny Chesney.) "Patsy Cline was killed in an auto accident." (False: It was a plane crash.)

CW Karaoke

Set up a karaoke machine along with popular country-western hits and let the future Shania Twain sing the blues.

Songwriter

Have the cowgirls make up their own heartbreaking country song, then sing—or read—the lyrics to the group. Award a prize for the saddest story.

Pimp Your Hat, Pardner

Set out craft supplies and let the guests decorate their cowgirl hats, with everything from sequins and feathers to glitter and bling.

Refreshments

Barbecue is popular at a country-western party—anything from chicken or steak to hot dogs or burgers—with a variety of tangy sauces. Offer plenty of sides: Cole slaw, baked beans, corn on the cob, creamed corn, mashed potatoes, macaroni and cheese, chili, garlic bread, and salsa and chips. Try to avoid green vegetables.

Favors, Prizes, and Gifts

The cowgirls can take home their hats and bandannas. You might also give them a small cactus plant, a stuffed horse or cow, a jar of jalapeño sauce or bottle of hot sauce with a funny label, such as "Ass-Kickin' Hot Sauce," "Fire Ant Juice," and simply "Death" (available online or at gourmet and gift shops).

Party Plus

Go to a country-western bar to learn the latest dances—and meet cowboys.

Ragin' Cajun Bon Temps Mardi Gras

You don't need to be in New Orleans to celebrate Mardi Gras. You can gather your friends, dress up in costume, and have your own colorful festival right in your own home. Mardi Gras is traditionally held on "Fat Tuesday" (the day before Ash Wednesday and forty days before Easter). It doesn't have to be Fat Tuesday to host a Mardi Gras Party.

Invitations

Decorate masks to use as invitations and send them to your amís. Or leave it plain, write the party details on the back, and ask the guests to decorate it and wear it to the party. Place the mask in a padded envelope or small flat box filled with gold coins, confetti, and Mardi Gras beads. Or use postcards of New Orleans for your party invitations, welcoming the guests to a mini-Mardi Gras at your house. Or make up a recipe card invitation featuring "Cajun, Creole, and Company."

What to Wear

Ask the revelers to come dressed in costume. Assign a theme, such as "Femme Fatales," "Women in History," "Glimpse into Your Future,"

"Literary Characters," and so on. Or suggest they come in masked Mardi Gras costumes, such as jesters or royalty, then greet them with purple, green, and gold beads as they arrive. Give them a mask to wear when they arrive, made from feathers, sequins, foam, or foil. Top them off with jester hats, jeweled crowns, and sparkling tiaras.

Decorations

Turn your party room into Bourbon Street, full of Zydeco and jazz, Hurricanes and Gumbo. Decorate using the brilliant Mardi Gras colors of purple, green and gold, with balloons, crepe paper streamers, costume jewelry, and confetti. Place masks around the room and hang them on the walls along with colorful beads and feather boas. Buy some posters of France or New Orleans and tape them to the walls. Write down New Orleans signs on posterboard, such as "French Quarter," "Bourbon Street," "Bon Temps," "Commander's Palace," "House of Blues," and "Madame Zydeco's Voodoo Shop," and place them around the room. Set the table with a colorful Mardi Gras-style tablecloth, sprinkled with costume beads, chocolate coins, and confetti. Place a few decorative masks in the middle as a centerpiece. Play jazz, Dixieland, or Zydeco music in the background and set out related musical instruments, such as accordions, rubboards, and spoons as props. Supply the guests with costume jewelry and noisemakers.

Games and Activities

Mardi Gras is just one big party filled with music, dance, costumes, and chance. Let the good times start rolling with Creole tunes, masked madams, and Lady Luck.

Let the Good Songs Roll!

Play music-related games and activities. Start with Name That Tune using jazz and Dixieland songs. Have the guests bring their musical instruments and strike up your own jazz band. Provide rented instruments and let the guests take turns performing for their fans.

Let the Lucky Dice Roll!

Make it a casino theme and set up a roulette wheel, poker game, and craps table, then gamble with Lady Luck and try to be a winner.

Who Was That Masked Mademoiselle?

If your guests come in costume as a specific character, such as Betsy Ross, Josephine Baker, Scarlett O'Hara, or Edith Piaf, have everyone try to guess who she represents. Award prizes for Best Costume, Most Obscure Character, Best Role Model, and Most Out of Place.

Make a Merry Mask

Provide plain masks for the revelers and have them decorate the masks with sequins, glitter, jewels, feathers, stickers, and so on. Award a prize for Most Creative, Most Beautiful, Strangest, Scariest, and so on.

Float Your Boat

Divide into teams, then design and create miniature parade floats from cardboard boxes, crepe paper, fake flowers, feathers, and small toys. Award prizes for Craziest Creation, Most Colorful, Most Exotic, Funniest, and Most Bizarre.

Parlez-vous Français?

Write out funny lines using a French phrase book, such as *Fermez la bouche* (shut up), *Cherchez la femme?* (Where's the woman?), and *Voulez vous couchez avec moi, ce soir?* (Would you like to sleep with me tonight?). Have players try to guess the translations.

Crown the Queen

Have the Queen wannabes state why they should be made Queen of Mardi Gras, then vote on the one with the best reason. Then have her make a speech that includes her plans for her reign.

Show Me Your . . . Beads

Write up stunts on index cards, such as "Cast a spell," "Do the Two-Step," or "Sing Happy Birthday with a French accent." Have players draw a card and perform the stunt to win a necklace. The person with the most necklaces wins an extra fancy necklace!

Go Zydeco

Turn on a Zydeco CD by Clifton Chenier, Queen Ida, Zydeco Force, or Buckwheat Zydeco, and dance the two-step.

Refreshments

Kick it up a notch with Cajun French food. Serve seafood, shrimp, and crawfish, and creole jambalaya, or gumbo with dirty rice and red beans. Cool down the spicy foods with a sweet Hurricane concoction. You can buy a pre-made mixture or make it yourself by combining one part dark rum, one part white rum, a dash of passion fruit syrup, and a dash of lime juice, then shake with ice and strain into a tulip-shaped Hurricane glass. Or serve mint juleps, iced tea, lemonade, or beer. For dessert, cut slices of key lime pie or pecan pie, or give the guests moon pies for fun. It's traditional to make a Mardi Gras King Cake, which makes an eye-catching centerpiece. Prepare a yellow cake mix and bake it in a bundt pan. When cool, insert a small plastic baby somewhere in the cake, then frost the cake with vanilla icing. Sprinkle purple, green, and yellow sugar in sections, to resemble a crown. Tell the guests that whoever finds the baby will have good luck all year!

Favors, Prizes, and Gifts

Send the regalers home with Mardi Gras memories! Give them bead necklaces, decorative masks, feather boas, gold crowns, pralines, moon pies, chocolate gold coins, and Zydeco or jazz CDs. Hand out Cajun cookbooks to recreate a Mardi Gras meal at home.

Party Plus

Choose a Bon Temps theme for a birthday party celebration, baby shower, wedding reception, prom night, or even a simple dinner party. Turn up the Zydeco music, Cajun food, and *Laissez les bon temps rouler*!

Disco Dance Your Pants Off Party

Hey, hot stuff! Boogie on over to the Funky Town Discothèque and shake your booty at a Disco Dance Party celebrating the silly '70s. Put on your *Saturday Night Fever* platform shoes and Austin Powers paisley pants, spin the disco ball, and head for the disco inferno to do the Hustle, baby!

Invitations

Write your party details on a scrap of loud print polyester fabric, cut in the shape of flared disco pants. Mail to guests with a cheap gold chain inside the envelope. Or cut out pictures of old '70s stars, such as *Charlie's Angels*, the original *Star Trek*, or *The Brady Bunch*, and use them as a background for your party invitation. Create speech balloons for the characters, and let them do the inviting. Or cut out a black circle about the size of a grapefruit and glue on a white circle the size of a walnut, to make the Magic 8 Ball. Write party details as a forecast inside the white circle, such as, "All signs point to a party."

What to Wear

Come as a classic icon from the '70s, such as John Travolta, Donna Summer, Michael Jackson from the Jackson Five, a BeeGee, a *Gilligan's Island* castaway, or one of the Village People. Or just wear polyester in psychedelic colors, in the form of miniskirts, disco boots, or platform shoes.

Decorations

Turn the party room in a disco studio, a psychedelic stage, or a replica of a '70s TV show set, such as *Charlie's Angels*, *The Partridge Family*, or *Gilligan's Island*. Put yellow smiley faces all around the room. Hang up posters of '70s rock stars, such as Kiss, Pink Floyd, Billy Joel, Led Zeppelin, and Patti LaBelle. Use lots of psychedelic colors, glow-in-the-dark accessories, and oversized jewelry. Play old TV shows or movies from the '70s in the background, such as *The Brady Bunch* or *Annie Hall*. Hang colored lights, black lights, and a large mirrored disco ball.

Games and Activities

It's disco a-go-go, with retro dances, trivia contests, and '70s-style songs and shows.

Disco, Disco Dance

Boogie down with disco music and dances, such as "Bad Girls," "Boogie Nights," "Night Fever," "Disco Inferno," "Funky Town," "Boogie Fever," "Shake Your Booty," "Hot Stuff," "Love Train," "Brandy," "Lady Marmalade," "American Pie," and "Dancing Queen."

Put on a Show!

Have a dance contest to see who can do the best John Travolta imitation. Provide costumes for the five Village People characters—the cop, Indian, construction worker, sailor, and motorcycle stud—and have five guests dress up. Then have them perform a lip-sync show for the rest of the party.

Play '70s Games

Direct the players in a game of Twister, pass around a Magic 8 Ball, Blast from the Past, and so on. There's even a game called The '70s Game you can buy.

Remember the '70s

Play '70s Trivia and ask questions about songs, TV shows, movies, and stars from the past, such as "Name the *Partridge Family* members," "What was the housekeeper's name on *The Brady Bunch*?" "What was John Travolta's name in *Saturday Night Fever*?" and "What's the opening line of the first *Star Wars* movie?"

Refreshments

Offer the guests '70s junk foods, such as Twinkies, Jell-O, packaged cheese 'n' crackers, and macaroni and cheese TV dinners. Serve Disco Balls—cheese balls with a side of crackers—or crackers with "Lady Marmalade" spread. For dessert, make or buy your favorite Miss American Pies. Make a Smiley Face cake by baking a round cake, then frost it with yellow icing, and dot on face details with chocolate tube icing.

Favors, Prizes, and Gifts

Pass out headbands, oversized sunglasses, and imitation gold chains to wear home. Buy mini disco ball key chains and give them to the partiers. Offer posters from the '70s. Pick up smiley face items for the guests. Give them Magic 8 Balls to keep. Send them home with *Saturday Night Fever* videos.

Kewl Karaoke Party

Sing your heart out to your favorite tunes—country, rock, hip-hop—whatever! Then capture it all on videotape and play it back for laughs—or the judges.

Invitations

Write the following details on square cards: "Are you the next American Idol? You've been selected by Paula, Simon, and Randy to appear on (date). To reserve your callback, contact the stage manager, (host's name), at (your number)." Add stickers or decals to make it look like a CD holder and mail to guests. Or write your party details on sheet music.

What to Wear

The performers should dress up like rock stars, in glamorous gowns, dramatic dresses, or sexy Spandex shorts and tops. Provide accessories when they arrive, such as fancy glasses, silky scarves, shimmery wraps, colorful tattoos, and spray on hair glitter. Have lots of extra makeup items available to use.

Decorations

Create a stage with a backdrop using sheets, blankets, or fabric. Set up a platform for the performances. Buy or rent a karaoke machine. Decorate the area with twinkle lights, a microphone and stand, and photos from previous *American Idol* contestants and rock stars. Provide instruments to pretend play, such as guitars or keyboards. Set up a table and chairs for the judges.

Games and Activities

Don't be put off by off-key singing—that's half the fun! Just let the guests open their mouths and belt out a barely recognizable tune—before they break into giggles and guffaws.

Dressing Room

Have all the performers prepare for their audition by gathering in front of mirrors to put on their makeup, costumes, accessories, and so on. Videotape "interviews" with each "contestant," and ask questions like, "How long have you been singing?" "Who are your own singing idols?" and "Why do you want to be the next American Idol?"

American Idol Auditions

Once everyone is dressed up for a performance, take turns singing karaoke (be sure to videotape the acts!). As each one "auditions," ask three others to be judges and make funny comments when the performance is over. Watch the video afterwards. Give out awards for Loudest, Funniest, Most Mistakes, Most Off-Key, and Winner of American Idol.

Refreshments

Serve a buffet of meats, fruits, breads, and cookies, much like you'll find in the "Green Room" backstage. If your karaoke party has a theme, such as Country Music, Broadway, or The '50s, match it to the foods, with Southern fried chicken and mint juleps, New York bagels and egg creams, tuna casserole and martinis. Ask the bakery to make a cake with a picture of Simon, Paula, and Randy on the top.

Favors, Prizes, and Gifts

Give the winners and losers copies of their performance videos, popular karaoke CDs, and their pictures superimposed with Simon, Paula, and Randy.

Party Plus

Some television cables offer access to karaoke on demand, so you might try that. Better yet, go to a karaoke bar and give a public performance.

CHAPTER 14

"As Seen on TV" Parties

"There are three things that you should know about me. One, my friends are the
most important thing in my life, two, I never lie, and three, I make
the best oatmeal raisin cookies in the world."

~ *Phoebe Buffay*, Friends

Television, whether we like it or not, has invaded our world. We're
hooked on our favorite shows, whether it's drama or comedy, and love
to watch the stories unfold over a bowl of popcorn. You can turn the
Big Screen into Big Time Fun with a party wrapped around your special
show. Just turn on the tube, surf the channels, and set up a screening
for screaming fans.

Red Carpet Review

Host an Oscar night or other awards party, dress as the stars, vote for
your winners, and rag on the outfits. Thanks to state-of-the-art TVs, pay-
per-view, and DVDs, the Movie/TV Party has become a popular way of
entertaining friends. For an Academy Awards Party, check out the official
Academy Awards Web site, *www.Oscar.com*, for great trivia about the
event ahead of time. Or get your friends together to watch it live! Your
guests can play along and try to guess the winners, while they wine and
dine in the style of their favorite stars! And now, on with the show!

Invitations

"The envelope please . . ." may be the three most exciting words
at the Academy Awards, so make your envelope just as exciting and
invite your guests to your glittering gala. You can buy inexpensive

plastic Oscars and mail them to guests in padded boxes, with party details written directly on the statues. Or cut out Oscar shapes from posterboard and spray paint them gold, or cover them with gold foil wrap. Write the party details in black felt pen and mail to guests in gold envelopes covered with silver star stickers. Include a list of the nominees for your guests to ponder ahead of time. Glue on pictures of the stars cut from magazines and add speech bubbles filled with lines from their nominated films.

What to Wear

Ask guests to come as their Hollywood "in-your-dreams" look-a-likes. Or have them come dressed as one of the nominated stars in the current flock of movies. Provide accessories when they arrive—boas, sunglasses, costume jewelry, tiaras, and so forth.

Decorations

Party stores sell festive "Hollywood theme" party packs you can use to dress up your party room. Greet the guests with a red carpet entry, flanked by giant cardboard or inflatable Oscars. Use a silver, gold, and black color scheme to decorate the party room, and hang balloons and stars from the ceiling. Set out director's clipboards and plastic Oscars. Hang up signs that read, "Opening Night," "Admit One," "Applause," "Lights! Camera! Action!" or use the names of the five nominated films. Buy posters of the stars and hang them on the walls near your TV screen. Make a large colorful chart of the nominees, with photos from the tabloids or movie magazines. Check off the winners with a felt pen or stars as their names are announced. Write out famous quotes from the nominated movies— or your favorite movies—on star-shaped paper, and tape them to the walls, such as: "Frankly, my dear, I don't give a damn," "Adriiieenn!", and "We're gonna need a bigger boat." Play the soundtrack from one or more of the nominated movies. Take paparazzi pictures of guests as they walk up the red carpet! Set the table with a gold or silver paper tablecloth and matching silverware, and add star candles and colorful champagne flutes. Make placemats out of large gold stars and place cards from inexpensive sunglasses with guests' names attached with a string. Create a centerpiece using symbols from the top five movies.

Games and Activities

Do you watch too much TV? Good! Then you're apt to be the big winner with the following channel-surfing challenges.

"And the envelope goes to . . ."

Print out ballots with all the nominees in all categories, and have players vote on the winners. Also make a giant scorecard from posterboard so the guests can see the winners and losers clearly. If you're game, place small bets on the nominees—poker chips, dollar bills, or fun trinkets.

"And the Most Trivial Winner is . . ."

After the show is over, vote on The Trivial Awards, such as "Most Embarrassing Speech," "Most Boring Speech," "Ugliest Outfit," "Most Risqué Gown," "Worst Hair Style," "Weirdest Walk to the Stage," and "Most Pompous Actor." Whoever gets the most points wins a prize.

Movie Star Gossip

Play a game of movie star trivia, such as "What is Tom Cruise's real name?" "How many times has Pamela Anderson been married?" and "Where does George Clooney live?"

What's My Motivation?

Write down memorable movie scenes, such as "The Shower Scene" in *Psycho*, "The Baby Birthin' Scene" in *Gone with the Wind*, or "You

Had Me At Hello Scene" in *Jerry McGuire*, on index cards and place them in a hat or bowl. Have the players choose a card and act out the scene for the others to guess.

Who Said That?

Write down some famous lines from movies, such as ". . . the stuff that dreams are made of," and have the players guess the speaker and the film.

You're Kidding Me!

Offer everyone rubber-tipped dart guns to shoot at the screen when they're unhappy about the winners!

Refreshments

No Awards gala is complete without popcorn, so serve it flavored with Parmesan cheese or Mexican spices in popcorn bags. Choose a food from one or more of the nominated films to serve to your guests, such as Italian food if the film takes place in Italy. Set up a candy concession stand, filled with theater candy, such as Jujubes, Jordan Almonds, Dots, Junior Mints, Raisinets, and Milk Duds. Offer a variety of foreign beers to honor the foreign films. Don't forget the champagne to toast the winners! Make a round Film Reel Cake that doubles as a centerpiece, or buy an iced cake and set an Oscar on top.

Favors, Prizes, and Gifts

Send the celebrities home with mini clipboard picture frames, star candles, movie theater candy, movie tickets, celebrity posters, film magazines, a box of microwave popcorn, a book on movie trivia, or small Oscar trophies with awards such as "Best Costume," "Best Guesser of Winners," "Biggest Loser," and "Most Like a Celebrity."

Party Plus

Before the event, rent the nominated videos or go to the theater as a group to see the nominated films so everyone has previewed the movies ahead of time.

Major Music Awards Night

Host a Music Awards Night for friends that features the Country-Western Music Awards, the MTV Music Awards, the Latin Music Awards, the Soul Train Music Awards, or the last episode of *American Idol*. Invite your girlfriends to a night of musical magic, then fill the party room with tunes, treats, and good times.

Invitations

Send out invitations written on sheet music or on homemade CD jackets, embellished with scrapbooking supplies. Or sing your invitation, capture it on tape, and mail to guests. Include ballots to vote for winners.

What to Wear

Ask guests to come dressed as the nominated singers or according to the style of music, such as western wear for the CMAs or rock stars for the MTV awards.

Decorations

Decorate the party room with sheet music placemats and musical notes hanging from the ceiling. Hang signs with song titles on the walls. Set out musical instruments, and offer guests maracas, kazoos, and hand clappers to play along with the show. Create a dance floor so the guests can dance to the tunes. Add details that coordinate with the music theme, such as plastic horses, cows, and boots for the CMAs.

Games and Activities

These games will be music to your guests' ears—unless they're tone-deaf and musically challenged!

Place Your Bets

Create a list of the nominees and print them out for the guests. Ask them to mark the ones they think will win, then award small prizes as each correct winner is announced, such as typical theater candy. Give the player with the most correct answers a big prize, such as a video or TV-related T-shirt.

Dance Contest!

Put the names of the players in a cowboy hat. When a song comes on, draw a name and have that player dance to the tune. Vote on her performance, and award a prize to the dancer with the best score when the awards are over.

Name That Tune

If you don't have a good collection of country songs on your iPod, tape record a few seconds of several country songs from the radio, especially those nominated for an award. During the commercials, play snippets of the songs and have players race to Name That Tune.

Karaoke Competition

Buy an inexpensive karaoke machine or rent a good one and let the guests show off their singing skills with a karaoke contest. Choose songs in keeping with the award show theme, and include a few silly songs for fun.

Refreshments

Serve food related to the theme, such as barbecue for the CMAs, soul food for the STMAs, and Mexican food for the LMAs. Make a sheet cake decorated like sheet music.

Favors, Prize, and Gifts

Send the musical guests home with maracas, kazoos, and hand clappers. Give them CDs of the most popular nominated songs. Award iTunes gift certificates to the game winners.

Party Plus

Create your own award show and have guests bring their favorite songs. Play them for the group and have them vote on their favorite songs by awarding points for each one. The song with the most points wins—and the player who brought the song gets a prize.

Sex and the City Party

Gather the girls for a night of sexy cosmopolitans and DVDs of the classic show. Join Charlotte, Miranda, Samantha, and Carrie in the Big Apple, and live the glamorous life of a city gal—if only for a night. Who knows—maybe Big will show up as a surprise.

Invitations

Download pictures of the four main characters—Charlotte the naïve one, Miranda the feminist, Samantha the sexy one, and Carrie the "normal" one—then superimpose the heads of your friends on their bodies, according to their matching personalities. Turn them into invitations, include a recipe for a Cosmopolitan, and mail to guests.

What to Wear

Ask the city girls to dress as a character from the show. If they need ideas, suggest a cashmere sweater or conservative pantsuit for Charlotte, red power suit for lawyer Miranda, short skirt and low top for Samantha, and a fashion fad for Carrie. When they arrive, have them guess who's who.

Decorations

Color the room pink and black—pink for girls and black for sophisticated New York. Put up neon bar signs, and New York street signs, such as "Fifth Avenue," "Greenwich Village," "Manhattan," and "Central Park." Make posters featuring Cosmopolitan recipes. Hang posters from Broadway shows, such as *Cats* and *The Lion King*. Decorate with anything New York—mini Statue of Liberty, shopping bag from Saks, subway tokens, apples (the Big Apple), and so on. Display designer shoes by Jimmy Choo and Manolo Blahnik. Play Frank Sinatra or Broadway show tunes in the background. Set the table in pink and black, with Cosmo glasses and the ingredients as a centerpiece, along with *Sex and the City* DVD covers.

Games and Activities

Fans of the popular TV show and movie will rule at these competitive games, so kick off your stilettos and get your game on.

Sex and the City *Game*

You can buy a *Sex and the City* game or create one yourself by writing down trivia questions about the show for guests to draw and answer, such as "What's Big's real name?" "Where did Miranda work?" "Why did Charlotte get divorced?" "What designer did Carrie model for?"

Cosmos and Cocktails

Teach the guests how to make their own Cosmos (see recipe below). Once they've mastered that, set out a variety of liquors, such as vodka, gin, vermouth, rum, along with some mixers and fruit juices, and have the guests try to create the ultimate cocktail. Give the best one a name, such as "Charlotte's Chastity Challenger," "Miranda's Multiple Martini," "Samantha's Sex Scandal," and "Carrie's Cure-All." Don't forget the olives, pearl onions, lemon twists, and fancy swizzle sticks and mini umbrellas.

Sex and the TV Screen

Have a marathon *Sex and the City* video viewing and watch your favorite episodes while you enjoy your Cosmos.

Refreshments

Make Cosmos, of course. Here's a great—and easy—recipe: Mix 1 ounce vodka, ½ ounce triple sec, and ½ ounce lime juice in a shaker and mix well. Serve in chilled plastic martini glasses in festive colors, with fancy stirrers and paper umbrellas. For snacks, go with classic New York food—bagels and cream cheese, potato knishes, roasted nuts, hot dogs, and pastrami sandwiches. Or go elegant with shrimp cocktails and fancy appetizers. For dessert, make it something decadent, such as chocolate soufflé, chocolate crème brulee, chocolate crêpes, chocolate lava cake, chocolate mousse, or triple chocolate brownies.

Favors, Prizes, and Gifts

Give each girl a *Sex and the City* DVD, a box of chocolates, a Cosmo glass and recipe, or a designer scarf to take home.

Party Plus

Take your party on the town. Dress up as the characters, go to some hot spots in your local city, and chat about men while you watch the eye candy around you.

Trading Spaces Makeover Party

Everyone could use a makeover now and then—a room makeover, that is. When it's time to update a look or spruce up a setting, surprise a special lady with a magical room makeover, then trade decorating tips and tricks with all the guests. Take turns providing the party at each girl's home so everyone has help with a needed project—painting, wallpapering, flooring, or redecorating.

Invitations

Search through a decorating magazine for a "before and after" spread and photocopy it for your invitation. Write the party details underneath the "before and after" and mail to guests with a few paint samples, fabric scraps, or magazine pictures of decorative accessories. Or use a computer program to design your own "before and after" layout and plans for the makeover to use as an invitation.

What to Wear

The party may get messy so tell your guests to wear old clothes they don't mind getting dirty. Provide them with special smocks, aprons, or T-shirts when they arrive to wear as coordinated cover-ups. Give them baseball caps to cover their hair, gloves to protect their hands, and shoe sleeves for their shoes.

Decorations

Keep the decorations simple and practical—tarps to cover the floor, masking tape for windows, paint brushes and wallpaper supplies, as needed for the project. Have a radio or CD player nearby for upbeat music to keep the energy high. Provide clean up supplies in a nearby bathroom—hand soaps, towels, and so on. At the snack table, set out decorative magazines to peruse ideas.

Games and Activities

Whistle while you work—and chat, gossip, laugh, tease, and play!

Room Redo

The primary purpose of the party is to make over the special guest's room. It may be she wants a fresh paint job, new wallpaper—

or removal—help with hanging art, rearranging the furniture, or suggestions for new decorator items. Whatever it is, have fun working together to complete the project.

Magazine Makeover

At break time, gather around the snack table with decorator magazines, large sheets of paper, markers, scissors, glue, and tape. Ask each player to create a "new room" for the special guest, using items from the decorator magazine. Draw the basic room on a sheet of paper, then add the objects you've cut from the magazine. Vote on the "Best Design," "Most Expensive Makeover," "Most Bizarre," "Most Suitable to the Guest of Honor," and "Most Cluttered." Give them to the special guest when you're finished.

Refreshments

Your designing women will be hungry, so keep a snack table open for munching and grazing. Set out cheese and crackers, DIY sandwiches with deli meats and rolls, popcorn, cut-up fruit, and macaroni or potato salad. Keep lots of drinks on ice, everything from water and sodas to beer and wine. For dessert, open a box of chocolates, make brownies, or serve a sheet cake topped with doll furniture!

Favors, Prizes, and Gifts

Give the helpers household tools for their own makeovers, copies of decorator magazines, cover-ups and hats, or items for a relaxing recovery bath after all that work. Or pick up a nice decorator item, such as a candle and holder, a fancy bowl, a picture frame, or an artificial plant.

Party Plus

Go as a group to a designer show, or visit several furniture stores and discuss the ideas you gather along the way. Or view some local model homes for great decorating tips.

Desperate Housewives Party

Homemaking and housewifery can drive a woman over the edge at times. Take a break from the household chores and host a party featuring the wives from Wisteria lane—gone mad. Ask the guests to come as their *Desperate Housewives* alter ego, stereotypical housewife, or their mothers!

Invitations

Create invitations by downloading pictures of the Desperate Housewives.

What to Wear

Ask the girls to come dressed as their favorite character from the show—Bree the "perfect" obsessive compulsive, Susan the klutzy flower child, Lynette the frazzled mother, Gabrielle the sexy spitfire, or Edie the conniving vixen. Or have them come as stereotypical housewives from the past, in housecoats, curlers, and slippers, or frocks, gloves, and pillbox hats.

Decorations

Recreate the Wisteria Lane set or set the mood with tacky household items from the past, such as ceramic ashtrays, odd lamps, antimacassars, throw pillows, and slipcovers. Lay copies of the tabloids and entertainment magazines around the room. Play music from the '50s. Set out cake boxes, canned vegetables, and Jell-O molds for a centerpiece. Put up posters of '50s movies, cars, stars, and products.

Games and Activities

You never knew homemakers had so much fun? You will, once you play these desperately funny games.

Desperate Details
Quiz the guests à la a '50s quiz show using questions from the TV series, such as "What is Susan's daughter's name?" "What kind of car does Gabby drive?" "Where does Lynette work?" and "Who killed Bree's first husband?"

Card the Guests
Play a round of "housewife" card games, such as Bridge or Gin.

Help Heloise
Have a Household Tips Bee and ask the guests questions related to housewifery, such as "How do you get blood out of the carpet?" and "Give three uses for baking soda."

Pimp Your Apron
Give the guests a white apron and craft items to embellish it, then let them create their own designs.

Recipe Bakeoff
Have the "housewives" bring favorite recipes to share, along with samples. Have a brownie or chocolate chip cookie bakeoff and vote for the winner.

Housewife Viewing
Watch the latest episode of the show, or rent a season's worth of the videos.

Refreshments
Share samples of your favorite recipes. Make classic "housewife" food, such as tuna casserole, deviled eggs, Waldorf salad, and coffee cake. Serve bonbons, martinis, and coffee.

Favors, Prizes, and Gifts

Let the guests take home their aprons. Give them pot holders, feather dusters, rolling pins, spatulas, or other household or kitchen items. You can also pass out *Desperate Housewives* items, ordered through the Web site.

Party Plus

Choose another favorite show and plan a party around that.

Video Vixens Party

For a unique evening that's sure to thrill your friends, set the theme around a favorite video and match the party details to the genre—adventure, thriller, horror, mystery, or romance. You'll find suggestions in the following text for your video party, everything from welcoming invitations to goodbye gifts. Lights, camera, party action!

Invitations

Make your own super-sized movie tickets and write the party details on the back. Or use popcorn bags to carry your party invitations. Or photocopy the cover of the DVD you're planning to show, and write your information there. Include an appropriate prop in the envelope, such as an eye patch for a pirate movie or plastic alien for a sci-fi film.

What to Wear

Characters from the selected movie make great costumes for the party, so encourage your guests to dress up for the role of the mistress, wife, daughter, and so on. Give them matching accessories to get them in the mood for the viewing, such as a cowgirl hat for a western movie, costume jewelry for a film about fashion, or an apron for a video that features gourmet cooking.

Decorations

Create a backdrop for your party, keeping in mind the theme. Write down quotes from the movies and post them on the walls. Hang movie posters, and use film star photos as placemats. Set up a candy and popcorn counter. Buy paper products to match the theme, such as grapes for a movie featuring wine, flowers for a romantic film, or just plates and napkins that feature the Hollywood sign.

Games and Activities

After you view the video, question the guests on their story savvy, then have them rehearse their favorite roles.

View a Video

Choose a favorite video—or one from the following list—pop it in the player, turn down the lights, and push "Play"! For suggestions, try: *My Big Fat Greek Wedding, The Wedding Planner, Divine Secrets of the Ya-Ya Sisterhood, Bridget Jones's Diary, What Women Want, Erin Brockovich, Runaway Bride, You've Got Mail, Titanic, Jerry Maguire, Fried Green Tomatoes, The Joy Luck Club, Sleepless in Seattle, Four Weddings and a Funeral,* and *The American President.*

There Will Be a Quiz . . .

Following the film, quiz the guests on the details, such as character names, significant quotations, the setting, and the actors. Award points and prizes for the winners.

Mixed Up Movies

Write down some famous characters on index cards, such as Sigourney Weaver's Ripley in *Alien*, Helen Mirren's Queen Elizabeth II in *The Queen*, or Keira Knightley's Lizzie Bennet in *Pride and Prejudice*, and place them in a hat or bowl. Write down some film titles and place them in another bowl, such as *Hairspray, The Devil Wears Prada*, or *Knocked Up*. Have two players each draw a card from the character bowl, then together draw one from the film title bowl. Have them create a scene with their characters in the film.

Audition

Search the Internet for sites that sell movie scripts, and purchase one for the video you'll be showing. After viewing the movie, have the guests audition for the featured roles by reading dialogue from the scripts. Be sure to videotape their screen tests and play them back for laughs.

Refreshments

Along with movie popcorn and candy, give the guests ice cream bars, nachos with melted cheese, and hot dogs—all foods you can buy at the theater these days. Make a cake centerpiece that fits the theme of the video, such as a wedding cake for *My Big Fat Greek Wedding*, a diary for *Bridget Jones's Diary*, or a ship for *Titanic*.

Favors, Prizes, and Gifts

When the movie is over, send them home with a DVD, flavored popcorn, movie memorabilia, or a gift certificate to the movie theater.

Party Plus
Get the gang together and go to the movies for a premiere showing!

Extreme Beauty Makeover Party

Every girl needs a beauty lift now and then, so summon your friends for a complete makeup and hair makeover. Keep the camera handy for those miraculous "Before" and "After" shots. And watch the drab ducklings turn into stunning swans, right before your lens.

Invitations

For a glimpse of the makeovers, cut out pictures of models, superimpose heads of the guests, and photocopy them. On the front of the invitation, glue on headshots of all the guests. Add warts, bad hair, freckles, and other funny face additions to their headshots, then write "Before . . ." at the bottom. Inside paste a photocopied picture of the guests with their heads superimposed on models, and write "After!" Enclose a makeup item in the envelope, such as a small lipstick, eye pencil, or makeup brush.

What to Wear

The girls should come without makeup on, so they can begin with a clean slate. Ask the guests to wear casual clothes, but to bring along a dressy outfit to change into when the makeover is complete. Encourage them to bring their own makeup items and equipment to the party.

Decorations

Set up a catwalk for the models, along with bright lights and a video camera. Tape up ads for cosmetics. Hang posters of supermodels with mustaches, glasses, and warts added, along with the word: "Before . . ." Set up makeup stations, such as "Eyebrow Shaping," "Lip Coloring," "Hair Styling," and so on with appropriate cosmetics and equipment. Include portable mirrors at each station. Take "Before" and "After" snapshots for the guests to take home after the party is over. Set a snack table with a centerpiece made of makeup items, or use a Styrofoam head (for a later game).

Games and Activities

Put on a magic makeover show, by sharing tips and tricks, games and activities, new looks, and lots of laughs.

"Before" and "After"

Start the party by taking "Before" pictures, without makeup. Ask the guests to make funny faces as well, for an extra laugh. Then send them off to different stations to experiment with different makeup items and equipment. Include some add-ons, such as false eyelashes, fake moles, false fingernails, and so on. Have them take turns making over each other. Try an exotic new look for fun, or choose a theme, such as "Slutty," "Egyptian," "Goth," "Stage Actress," "Aging Matron à la Betty Davis," and have fun with the makeup and hair styles. At the end of the makeovers, when everyone is all glammed up, change into fancy clothes and take "After" shots.

I'm Too Sexy for the Catwalk

Roll out a red carpet or set up a stage and have the models walk the catwalk to show off their new looks. Tell them to vamp it up a bit, then videotape the performances and play them back during refreshments.

Beauty Supply Shop

Cut out products from beauty magazines, omitting the names of the products (or blacken the names out with a felt-tip pen). Glue the pictures onto construction paper, with the names of the products written lightly on the back of each. Hold up one picture at a time and have the players write down the names of the products. When all the pictures have been displayed, read the answers out loud to see who guessed the most correct answers.

Talk to the Camera

Have a photo shoot and take turns posing for the camera or posing as the photographer. Encourage them to sex it up. Print out the best—or funniest—shots using a digital camera.

Refreshments

Serve elegant finger foods, such canapés, veggie trays, fruit bites, and champagne, using your best dishes. Make a "Makeover Cake" by baking a rectangular cake. Frost it white, lay a mirror flat in the middle, and outline the edges to look like a frame. Set makeup items around the base of the cake. Tell the guests to look in the mirror to see the Makeover Cake.

Favors, Prizes, and Gifts

Send the models home with a copy of the catwalk videotape, some makeup and fashion accessories, small mirrors, beauty magazines, hair products, and double frames for their "Before" and "After" photos.

Party Plus

Hire a stylist or esthetician to come and offer beauty tips. Or head for a salon as a group to get professional makeovers.

CHAPTER 15

"Just Because" Parties

"There's nothing better than a good friend, except a good friend with chocolate."
~ *Linda Grayson*

Girls don't need an excuse for a get-together—they can have fun anywhere, any time, for any reason. But in case you want a reason, here are some suggestions for "whatever" themes, everything from ghostly gatherings to laugh factories. You'll find even more excuses at the end of the book!

Soak and Spa Party

Invite a masseuse to your Soak and Spa party and enjoy a luxurious day of pampering and pleasure with friends. Tell them to slip on their velour robes, and bring those broken nails, that dry skin, and that stressed body to a hot and steamy spa escape!

Invitations

Send the guests a small tube of massage cream in a padded envelope, with the party details written on scented paper cut into a body shape. Or include a tube of red lipstick in a padded envelope, along with party details written in red marker on lip-shaped paper. Or mail an envelope of bubble bath with details written on a small sheet of paper glued to the back of the bubble bath. Include a brochure from the spa.

What to Wear

Suggest the guests wear their bathrobes and slippers, a hair wrap, and no makeup. They might want to wear grungy clothes for arrival and a nice outfit for departure.

Decorations

Low lighting with candles, soft music, lots of pillows, and vases of flowers will create a soothing atmosphere for your spa day. Don't forget to set out a box of chocolates.

Games and Activities

Try these girly games to spice up the spa day, and learn more than you wanted to know with a TMI (Too Much Information) game!

Spa Fun

Set up stations for your spa, such as a bubble bath, hot tub soak, massage table, facial chair, manicure and pedicure area, and waxing station. Assign each guest to one aspect of a spa and have her bring along the necessary equipment or materials. Then take turns moving from station to station, as you help each other get a treatment. You might assign each guest to begin at a different station, then have them rotate so everyone gets to do everything in turn.

Sexual Preference

While you're getting your makeovers or soothing treatments, play an eye-opening game with your gal pals and find out their sexual preferences—if you dare. Think up two sex-related activities such as, "Would you rather be licked on the foot or the underarm?" or "Would you rather be caught having sex by your parents or your teacher?" Have all the players respond—or they have to give someone a foot massage.

Feeding the Flame

When you all get a chance to gather together over lunch, during a massage, or in the hot tub, have everyone take a turn sharing one of her secrets for keeping love alive over the years, such as "We never go to bed mad—and when we make up, we have hot makeup sex afterward!"

Refreshments

Most spas supply some sort of food options, so follow suit by setting up refreshment stations to quench the guests' hunger and thirst. Place snacks in picnic baskets, large tubs, or festive trays, and include light and healthy snacks, such as salad makings, cut-up fruit, veggies and dips, cheese and crackers. Make sure all the snacks are low fat, low-sugar, and low salt. Bring energy drinks, bottled water, even champagne, if it's allowed, with your own plastic champagne glasses. Mimosas—orange juice mixed with champagne—are a great way to enjoy the day.

Favors, Prizes, and Gifts

Set out disposable cameras, hair wraps or scrunchies, inexpensive terrycloth robes, printed beach towels, flip-flops or fuzzy slippers, chocolate truffles, gift certificate for another day at the spa, do-it-yourself manicure and pedicure kit, edible underwear, jar of chocolate massage spread, sexy panties or lingerie, makeup bag filled with the latest lipstick, polish, and shadow colors.

Party Plus

Visit a day spa and spend the afternoon getting massages, manicures, and makeovers.

Ghost Whisperer Party

So you want to chat with Elvis? No problem—even though he's been dead for decades. Just host a séance, hold hands around a crystal ball, and wait for the spirits to appear. . . . Ideally, at the circle you'll want a few true believers, a couple of skeptics, and one or two who are open to the possibility of the supernatural. And don't forget the medium—real or not.

Invitations

Invite the skeptics and believers with "Message from the beyond . . ." Cut out a white circle, glue the top edge to a black card, and write "The Spirits Are About to Speak . . ." on the outside. Underneath, glue another white circle and include the party details. Or draw a ghost on a white card with a speech bubble providing the information. Or outline your palm, draw lifelines, and write the details along each line, indicating their "future" at the party. Include a Tarot card or a lucky rabbit's foot.

What to Wear

As the hostess, you might dress up as a gypsy or wear all black, with a lacy scarf. Tell the guests to come in costume, dressed as a character from the '20s, when the séance was at its heyday. Or suggest they come as witches, sorcerers, or fortunetellers.

Decorations

You'll need a dark room to host the séance, one with drapes that will keep out the light from outside. Set a round table in the middle of the room, and drape it with a black lace tablecloth. Set a crystal ball (or an upside-down fishbowl) in the center of the table. Light candles around the room, and play spooky Halloween music in the background. Set hanging pictures at an angle, and string fake cobwebs along the lights and furniture, or in the corners of the room. Download creepy pictures from the Internet and frame them, then set them on tables or hang them on the walls. Get an accomplice to help you with some simple séance gimmicks while you summon the spirit world. (See Games and Activities for examples.)

Games and Activities

Scare the goose bumps out of your guests with a few ghoulish games and spooky surprises!

Summon the Spirits

Have a real séance with a hired medium. Or put on your own séance and set the scene with lots of spooky gimmicks. Have the attendees sit at the table and hold hands. While you close your eyes and mumble to the spirit world, have your accomplice do some of the following tricks. Tie fishing line to a picture on the wall and move it slightly. Do the same to the drapes. Knock softly, then louder, on the wall. Turn on a fan and blow out a candle or two. Start up a fog machine. Spray the guests with a sudden blast from a squirt gun. Have a sheeted ghost pass through the room. Use a speaker or karaoke machine to create the voices.

Channel the Spirts

After the guests are thoroughly spooked by the unseemly spirits, it's time to channel the dead. First tell a little background story to continue the spooky mood and put on a theatrical performance as you call the spirits. Then bring back someone famous from the past that everyone knows, such as Elvis, Queen Victoria, or Marilyn Monroe. Have the accomplice imitate the voice, and answer questions from the attendees, such as "Elvis, how did you die?" "Ah ate too many pork rinds, thank-you-verah-much."

Ouija Board

Get out the Ouija Board, choose a couple of guests to sit opposite each other, and ask questions. Take turns so everyone gets a chance to hear answers "from the other side." You might even include some pre-formed questions the players must ask, such as "Who will meet the man of her dreams next?" or "Who in the room is keeping a deep dark secret?"

It's in the Cards

Read up on fortune-telling with Tarot cards, then predict each guest's future using the cards.

Predictions

Have the guests make up predictions for each guest. When everyone is finished, choose one guest to read her predictions—then guess who created it.

Movie Madness

Rent creepy movies that feature ghosts and other strange creatures, such as *The Others, The Ring, Thirteen Ghosts, Ghost Ship, Ghostbusters, The Haunting, The Legend of Hell House, Poltergeist, The Shining, What Lies Beneath*, or *Ghost*. Share them with the group.

Refreshments

Make your own fortune cookies. Buy prepackaged sugar cookie dough. Roll out the dough as thinly as possible, cut into circles, fold the circle, curve it into a "C," and pinch the ends, leaving a small opening. On small strips of paper, write down funny fortunes, such as "You will learn to play the violin," "You will marry a clown," or "You will come back as a mule." When the cookies are lightly browned, let them cool, then insert the paper predictions. Make a devil's food cake for a centerpiece, topped with Tarot cards or the crystal ball.

Favors, Prizes, and Gifts

Tarot decks make great prizes and favors, along with lucky charms, scary movies, a book of ghost stories, creepy soundtracks, and astrology books.

Party Plus

Invite a "real" medium, psychic, or tarot card reader to your party to lead the séance or predict the future.

Last Laugh Party

If your group has a sense of humor, create your own comedy club for some hilarious hoots and howls. Before you know it, the wine you're drinking will be coming out of your nose, you'll be laughing so hard! Clean up on aisle four!

Invitations

Make a card featuring a giant smile on the front. Or use a clown face for the cover of your invitation. Underneath write, "What's funnier than a clown?" Inside give the punch line—"A Last Laugh Party!" Add a few one-liners here and there, then mail to guests. Include a foam or rubber clown nose in the envelope.

Decorations

Add humor to your party room with pictures of clowns, jesters, or famous comedians. Hang signs that read "Wet Paint," "Beware of Banana Peels," and "Giggle Zone." Set out clown gags, such as joy buzzers, Whoopee Cushions, and "spilled" drinks made from resin. Cut out giant smiles and laughing mouths full of teeth and use them as placemats. Set up a stage for comedy performances, and gather props you plan to use during the skits (see the next section).

Games and Activities

There are laughs-a-plenty listed below so try out the ones that work best for your group, then go after those gags with girly giggles and gut-busting guffaws.

Improv Comedy

Choose some skits from the list below that you think will work best with your group. Write them on index cards and place in a bowl or clown hat. Have the comedians take turns choosing from the bowl and performing the skits for the rest of the group. Videotape the performances and play them back during refreshments.

- "Addicts Anonymous." Two players attend a meeting run by a third, and each one has a different—and strange—addiction, such as Chocoholism, Obsession with Jerry Springer, Fear of Doorways, etc.

- "Alphabet Scene." Players choose a theme, such as "Going to a Cocktail Party" or "First Day of School." They must act out a scene using a sentence that begins with consecutive letters of the alphabet. For example, player one might say, "Amy's having a cocktail party." Player two might follow with, "But I thought you wanted to go to the movies." Continue through the alphabet. To make it more exciting, set a timer for 90 seconds.

- "You Got the Part." Players must offer terrible auditions for a role, such as the last scene in *Gone with the Wind* or something from Shakespeare.

- "Back to the Beginning." Two players act out a scene, such as "Getting Ready for Bed" or "A Day at the Office," but perform it backwards, from the end to the beginning. Have the other players guess the theme.

- "Apply Within." Players take turns applying for a job, such as "Sanitary Worker," "Postal Delivery," or "Zookeeper," without knowing what the job is. (Hold a sign up for the audience to let them know the job title.)

- "Ballad of My Best Friend." Two players take turns singing lines from a ballad about someone in the audience.

○ "Crazy Couples." Two players act out a suggested scene, such as a car collision, a first date, or a job interview, but must change into different couples when the audience shouts out names, such as Britney Spears and Martha Stewart, Marilyn Monroe and Jackie Kennedy, Oprah and Queen Elizabeth.

○ "Who Done It?" One player acts as the prosecutor in a murder case such as "Who Killed Elvis?" and questions audience members as witnesses. Each witness must present a piece of evidence, such as a rubber snake, a dirty sock, a lipstick, and so on, and use it in her testimony.

○ "Match a Mate." Players take turns introducing themselves for a video dating service—wearing a hat, such as a fedora, knitted cap, sailor's hat, and so on.

○ "Ms. Know-It-All." One player interviews another player who's an "expert" on a strange topic, such as "Mating Habits of Elephants," "How a Remote Actually Works," and "The Ingredients for Making a Nuclear Reactor."

○ "What Did She Say?" One player speaks in another language (or makes one up), while the second player makes up a translation.

○ "Dub the Speech." Turn on a video, turn off the sound, and have one or more players dub the speech for the actors on the screen.

○ "Dear Departed." Players take turns giving eulogies for a strange person's death, such as a clown, a hypnotist, a window washer, or a birdwatcher.

- "Girlsta Rap." Two players take turns rapping about a subject, such as spaying your pet, trying out for a game show, or competing in an eating contest.

- "Handy Gestures." One player stands facing the audience, with her hands behind her back. Another player sits behind her and slips her hands through the gap at the waist. The first player must give a talk on a subject, such as global warming, how to cook a turkey, or makeup tricks, while the second player provides the hand gestures.

- "Quirks." Four players stand at the front of the stage, in pairs. One pair—players one and two—discuss the quirks of the other pair—players three and four. As the quirks of players three and four are mentioned by players one and two, players three and four must perform those quirks. For example, if player one says, "Susan (player three) is always crossing her legs, even when she's standing up," player three must perform that quirk. Other quirks might be, scratching her butt, biting her nails, burping repeatedly, performing ballet steps, and so on.

- "Home Shopping Network." Two players must try to sell a strange product, such as a baton, some loose change, an empty candy box, to the television audience.

- "Human Props." Two players act out a scene, using two other players as their props. For example, if the scene is getting a driver's license, the driver being tested might use a player as her car, while the DMV official might use the other player as her scoreboard.

- ○ "Split Personality." A player gives a talk on a subject, but cannot move until moved by another player. For example, if she's giving a talk on exercise, a second player might put her in a strange exercising position.

- ○ "Say It in Threes." Two players are given a topic to discuss, such as how to bake a cake, what's up with the latest tabloid stars, or where to find the best bargains, but they can only speak three words at a time.

- ○ "Props to You." Two players take turns figuring out how to use random props they are given, such as giant underwear, an empty beer can, a rubber snake, and so on.

Refreshments

Serve fun foods at your funny party, such as Hostess Cupcakes, cheese and cracker packages, DIY spray can whipped cream on brownies, caramel popcorn, and so on. For added fun bake a rectangle cake. While it cools, tie ribbons to small joke or novelty items and insert them into each potential serving piece. Frost around the ribbons, lay them decoratively on top, and add more joke items, then display as a centerpiece. At serving time, carefully cut the cake so the hidden toys don't show, and serve to guests. Tell them to pull the ribbon to reveal the surprise. Have a real backup cake ready to serve so they don't have to eat the one that's rigged.

Favors, Prizes, and Gifts

Send the jokesters home with silly novelties, joke books, clown noses, and videotapes of their performances.

Party Plus

Go to a comedy club with the girls and have a good laugh. Or buy the *New Yorker* Cartoon Caption Game and have the guests make up captions for the cartoons.

Personals Party

have you got a single friend who desperately needs a date? Don't let her sit home watching TV and waiting for the phone to ring. Gather the girls and write your own personal ads—the winning ad gets submitted online. And your friend might just get a date!

Invitations

Create your own ad to use as an invitation. For example, you might write something like, "Wanted: Attractive, intelligent women for a fun and festive evening. Age doesn't matter. Must love wine and chocolate." Type it up to look like an ad and mail to guests. Mark envelope "Personal!"

What to Wear

Dress up for your interviews so you'll look good for the video camera. Ask the girls to bring along props that symbolize parts of their personalities, such as a tennis racket, shopping bag, or gardening tool.

Decorations

Set up a chair with a plain background behind to serve as the interviewee's seat, and place the video camera in front to capture the interview. Hang up photos of various types of men—cowboys, bikers, businessmen, clergy, athletes, hippies, and so on. Get out copies of personal ads to use as examples for the activity.

Games and Activities

The goal is to get a date for your special guest, so get busy with that personal ad, and show the world how great she really is!

Get a Date!

1. Write a Personals Ad

   Give all the girls a sheet of paper and a pen. Read a couple of personals ads aloud, to get them started, then ask them to write an ad for one of the single girls at the party. For example, they might write, "My name is Jennifer. I love long walks in the desert, playing Frisbee with my dog, and dining on vegetarian food . . ." You can make the ad real, based on the single girl's interests, or just have fun with it, and exaggerate the claims.

2. Tape an Interview

   Have the single girl sit in the interview chair, facing the video camera. Hand her one of the personals ads created by a guest, and ask her to read it to the camera. Follow that with another ad, and so on, until all the ads have been read.

3. Play the Tape

   After the single girl is finished reading all the ads to the camera, play back the tape and watch the interview.

4. Time to Vote

   Ask the guests to vote on the best ad, then submit it to a personals site, such as Match.com (with the single girl's permission!).

Match Up the Stars

Assign a pair of movie stars or famous people to each player, such as Brad Pitt and Julia Roberts, Britney Spears and George Clooney,

George Bush and Hillary Clinton. Ask them to write up a personals ad for one of the pair, with the other one in mind. For example, Brad Pitt might write his personals ad like this: "Hunk of a male, often blond, with boyish charm, seeks woman with large mouth, big box office, and twins with odd names." Have the others guess who's who.

Refreshments
Serve matching food, such as cheese and crackers, chips and dips, peanut butter and jelly sandwiches, milk and cookies, gin and tonic, and cake and ice cream.

Favors, Prizes, and Gifts
Give them copies of personal ads, books on dating such as *1,001 Places to Meet Mr. Right* or *Why Men Love Bitches*, and beauty aids. Or offer makeover coupons at the local beauty salon.

Party Plus
Ask a professional dating counselor to come speak to the group on how to find Mr. Right.

PMS Pamper Party
Feeling cranky? Bloated? Tired and depressed? Cheer yourselves up with chips and chocolate, games and goodies, and turn PMS into FUN. This is the perfect time to pamper yourself with a relaxing afternoon or evening.

Invitations
Hand-deliver a mini box of chocolates to each guest with the party information attached to the top of the box. Or mail a spa sample, such as an envelope of bubble bath or a nail file, with party details attached.

What to Wear

Grunge wear, baggy clothes, pajamas, sweats—anything comfortable and cozy. Keep the makeup minimal and let your hair down—or twist it up in an unkempt knot. Bring slippers or socks to change into.

Decorations

Begin lifting those low spirits with a festively decorated party room. Use lots of balloons, crepe paper streamers, and banners in bright colors. Cover the party table with a cheery tablecloth and paper products. Fill candy bowls with chocolate candies, such as M&Ms, malt balls, and chocolate-covered raisins. Place pillows around the room for extra comfort, and soft blankets and throws to cuddle up in. Light scented candles for aromatherapy. Hang up posters of inviting vacation spots. Play relaxing music.

Games and Activities

It's all about pampering—yourself and your friends! And you deserve it!

Pamper Yourselves, People!

While you chat about men, discuss new diets, or gossip about neighbors, pamper yourselves with manicures and pedicures, foot massages, makeovers, leg waxes, and so on.

Mushy Movies

Rent some romantic videos and share them with the group. Feel free to shout at the characters, boo the cads, or vent about similar situations throughout the film. At the end, let each guest talk about how she might have done things differently from the couple in the video.

Chocolate Test

Unwrap a variety of candy bars, cut them up, and place the pieces in separate paper bags. Pass the bags around, have the players taste a candy (without looking at it), and guess what it is.

Junk Food Exposed

Buy some popular junk foods, such as potato chips, Oreo cookies, Twinkies, and so on. Read the ingredients to the group (without letting them see the product), and have them guess what it is.

Dessert Draw

Get out a few of your favorite dessert recipes and gather the ingredients. Divide the group into teams, and have them prepare the desserts, without knowing the end product. When everyone has finished, gobble up the yummy desserts.

Refreshments

All things chocolate belong at this party—chocolate cookies, chocolate candy, chocolate-covered pretzels. And don't forget the junk food—chips and dips, cheesy nachos, glazed donuts. But before you overdose, offer some alternatives, such as cheese and crackers, veggies and dips, fruit salad, deli sandwiches.

Favors, Prizes, and Gifts

When the party is over, keep the guests happy with bags of chocolate candy, a stress-release ball, a sweet stuffed animal, a relaxing CD, some beauty products, bath items, and soft fuzzy socks.

Party Plus

Hire a manicurist to attend the party and do everyone's nails. Or head out for a night on the town, a day at the spa, a new movie, a fancy dinner at a restaurant, or a trip to the wine country.

Girls' Game Night!

Board games never go out of style, even with all the video and Internet games available. There's nothing like gathering around a table with your girlfriends, rolling the dice, collecting points, and chatting in between exciting plays. Have the guests bring their favorite games from the good old days, such as Monopoly, Clue, or Passout, or games that are popular today, such as Outburst, Scattergories, or Cranium, and play one game after another. Or take turns hosting Game Night and let the hostess share her favorite game for the evening.

Invitations

Buy some play money and write the party details on the back. If you're sharing games, don't forget to ask the guests to bring a favorite game. Place the money invitations in a padded envelope along with a couple of dice. Or make your own spinner from white posterboard and fill in the pie-slice divisions with the party details, such as the time, place, and theme of the party.

What to Wear

Have the guests come dressed in their favorite game-related outfits. For example, a guest might wear red from head to toe as Miss Scarlet from Clue, or sport a phony mustache and a top hat like Mr. Monopoly, or come as an artist from the game of Pictionary. Or ask the girls to dress up as tacky game-players wearing mismatched clothing, heavy makeup, and bizarre accessories.

Decorations

If you've selected a particular game for the evening, decorate with symbols from the game. Photocopy the game board and have it enlarged, then hang it on the wall or use it as a table cover. Enlarge the game icons, such as the characters from Clue, and set them at the table as placemats. Put out game pieces, play money, and lots of dice. Write up phrases from the game, such as "Do Not Pass Go!" and "Mr. Green did it with a candlestick in the library." Tape them to the walls. Make your own personalized game pieces by photocopying your guests' pictures, then glue them to thick posterboard, and set them around the table for each player. Use paper products and balloons that match the color scheme of the game.

Games and Activities

The board games will provide most of the entertainment. To prepare, set up the first game ahead of time so it's ready to go. If there are tokens in the game for the players to use, exchange them for something more fun. For example, if you're playing Monopoly, use costume rings, small chocolates, or tiny figurines so players can choose the ones that suit their interests or personalities.

Mixed Up Monopoly

Instead of playing the number one bestselling game of Monopoly according to the rules, give it a twist by playing with real one-dollar bills (contributed by all the players), or by playing the game backwards (by moving around the board in reverse), or by having the players lose money instead of gain money (with the richest—or poorest—player as winner). See how creative the players can be with other board games, and try racing to the end instead of having the most money or drawing a picture blindfolded.

Game Guess

Write up trivia questions about various popular games and have a Guess-Off. For example, you might write "What's the space opposite the 'Go!' square on the Monopoly board?" "What color are the triangles in Trivial Pursuit?" "Name the characters in Clue," and "What are the four games in Cranium?" Keep score and award a prize to the Game Master.

DIY Game

Divide the group into teams of three or four players. Give each team a large sheet of white posterboard and some markers, and have them design their own board game! When everyone is finished, set the games up around the room and have the teams take turns playing the newly created games. Award a prize for best game.

Sensory Deprivation

Play a board game, but tell the players they cannot talk during the play—they can only communicate by using gestures instead of speech. The silent expressions of the guests provide extra laughs for any game. Each time a player accidentally speaks, she loses a point. The one with the fewest negative points wins a bonus prize, in addition to the winner of the game.

Refreshments

Have lots of snacks in bowls and on trays at the game table so players can munch while they play. Serve strawberries, grapes, cut-up pineapple, cheese slices, crackers, trail mix, flavored popcorn, veggie and dips, triangle sandwiches, mini-pizzas, and chocolates. Wash it all down with wine coolers, beer, or fruit drinks. Make a cake decorated like a board game, a game spinner, or a giant die.

Favors, Prizes, and Gifts

Send the winners—and losers—home with a travel board game, a card game like Zobmondo or UNO, a deck of cards, or an object related to the game, such as a can of Play-Doh for Cranium, an art pad for Pictionary, or a bag of apples for Apples to Apples.

Party Plus

Learn how to play a retro game, such as bridge, mah jong, or bunco. Or set up game stations with one-on-one games at each site, such as checkers, chess, Stratego, Battleship, and Risk, then have everyone rotate when a timer rings. Or host an old-fashioned BINGO Game Night!

Why Not Have a Wii Party

Everyone seems to be playing Nintendo's Wii (pronounced "we") games these days. The system comes with a remote that is used as a racquet, bat, pool cue, bowling bowl, and dozens of other types of sports equipment, and simulates playing games like football, basketball, even carnival games. If you or a friend has a Wii system, why not invite the girls over for some indoor athletic fun? You can play in teams or compete individually against each other in everything from bowling, tennis, and golf to duck hunting, pool, and archery. It's a great way to learn new sports, get some exercise, and even stay in shape when the weather's not cooperating. So turn on your Wii and get your game on!

Invitations

Since you'll be playing electronic games, gather the guests electronically by e-mailing your invitation. Download an advertisement for a Wii system onto your word processing program, add party details and clip art to match, and send as an attachment to your online friends. You can also use one of the electronic invitation services available on the Internet, such as eVite.com, Sendomatic.com, or CardFountain. com. If you prefer snail mail invitations, print out your creations and send them through the postal service.

What to Wear

Ask guests to dress in sporting outfits, such as jerseys of their favorite teams, golfing or tennis clothes, boxing shorts and tank tops, or tacky bowling shirts and shoes. Or divide them into teams ahead of time, and in the invitation, ask the guests to wear T-shirts with assigned team colors. Give the teams names, such as "The Danville Debs" or the "Greenville Girl Gang," then mail iron-on letters with the team name to the guests and ask them to apply the letters before the party. Offer sweatbands when the guests arrive, or Survivor-type "buffs" (bandanas) that match their team colors, and whistles to wear around their necks.

Decorations

Set out sports equipment, hang up banners, and write slogans such as "Go Team!" to put around the room. If you have any sports jerseys or caps, set them out in strategic locations. Move the furniture out of the way so there's plenty of room to swing and shoot, and arrange the chairs in a semi-circle so the audience can watch the players. Turn on sports-related songs in the background, such as "We Will Rock You" by Queen, "Whoop There It Is," by Tag Team, "Celebration Time!" by Sly Stone, and "Get Ready for This!" by 2 Unlimited.

Games and Activities

Spend the party time playing a variety of Wii games, and cheering on your team or the individual competitors.

Create Your Alter Ego

First, give each player a chance to design her own Mii (online character). She can choose from a number of options, such as hair style, type of eyes, glasses, skin color, and approximate age. Have her give her avatar a nickname or initials. Award a prize for the character that looks the most like the player, as well as the funniest looking character and the character that looks the least like the player.

Start the Tournament

Next decide what games you want to play, then set up a tournament. Write the players' names on a large sheet of posterboard or a dry-erase board, and keep score during the competition.

Have players who are sitting out guess who will win each event. When the games are over, award prizes for the player who gets the most points of all (and who gets the least), who has the best form (or the funniest), who's the loudest (or quietest), who cheats the most (or maybe should have), and who should never pick up a Wii remote ever again.

Step Out of Your Comfort Zone

Have players try their hands at sports they've never played before, such as duck hunting, boxing, ping-pong, or football. Award prizes for how quickly they learn the game, how funny they look while playing, and what their best virtual sport is.

Refreshments

Serve casual sports-related food such as hot dogs, chili, nachos, pizza, popcorn, and peanuts. Set out bowls of trail mix and energy bars, sport drinks, and energy sodas to keep their energy up. Or do the opposite and make elegant food, such as fancy appetizers, a salad bar, truffles, and upscale drinks, along with lots of bottled water to replenish fluids. Bake cupcakes and decorate them to look like tennis or golf balls.

Favors, Prizes, and Gifts

Send the sports fans home with Frisbees, tennis balls, baseball caps, team shirts, and containers of trail mix to thank them for coming, or give them out as prizes. For the grand prize, give tickets to a sports event, a sports CD, a DVD featuring a sports theme, or a special jersey.

Party Plus

Instead of playing the athletic games, put your own girl band together and play Guitar Hero. Take turns playing different instruments, and add a karaoke mic to the mix for the lead singer and her backup singers.

The party's never really over, so after you've hosted all the parties in *Ladies' Night*, just check out the bonus themes in the Appendix and design your own special event, from the invitations, decorations, and costumes, to the games, goodies, and goodbye gifts. All you need is a little creativity and imagination to personalize your party—and a great gang of girlfriends to share the fun! Party on, ladies!

Appendix A: Extra Party Ideas, Games, and Activities

Party On! More Ideas for Super Showers

○ Build a Basket Shower—Gather themed baskets filled with gifts and goodies.

○ Cupid's Champagne & Candlelight Shower—Create a romantic night for bride and buddies.

○ Decadent Dessert Shower—Indulge your decadent dreams with delicious desserts.

○ Designer Decorator Shower—Supply the bride with designer ideas and decorator items.

○ Dr. Ruth's Sex Advice Shower—Share your secrets for a scintillating marriage with sex tips.

○ Fifties Housewife Shower—Bring the stereotypical housewife to life for a trip to the past.

○ Gala Gallery Shower—Set up a gift gallery and host a reception for the art patrons.

○ Gizmos and Gadgets Shower—Make the bride guess the gizmos and gadgets galore.

○ Gourmet Goodies Shower—Help the budding gourmet fill her pantry with gourmet foods.

○ Helping Hand How-To Shower—Offer household tips and services, along with special supplies.

○ Love and Lattes Shower—Host an espresso extravaganza with gifts and gab on the side.

- Make a Plate Shower—Take the group to a ceramics shop and paint a place setting.

- Marriage Menu Shower—Write up menus for marriage and serve a sampler spread.

- Powder Room Shower—Shower her with shower stuff and beautify the bride's bath.

- Room by Room Shower—Assign a room to each guest and fill the bride's new home.

- Something Old, Something New Shower—Guests create something new, bring something old.

- This Was Your Life Shower—Show the bride life "before" and "after" the upcoming date.

- Twenty-Four-Hour Shower—Assign the guest a time of day and bring a gift to match the hour.

- Victorian Tea Party—Host a High Tea with your best finery to honor the bride-to-be.

More Bridal Shower Games and Activities

- Beautiful Bride—Identify obscured beauty ads from magazines.

- Bridal Bingo—Write down typical gifts on card; when bride opens gifts, see if they match.

- Bride's Purse—Guess what's inside the bride-to-be's purse; see if you can match.

- Clothespin Capture—Guests have five pins; if they say a certain word they lose a pin.

- Dance Your Ass Off—Play dance videos; try to copy, i.e., Two-step, Crunk, Waltz.

- Dress the Bridesmaids—Use colorful crepe paper to design outfits.

- Guess the Gizmos—Give each person an odd cooking tool; make up how to use it for sex.

- Hyphenated Honeymooners—Match up famous names to make funny new ones.

- Love Bites—Write down famous love quotes; guess who said them.

- Love Lines—Write down famous lines from romantic movies; guess film.

- Love Match—Write prompts like, "something found in bedroom"; match bride-to-be's answers.

- Love Stinks—Think up phrases using word "love."

- Madison Avenue Love—Name commercials with romance themes.

- Makeover Bride—Bride gets a beauty makeover.

- Marital Millinery—Make wild hats out of crepe paper and funny objects.

- Marriage Advice—Write funny advice for bride-to-be.

- Memorable Bride—Bride leaves room; ask questions about her outfit.

○ Newlywed Game—Ask questions about bride and groom; see who's most correct.

○ Perfect Marriage—Fill in the prompts for marriage suggestions.

○ Predict the Future—Guests answer questions about bride's future.

○ Recipes for Romance—Guests write recipe-style tips for romance.

○ Romantic Memories—Guests remember special times of couple.

○ Romantic Serenades—Play bits of romantic music, name that tune.

○ Scavenger Hunt—Find wedding-related items hidden in party room.

○ Sense of Touch—Feel romantic things in bags; guess what they are.

○ Sing It Out—Start first line of love song, have player finish it.

○ Wedding *Jeopardy!*—Answer category questions related to wedding.

○ What If…—Make up what could go wrong at wedding, and what bride-to-be would do.

Party Plus: More Creative Bachelorette Bashes

○ Big Girl Pajama Party—Slip on your sexy lingerie or old PJs for a grownup sleepover.

○ Chocoholic Orgy—Eat it, drink it, spread it, lick it—it's a chocolate marathon.

○ Dancin' with the Girls—Cut loose and show your stuff on the dance floor.

○ Full Monty Stripper Party—Surprise the bride, and the guests, with a sexy striptease.

○ Getaway Weekend—Escape the rat race and take a road trip with the girls.

○ Margaritaville! Party—Mix up tropical treats for your party people and shake well.

○ Peter Party—Stage a smutty soirée to celebrate Peter, Dick, and Big Johnson.

○ Shopping Spree Party—Take the bride on an all-day mall marathon.

○ Sing Your Heart Out Karaoke Party—Sing along to some steamy love songs—on or off key.

○ Stud and Stogies Night—Guzzle beer, play poker, choke on cigars, and burp like the boys.

○ Venus vs. Mars Party—Test your Men-Q while you try to figure out those Martians.

○ Victorian Virgins Tea Party—Repressed ladies—pure or pro? Watch out for steaming sexpots.

○ Viva Las Vegas Night—Roll the dice and hope you get lucky at the tables.

Party On!: More Bouncy Baby Shower Themes

○ ABC Shower—Turn the alphabet into a complete A to Z shower.

○ Angel Baby Shower—Let the angels be your guide and have a heavenly time.

○ Babes in Toyland Shower—Set up Toyland and shower the baby with playthings.

○ Baby Animals Shower—Invite baby lions, tigers, and bears to the baby party.

○ Beautiful Baby Shower—You can just picture the most beautiful baby shower.

○ Bib and Booties Shower—Provide all the basics for baby's layette.

○ Brilliant Baby Shower—Welcome the baby genius with gifts for the mind.

○ Bubbles and Balloons—Fill the room with colorful balloons and blustery bubbles.

○ Calendar Kid Shower—Mark the calendar for baby's developmental milestones.

○ Cartoon Characters Shower—Invite a Baby Muppet or Disney kid to the party.

○ Diaper Duty Shower—101 things you can do with a diaper—and more.

○ Dolly's Tea Party Shower—Invite baby's new dolls to a mother-baby tea party.

- Good Advice Shower—The MTB to be gets advice and a gift to go with it.

- Pamper the Pregger Shower—Give the gift of self-indulgence to perk up the pregnant mom.

- Pink and Blue Shower—It's all pink (or blue) with lots of creative color use.

- Makeover Mom Shower—Give MTB a makeover and lift her pregnancy spirits.

- Make Room for Baby Shower—Have the guests bring gifts and gadgets for the baby's room.

- Making Memories Shower—Put together a scrapbook and start mom collecting memories.

- Mystery Baby Shower—The shower is a surprise, and the gifts and games are mysterious.

- Mother Goose Shower—Make Mother Goose and her nursery rhyme friends the party theme.

- Storybook Shower—Turn a favorite book into a party, such as *Pat the Bunny.*

- Teddy Bears' Picnic Shower—Lay out a spread and invite baby's teddies to join you.

- Time of Day Shower—Give the guests baby's time of day for gifts and gadgets.

Appendix B: More Excuses for a Party

January 3—Fruitcake Toss Day

January 4—Trivia Day

January 5—National Bird Day

January 8—Male Watcher's Day

January 14—Dress Up Your Pet Day

January 15—National Hat Day

January 16—National Nothing Day

January 19—National Popcorn Day

January 23—National Handwriting Day

January 25—Opposite Day

January 27—Chocolate Cake Day

January 29—National Puzzle Day

February 2—Groundhog Day

February 7—Send a Card to a Friend Day

February 8—Kite Flying Day

February 11—Make a Friend Day

February 15—Singles Awareness Day

February 17—Random Acts of Kindness Day

February 23—Tennis Day

February 26—Carnival Day

February 29—Leap Day

March 1—Peanut Butter Day

March 2—Old Stuff Day

March 5—Multiple Personality Day

March 8—Be Nasty Day

March 9—Panic Day

March 12—Girl Scouts Day

March 13—Jewel Day

March 14—National Potato Chip Day

March 17—National Quilting Day

March 17—St. Patrick's Day

March 18—Goddess of Fertility Day

March 20—International Earth Day

March 21—Extraterrestrial Abductions Day

March 21—Fragrance Day

March 22—National Goof-Off Day

March 25—Waffle Day

March 26—Make Up Your Own Holiday Day

April 1—April Fool's Day

April 1—National Peanut Butter and Jelly Day

April 4—Tell a Lie Day

April 6—Plan Your Epitaph Day

April 6—No Housework Day

April 6—Golfer's Day

April 10—National Siblings Day

April 13—Blame Someone Else Day

April 13—Scrabble Day

April 14—International Moment of Laughter Day

April 18—International Juggler's Day

April 19—National Garlic Day

April 20—Look Alike Day

April 22—National Jelly Bean Day

April 23—Lover's Day

April 23—Take a Chance Day

April 27—Tell a Story Day

April 28—Great Poetry Reading Day

April 30—Hairstyle Appreciation Day

April 30—National Honesty Day

May 1—May Day
May 1—Mother Goose Day
May 4—Renewal Day
May 4—Cinco de Mayo
May 4—Beverage Day
May 6—National Tourist Appreciation Day
May 6—No Diet Day
May 10—Clean Up Your Room Day
May 10—Eat What You Want Day
May 10—Twilight Zone Day
May 12—Limerick Day
May 15—National Chocolate Chip Day
May 18—International Museum Day
May 26—International Jazz Day

June 1—Dare Day
June 1—National Doughnut Day
June 4—Old Maid's Day
June 4—National Chocolate Ice Cream Day
June 4—Best Friends Day
June 8—Name Your Poison Day
June 10—Iced Tea Day
June 12—Red Rose Day
June 16—Fresh Veggies Day
June 18—National Splurge Day
June 21—Go Skate Day
June 23—National Pink Day
June 26—Beautician's Day

June 29—Camera Day

July 1—Build a Scarecrow Day
July 1—Creative Ice Cream Flavors Day
July 1—International Joke Day
July 4—Independence Day
July 4—National Country Music Day
July 6—National Chocolate Day
July 9—National Sugar Cookie Day
July 11—Cheer Up the Lonely Day
July 12—Embrace Your Geekness Day
July 12—Bastille Day
July 14—Pandemonium Day
July 14—National Ice Cream Day
July 20—Moon Day
July 21—National Junk Food Day
July 26—Culinarian's Day
July 30—National Cheesecake Day

August 4—Friendship Day
August 5—Sisters Day
August 9—Book Lover's Day
August 10—Lazy Day
August 15—Relaxation Day
August 15—National Tell a Joke Day
August 18—Bad Poetry Day
August 26—National Dog Day
August 27—Just Because Day
August 30—Frankenstein Day

September 4—Fight Procrastination Day
September 6—Read a Book Day
September 10—Sewing Machine Day
September 10—Swap Ideas Day
September 10—Defy Superstition Day
September 13—Positive Thinking Day
September 15—Make a Hat Day
September 16—Mexican Independence Day
September 16—National Women's Friendship Day
September 19—International Talk Like a Pirate Day
September 21—Miniature Golf Day
September 21—World Gratitude Day
September 22—Business Women's Day
September 25—National Comic Book Day

October 1—World Vegetarian Day
October 5—Do Something Nice Day
October 8—Columbus Day
October 11—It's My Party Day
October 11—National Dessert Day
October 16—Dictionary Day
October 18—Wear Something Gaudy Day
October 19—Evaluate Your Life Day
October 21—Sweetest Day
October 25—World Pasta Day
October 31—Increase Your Psychic Powers Day

November 1—Saint's Day
November 2—All Soul's Day
November 4—Housewife's Day

November 5—Guy Fawkes Day

November 7—Cook Something Bold Day

November 10—Forget Me Not Day

November 13—Sadie Hawkins Day

November 16—National Philanthropy Day

November 17—Take a Hike Day

November 18—Occult Day

November 19—Have a Bad Day Day

November 19—Absurdity Day

November 20—Beautiful Day

December 4—Letter Writing Day

December 4—National Brownie Day

December 10—National Chocolate-Covered Anything Day

December 18—Bake Cookies Day

December 20—Go Caroling Day

December 21—Humbug Day

December 23—Look on the Bright Side Day

December 25—Christmas Day

December 26—Boxing Day

December 27—National Fruitcake Day

December 28—Card Playing Day

December 28—National Chocolate Day

Appendix C: Resources

www.1partysuppliesandfavors.com

www.amazon.com

www.americanpartyoutlet.com

www.apronpromotionaloutlet.com

www.atlasquest.com

www.babybar.com

www.balloontime.com

www.bellymasks.com

www.brides.com

www.bulkpartysupplies.com

www.bulwer-lytton.com

www.cafepress.com

www.chroniclebooks.com

www.circleup.com (online invitations)

www.clothingswap.org

www.custompromotionproducts.com

www.drinkalizer.com

www.engravedgiftcreations.com

www.epromos.com

www.evite.com (online invitations)

www.geocaching.com

www.Googleearth.com

www.gotparty.com

www.herecomestheguide.com

www.iparty.com

www.letterboxing.org

www.literaryluminaries.biz

www.mypunchbowl.com (online invitations)

www.NancyDrewSleuth.com

www.OrientalTradingCompany.com

www.Oscar.com

www.party411.com

www.partyadventure.com

www.partyandpaperwarehouse.com

www.partybanners.com

www.partycity.com

www.partyoptions.com

www.partyperfection.com

www.partysupplies.com

www.personalizationmall.com

www.personalizedpartyfavors.com

www.pennywarner.com

www.redenvelope.com

www.redhatsociety.com

www.renkoo.com (online invitations)

www.rubbergrams.com

www.shindigz.com

www.sisterhoodcircle.com

www.sweetpotatoqueens.com

www.thepartyworks.com

www.theknot.com

www.webbabyshower.com

www.weddingchannel.com

About the Author

As the Premiere Party Queen, Penny Warner writes party tips for several Web sites, including Oriental Trading Company, iParty.com, Party411.com, ToysRUs.com, DrSpock.com, BalloonTime.com, and Fisher-Price.com. She has sold more than forty books for parents and kids, featuring ideas for parties, games, activities, snacks, and fun. Her bestselling books include *The Best Party Book* and *Games People Play*, along with *Kids' Party Games & Activities*, *Kids' Pick-a-Party*, *Kids' Holiday Parties*, and *Slumber Parties*. Warner was a regular guest on several San Francisco Bay Area television talk shows, including *People Are Talking* and *A.M. San Francisco*, and has appeared on national television presenting party and activity tips for parents and kids, including HGTV's *Smart Solutions* and *Later Today*. She has done numerous television media events and satellite media tours for party companies; participated in hundreds of radio interviews; worked with dozens of public relations firms including Ketchum, HL Marketing, McKee Products, Amann & Associates, Southard Communications, Edelman, and Zeno Group; promoted party products; and provided numerous newspaper, magazine, and Internet interviews.

Warner's party articles have appeared in dozens of magazines and newspapers, including *Martha Stewart's Kids*, *Family Fun*, *Nick Jr.*, *Woman's Day*, and *Parenting* (copies available upon request). She does promotion work for party products for large corporations and gives workshops on party tips, including at the annual Halloween and Party Show in Chicago. She has written and sold more than 400 mystery parties.

Other Party Books by Penny Warner:

Storybook Parties, Meadowbrook Press

Baby Birthday Parties, Meadowbrook Press

Kids' Outdoor Parties, Meadowbrook Press

Big Book of Party & Holiday Fun, Meadowbrook Press

Kids' Party Cookbook, Meadowbrook Press

Birthday Parties for Kids, Prima Publishing

Murder Mystery Parties, St. Martin's Press

Penny Warner's Party Book, St. Martin's Press

Happy Birthday Parties, St. Martin's Press